ADVERTISEMENT

THIS series of ten volumes, each complete in itself, is designed to constitute a connected treatment of the entire range of Catholic Doctrine.

It is hoped that the remaining volumes will be published at intervals of about eighteen months.

THE BEING AND

ATTRIBUTES OF GOD

THE BEING AND

ATTRIBUTES OF GOD

BY THE

REV. FRANCIS J. HALL, D.D.

PROFESSOR OF DOGMATIC THEOLOGY IN THE GENERAL THEOLOGICAL
SEMINARY, NEW YORK CITY

NEW IMPRESSION

LONGMANS, GREEN AND CO.

FOURTH AVENUE & 30TH STREET, NEW YORK

39 PATERNOSTER ROW, LONDON

BOMBAY, CALCUTTA, AND MADRAS

1918

Copyright, 1909

BY

LONGMANS, GREEN AND CO.

First Edition, March, 1909
Reprinted, April, 1918

PRINTED BY BRAUNWORTH & CO., BROOKLYN, N. Y.

PREFACE

THE writer's sense of the difference between his ideal and his execution has been intensified during the production of this volume. To write worthily of God, and to induce men in this over-busy age to turn once more to a direct and systematic study of Him, is an undertaking quite too formidable to be faced, except under a sense of necessity and of divine prompting. That it is peculiarly necessary at this time to do what one can to revive the love of the study of God is certain. The common view is that the greatest subject for man's study is man. The truth which needs reassertion is that the greatest subject for human study is God. We cannot understand man, unless we study him as made in the image of God; and we cannot realize adequately what this means, until we have studied carefully the nature of God, in whose image we have been created.

Much theistic literature is appearing, but it is almost exclusively apologetical. We need also a systematic study of God Himself. The key-note of this volume is contained in our Lord's assertion that life itself consists in knowing God. (St. John, xvii. 3.) Furthermore the knowledge of God is not adequate—not as adequate as it can be made under

Christian conditions,—unless we reckon with the
revelation of His dispensation of redemption and
grace which is preserved in catholic doctrine and
Holy Scripture. Accordingly we have sought in
this volume to interpret the self-revelation of God
in the light of its full context, and to deal with the
doctrine of God as part of a larger constructive
theology, rather than as a detached study of theism.

God is our life; and His character, when translated into human terms in Jesus Christ, constitutes
the pattern of human perfection and the form of
human self-realization. To study His works is a
joy forever, but to face and to study Him is the
most important and most satisfying labour of all.
God is the solution of every problem, the chief end
of man, the basis of all true philosophy.

New York,
March, 1918.

CONTENTS

CHAPTER I

INTRODUCTION

PART I. *Some Preliminaries*

PART II. *The Doctrine of God*

CHAPTER II

THEOLOGICAL AGNOSTICISM

PART I. *Nature and History*

X CONTENTS

CHAPTER III

CHRISTIAN THEISM

CHAPTER IV

THE STATE OF THE QUESTION

PART I. *Consent and Experience*

PART II. *The Burden of Proof*

CHAPTER V

THE COSMOLOGICAL ARGUMENT

PART I. *Positive Statement*

PART II. *Objections*

PART III. *Teachings*

CHAPTER VI

THE TELEOLOGICAL ARGUMENT

PART I. *Statement*

Part II. *Objections*

Part III. *The Wisdom of God*

CHAPTER VII

THE MORAL ARGUMENTS

Part I. *Conscience and History*

Part II. *Truth, Beauty and Religion*

CHAPTER VIII

THE ONTOLOGICAL ARGUMENT

CHAPTER IX

ANTI-THEISTIC THEORIES

CHAPTER X

MONOTHEISTIC DOCTRINE

PART I. *Its Formal Development*

PART II. *Primary Attributes*

CHAPTER XI

QUIESCENT ATTRIBUTES

PART I. *Self-existent and Eternal*

PART II. *Transcendent Spirit and Life*

CHAPTER XII

ACTIVE AND MORAL ATTRIBUTES

PART I. *Active Attributes*

PART II. *Moral Attributes*

PART III. *Divine Excellence*

THE
BEING AND ATTRIBUTES OF GOD

CHAPTER I

INTRODUCTION

I. *Some Preliminaries*

§ 1. Inasmuch as theology is the "science of things divine," and treats of every thing with which it is concerned, in relation to God,[1] *The Being and Attributes of God* ought obviously to occupy the first place in any systematic treatise of doctrine. Until we have given due consideration to this subject it is not to be expected that we shall be able intelligently to investigate the other contents of Dogmatic Theology. The doctrine of God affords the standpoint from which all other doctrines are to be understood. The pro-profundity of the subject must not deter us, therefore, from considering it first.

§ 2. The beginnings of human knowledge of God are prehistoric, and lie beyond the range of things which modern investigators can successfully investigate. The second chapter of Genesis must be assumed, at least by those who believe in the catholic doctrine of inspiration, to possess a true meaning. But whether

[1] Hooker, *Eccles. Polity*, III. viii. 11; St. Thos., *Summa Theol.*, I. i. 7. Cf. *Introd. to Dog. Theol.*, ch. i. § 9.

this meaning is properly historical or symbolical has always been an open question in the Church.[1] Modern scholars usually deny that the narrative has historical value.[2]

In any case the Book of Genesis teaches that primitive man received some sort of supernatural revelation from God — of a kind, no doubt, suited to the receptive capacity of those who were childlike in their lack of experience and mental culture. The Bible also clearly teaches that mankind was originally monotheistic,[3] and this teaching appears to be confirmed by what little the science of the history of religion can tell us that is relevant.[4]

Sin intervened,[5] and the primitive state of innocence

[1] Sanday gives some suggestive thoughts on symbolical interpretation, in a paper on the Symbolism of Scripture in his *Life of Christ in Recent Research.* The ancient fathers usually regarded the narrative as truly historical, although susceptible of allegorical treatment as well. The early Alexandrians (see Bigg, *Christian Platonists of Alex.*, pp. 57, 58, 131–151), St. Irenæus (*Adv. Haer.*, v. 5), St. Hilary (*De Trin.* vi), and St. Ambrose (*De Paradiso*, § 1) do not take it historically. St. Augustine prefers a historical interpretation, but not dogmatically (*De Gen. ad Lit.*, i. 1; xi. 2; viii. 1). Darwell Stone gives a useful note, *Outlines of Dogma*, note 10.

[2] *E.g.* S. R. Driver, *Genesis*, pp. 51–57; and Ryle, *Early Narratives of Genesis.* Many critics are inclined to regard the narrative as mythical — a view which would have startled the ancients. Cf. on the whole subject, *Authority Eccles. and Biblical*, ch. vii. §§ 5, 6, 14, 15.

[3] Cf. Jas. Orr, *Problem of the Old Test.*, pp. 123 *et seq.*

[4] Numerous references to the foremost authorities in comparative religion are given in support of this contention by Driscoll, *God*, pp. 29–42.

[5] The fall of man is to be considered in the fifth treatise of this

and grace rapidly degenerated into wide-spread savagery. Whether this savagery became universal or not, the teaching of Scripture and the earliest traces now discoverable of human society alike show that, when men began to leave permanent evidences of their condition, they were generally barbarous, superstitious, and alienated from the true God. The earth was filled with violence.[1]

§ 3. The development of men's knowledge of God has been slow, and has pursued two distinct lines — natural and supernatural. The nations at large were suffered for many ages to seek after God without other revelation of God than is contained in Nature's teaching, although not without providential assistances and promptings. Climatic conditions, material resources, and civilization helped on the more progressive races; and at certain critical epochs — notably in the age of Confucius, Gautama, Zoroaster and Socrates — special and upward impulses were

series. The modern view is set forth by F. R. Tennant, *The Origin and Propagation of Sin;* and *The Sources of the Doctrines of the Fall and Original Sin.* The modern view is criticised from a traditional standpoint by Jas. Orr, *God's Image in Man.* Macculloch's *Comparative Theology,* ch. vii., will be found to be instructive.

[1] Gen. vi. 11. It is hardly to be disputed that man is much more ancient than any remains which indicate his condition. Whether the savage state out of which he appears to have been emerging, when he began to fashion tools and to build permanent structures, was his original state is not determined by any remains which we can discover. Archæology can neither prove nor disprove catholic doctrine as to a primitive state of holy innocence and grace. Cf. Fairbairn, *Philos. of the Christ. Religion,* p. 204; De La Saussaye, *Manual of the Science of Religion,* pp. 28, 29.

felt, and choice souls were able to draw nearer to the God whom many were seeking. That these impulses came from above, can hardly be denied.[1]

But the more determinate and supernatural self-manifestation of God was made to a special race, which was separated from the nations at large, and trained under the conditions of theocratic government, in order that, in the fulness of time, it might become capable both of receiving the revelation God in Christ, and of publishing the Gospel to the rest of mankind. The Israelites were chosen and put to school that they might become teachers of the rest in the knowledge of God.[2] God taught them in many portions and in many manners in His prophets;[3] and established a dispensation and ministry for the preservation of what was gradually revealed, and for its embodiment in religious institutions of prophetic meaning.[4]

In spite of many backslidings, visited with divine

[1] Cf. our *Introd. to Dog. Theol.*, chh. ii. § 9; viii. Pt. IV. Newman discusses the "dispensation of paganism" in *Arians*, ch. i. § iii. 5.

[2] Cf., in the order given, Ephes. i. 9, 10; Gen. xii. 3; xxii. 18; Deut. vii. 6; Rom. ix. 4, 5; Isa. xlix. 6; Acts ix. 15; xxvi. 17, 18; Ephes. iii. 6; Gal. iii. 16, 26–29. For prophecies that the Gentiles should in due season share in the inheritance of Israel, see, among others, Psa. xxii. 27; lxviii. 31; Isa. ii. 2–4; xlix. 6; lx. 3–14; Jer. iii. 17; Mal. i. 11; St. Matt. viii. 11; xii. 18–21; St. Luke xiii. 29; St. John x. 16.

See Gore, *The New Theol. and the Old Relig.*, pp. 45, 46. St. Athanasius says, *De Incarn.*, xii, that the Jews "were for all the world a holy school of the knowledge of God."

[3] Πολυμερῶς καὶ πολυτρόπως . . . ἐν τοῖς προφήταις: Heb. i. 1.

[4] Heb. viii. 5; ix. 9, 10; x. 1, 2; Gal. iii. 24.

punishments, the chosen race came at last to a secure knowledge that there is but one God and Judge of all mankind, righteous, strong, and patient; of infinite knowledge and wisdom, the Controller of history, and the joy, where rightly known, of all the earth.

Some in Israel had come to understand that the real evil in the world was sin, and that no remedy for this could be had, except through the intervention of God Himself. The coming of a Messiah became the great hope of Israel in the midst of political disaster;[1] and although many were looking merely for an earthly warrior who should conquer the world and make earthly Jerusalem the mistress of a world-wide empire,[2] others had profited by divine tutelage and were ready to recognize Him who came to die, and to triumph in human hearts rather than over men's bodies.[3]

In Christ dwelleth all the fulness of the Godhead bodily.[4] His mission on earth had, so far as our present subject is concerned, two results: a direct revelation of God in Person, and the establishment of a visible society, the Catholic Church, wherein, among other blessings, men's spiritual understandings are sanctified and enlightened, and their knowledge of God becomes determinate and is preserved and

[1] Cf. Schürer, *Jewish People in the Time of Christ*, Div. II. Vol. II. § 29; Drummond, *The Jewish Messiah;* Edersheim, *Life and Times of Jesus the Messiah*, Bk. I. ch. vi.

[2] St. John vi. 15. Cf. xii. 37–43; xviii. 33–39; St. Matt. ii. 2, 3.

[3] St. Luke ii. 25–39. Cf. St. Matt. ii. 1–12; xxvii. 54; St. Mark xv. 39; St. Luke xxiii. 39–43, 50–51.

[4] Col. ii. 9.

propagated. In the light of this knowledge the New Testament Scriptures were written, and became the Church's divinely inspired thesaurus, from which to illustrate and confirm ecclesiastical teaching. In the New Testament the truths of God, which are latent and obscure in the Old Testament, are patent and clear.[1]

The self-manifestation of God in the supernatural order has enabled men to understand more adequately and clearly His self-manifestation in the natural order. As will be shown in a later chapter, although theistic forms of thought were developed by ancient philosophers, no determinate theism was, or could be, developed by them.[2]

II. *The Doctrine of God*

§ 4. It is well at this point to define in a summary way the contents of the Christian doctrine of God, and to indicate the manner in which the knowledge of God is normally acquired.

In contrast to anti-theistic theories, Christian doctrine declares the existence of one supreme and personal God, of infinite glory, power, knowledge, and wisdom, just and merciful, loving and righteous in all His ways. This God transcends all else in nature and attributes, and is not contained in or measured

[1] St. Augustine, *Quest in Ex.*, 73: "The New is latent in the Old, and the Old is patent in the New." Cf. *Authority, Eccles. and Bib.*, pp. 246, 247, note 2.

[2] See ch. iii. § 10, below.

by the spatial or temporal; although He is immanent in all the universe, so that nothing can escape His immediate presence and energy. He is, by virtue of His will, the First-Cause of all things, and nothing can come into being, develop, or continue in any condition, apart from His will and operation. And He is at once the Designer and End of all things, by whom and for whom they are made. Beauty has its source in Him; and the course of events is the unveiling of His purposes, which are holy and cannot be altered or defeated. To Him all moral agents are accountable as to their Supreme Judge; and His will, as the expression of a nature which is the source of rectitude, is the standard of righteousness for all.

Christian doctrine teaches that God reveals His nature and will partly through natural phenomena, but more adequately and definitely by supernatural manifestations culminating in the Incarnation. From God we derive our being and every blessing, and to Him we owe entire obedience, worship, and love. In the knowledge of Him, and fellowship with Him, consists eternal life and our chief end. He is the Cause and explanation of the universe, and the knowledge of Him and of His ways is the highest wisdom, the sum of philosophy and the crowning joy of mankind.[1]

[1] Cf. Newman, *Grammar of Assent*, ch. v. § 1. In a note, *Philos. of Relig.*, pp. 10, 11, Caldecott gives definitions of the idea of God of various modern philosophers and theologians. Cf. also Ellicott, *Foundations of Sacred Study*, vol. I. pp. 117-124; and, on very modern lines, Royce, in *The Conception of God;* Fiske, *The Idea of God.*

Of works on the doctrine of God may be mentioned the following:

§ 5. This knowledge is utterly inadequate apart from the doctrine of the Trinity, by which the truth of God is distinguished from unitarian and tritheistic errors. God is one in being, essence, and nature, altogether unique, and without parts or possibility of division. But He is not a barren or distinctionless

PATRISTIC: Origen, *De Principiis;* St. Augustine, *De Trinitate; De Civitate Dei;* Pseudo-Dionysius, *De Divinis Nominibus;* St. John of Damascus, *Expos. Fidei Orthodoxae.* Much material can be found in the apologies and anti-Arian treatises.

MEDIÆVAL: St. Anselm, *Monologium; Proslogium;* Peter Lombard, *Sententiarum libri quattuor,* Bk. I; St. Thomas Aquinas, *Summa Theologica,* Part I; *Summa contra Gentiles;* St. Bonaventura, *Breviloquium.*

MODERN ROMAN: Estius, *Commentary on the Sentences;* Suarez, *De Deo Uno et Trino;* Ruiz, *De Deo;* Petavius, *De Deo Uno et Trino;* Thomassinus, *De Deo Uno* (These last two are rich in patristic citations): Perrone, *Praelectiones Theologicae;* Franzelin, *De Deo;* Tanquerey, *Theologia Dogmatica Specialis;* Schouppe, *Elementa Theologiae Dogmaticae,* Tract V; Scheeben, *Dogmatik,* Vol. II; Wilhelm and Scannell, *Manual of Cath. Theol.,* Bk. II.; Humphrey, *His Divine Majesty;* Driscoll, *Christian Philosophy: God.* Lacordaire, *Conferences: God.*

ANGLICAN: Thos. Jackson, *Works* (esp. Vol. V.); Bishop Pearson, *Apostles' Creed,* Art. I; *De Deo;* Forbes, *Nicene Creed,* Art. I; Browne, *Thirty Nine Articles,* Art. I; Gibson, *idem;* R. Owen, *Dogmatic Theology,* ch. iv; Darwell Stone, *Outlines of Christian Dogma,* ch. ii; W. J. Sparrow-Simpson, *Christian Doctrine of God;* F. J. Hall, *Doctrine of God.*

OTHERS: Macaire, *Théologie Dogmatique Orthodoxe* (Eastern); A. H. Strong, *Systematic Theol.* (revised edit.), Vol. I.; Weidner, *Theologia* (the last two rich in modern references); Chas. Hodge, *Systematic Theol.,* Vol. I; A. A. Hodge, *Outlines of Theology;* W. N. Clarke, *Outline of Christian Theol.*; Dorner, *System of Christian Doctrine,* Vols. I, II; Martensen, *Christian Dogmatics;* W. A. Brown, *Christian Theol. in Outline.*

monad. He has within His indivisible essence the self-sufficient grounds of abundant life, and of personal activity and relation. The manner of His unity is tri-personal. That is, He subsists in three Persons, the Father, the Son and the Holy Spirit, who are co-eternal and co-equal; possessing, and being distinguished by the manner in which they possess, the one eternal, immutable, and indivisible Godhead.

Of these Persons the Father is the source, so to speak, and principle of origin in the Godhead, from whom the Son and the Holy Ghost eternally proceed. The Son is eternally begotten of the Father; and is His personal Word, the express image of the Father's substance, and the Mediator between God and all else. The Holy Ghost proceeds from the Father by an eternal spiration, in which the Son has essential and active share. He is the bond of unity, so to speak, in the Godhead, by whose operation all divine purposes are brought to their perfect end. These three are real Persons [1] — not mere aspects of one Person — and their difference is grounded in the very essence of God. Yet they are not separate individuals, but three inseparable subjects of one indivisible essence.

By reason of this trinity of Persons God possesses an infinite and eternal sphere of knowledge, will, and love; and He possesses this independently of things

[1] That is, three distinct Egos, possessing intelligence and will. Cf. p. 239, note 1, below, where scholastic and modern definitions are given.

temporal and spatial. He is, in His own essence, almighty Goodness and Love.[1]

§ 6. Men do not acquire the true idea of God in a uniform manner, nor are they equally successful in obtaining it. Yet it is possible to discern normal methods of its acquisition, and the sources from which men in general derive the idea.

Men enter this life with a native mental constitution, with innate forms of thought, by reason of which they unavoidably think, speak, and act as if with a theistic presupposition. And this holds true, however unconscious they may be of it, or however defective and perverted their resulting convictions concerning God may be.[2]

§ 7. With the dawn of conscious reflection children begin to enter upon a theistic heritage, derived largely, perhaps, from the instruction of parents and teachers, but imbibed in any case from contact with the thought and theistic ways of those who survive from the previous generation. There is an unbroken tradition of theism, handed on through a multitude of channels, so that each new generation inherits and transmits the idea of God as it has been held by previous generations. No man wholly escapes the influence of traditional ideas, even though he seeks to overthrow them. The intellectual atmosphere which he must breathe is too heavily charged with them.

[1] The doctrine of the Trinity is to be treated of at length in our next volume. For a brief treatment, see the writer's *Doctrine of God*, Young Churchman Co., Milwaukee. [2] Cf. pp. 209, 210 below.

§ 8. The traces of divine operation which appear on the face of nature are multitudinous, and contain manifestations of the divine nature which are none the less real because partial and indirect.[1] A moderate amount of reflection enables men to detect these traces and indications as verifying and illustrating the theistic tradition. Men are not compelled to engage in profound study of the implications of natural phenomena in order to profit theistically by natural experience. The visible order forms the minds even of the most ignorant and unreflecting, and no one is wholly blind to the theistic meaning of natural phenomena except through wilful shutting out of the light. One may, indeed, be tormented by doubt; but theistic doubt presupposes some perception of the theistic implications of the contents of experience. Were no evidence of God discerned, doubt would be displaced by indifference.[2]

But those who profit by the theistic teaching of nature, and strive to make the most of it, are never really satisfied with the knowledge of God thus acquired; and the belief that God does not leave men groping, but supernaturally reveals Himself and His purposes, is not only very general but inevitable.[3] Whether, and to what extent, God has thus revealed His nature and designs to the heathen need not con-

[1] Psa. xix. 1–6; Acts xiv. 17; Rom. i. 20. The fathers give abundant acknowledgments of this. Cf. the passages cited by Illingworth, in *Divine Immanence*, pp. 41–44.

[2] On the subject of doubt, see ch. iii. § 9, below.

[3] Macculloch, *Comparative Theol.*, pp. 293 *et seq.*

cern us at this point.[1]   In any case the only authentic
and really satisfying self-manifestation of God is
that which is brought to our knowledge by the Church
of Christ, and by the Sacred Scriptures [2] which the
Church has preserved for our use. The higher and
more definite knowledge of God thus made available
does not in fact come to all men, but only to those
who are reached by Christian teaching, and who come
under the influence of a Christian environment. Men
acquire the Christian idea of God variously — by
early instruction or by subsequent contact with Christianity. But, however acquired, it is the Christian
idea of God that alone enables men to fill out and interpret correctly the idea of God which is derived from
natural experience. Supernatural revelation is the
clear light by which to discern more accurately the
teaching of nature.

§ 9. Intelligent thinkers are naturally and reasonably impelled to formulate the contents of their
knowledge and belief in precise and more or less
philosophical terms. Their idea of God is one which,
if taken seriously, must determine their view of life in
all its manifold ramifications. It is inevitable, therefore, that attempts should be made to define this idea
as adequately and precisely as possible. Speaking
summarily, the idea of God is formulated in three
ways: by way of causation, negation and eminence.

Thus, by way of causation, the nature and attri-

[1] Cf. § 3, above.
[2] Cf. Acts xvii. 23; 1 Thess. iv. 5; Ephes. iii. 9; Rom. iii. 2.

butes of God are inferred from the nature of His operations, whether in the natural order or in the supernatural. By way of negation men refuse to predicate external limitations or finite attributes of God. By way of eminence every attribute which the way of causation leads men to predicate of God is described as supremely perfect and infinite, transcending the finite terms and forms of thought by which our conceptions are limited.[1]

The idea of God thus derived, and thus formulated, is a finite idea and anthropomorphic; but it is a true idea of the infinite and triune God. Its truth is confirmed by its working value, by the multitude of problems which it solves, and by the mental and spiritual emancipation which is enjoyed by those who adopt it and guide their lives by its light. The personal experience of those who with divine assistance accept and apply the Christian idea of God dissolves doubt and develops belief into knowledge.

[1] Cf. ch. x. § 3 *fin.*, below, where references are given.

CHAPTER II

THEOLOGICAL AGNOSTICISM

I. *Nature and History*

§ 1. Theological agnosticism is the theory which asserts the *a priori* impossibility of any knowledge on man's part of the nature of God. If such a position is valid, the attempt to develop a scientific theology is obviously futile. It is desirable, therefore, before undertaking to treat of the doctrine of God, to consider the arguments which are advanced in support of agnosticism.[1]

The late Herbert Spencer was the leading expounder of the theory. He says that "the Power which the

---

[1] On agnosticism see, *Introd. to Dog. Theol.*, ch. v. Pt. II; Flint, *Agnosticism; Christianity and Agnosticism* (containing papers by Wace, Huxley and others); Calderwood, *Philos. of the Infinite;* Fisher, *Grounds of Theistic and Christian Belief*, pp. 72–88; Martineau, *Study of Religion*, Bk. I; Ladd, *Philos. of Knowledge;* Ward, *Naturalism and Agnosticism;* R. A. Armstrong, *Agnosticism and Theism;* Baldwin, *Dic. of Philos.*, s. vv. "Epistemology" and "Scepticism"; *Catholic Encyclopedia*, s. v. "Agnosticism"; Spalding, *Religion, Agnosticism, and Education.*

Among pro-agnostic classics are Kant, *Critique of Pure Reason;* Sir Wm. Hamilton, *Discussions on Philos.*, and *Lecs. on Metaphysics;* Mansel, *Limits of Religious Thought*, and *Philos. of the Conditioned;* Spencer, *First Principles;* Leslie Stephens, *An Agnostic's Apology;* Ritschl, *Theologie und Metaphysik;* Prof. James, *Pragmatism.*

universe manifests to us is inscrutable." [1] He adds, "Very likely there will ever remain a need to give shape to that indefinite sense of an Ultimate Existence, which forms the basis of our intelligence. We shall always be under the necessity of contemplating it as *some* mode of being; that is — of representing it to ourselves in some form of thought, however vague. And we shall not err in doing this so long as we treat every notion we thus frame as merely a symbol. [2] . . . By continually seeking to know and being continually thrown back with a deepening conviction of the impossibility of knowing, we may keep alive the consciousness that it is alike our highest wisdom and our highest duty to regard that through which all things exist as The Unknowable." [3]

The word "agnostic" was coined by Thomas Huxley to describe a different position, although one which is equally fatal to theology. He says, "Positively the [agnostic] principle may be expressed: In matters of intellect, follow your reason as far as it will take you, without regard to any other consideration. And negatively: In matters of intellect do not pretend that

[1] *First Principles*, p. 39. In his 1st edition he said "altogether inscrutable."

[2] Spencer uses the word "symbol" to signify a term which, like the algebraic x, stands for an unknown quantity. It is not *descriptive*. In theology a symbolic term is treated as descriptive of reality, but not as adequately so. It is true so far as it goes, and permanently so; but that which is signified transcends our description of it. The symbol becomes untrue when considered to be adequate to the reality. Cf. p. 47, and ch. x, § 4, below.

[3] *First Prins.*, pp. 96, 97.

conclusions are certain which are not demonstrated or demonstrable." [1] It ought to be added that Huxley was speaking with reference to theistic knowledge; and that he was not intending to assert the unknowability of God in the abstract, but the absence of rational demonstration of His being and attributes. It ought also to be added that he viewed theistic problems from a purely intellectual standpoint, excluding from consideration the emotional and volitional factors of knowledge.

Romanes defines the two kinds of agnosticism in a summary way. He says, "By its originator . . . [the word] was coined to signify an attitude of reasoned ignorance touching everything that lies beyond the sphere of sense perception — a professed inability to found valid belief on any other basis. . . . But the other, and perhaps more popular sense in which the word is now employed, is as the correlative of Mr. H. Spencer's doctrine of the Unknowable . . . . implying important negative knowledge that, if there be a God, we know this much about Him — that He cannot reveal Himself to men. *Pure* Agnosticism is as defined by Huxley.[2]

Huxley did not really escape from the combination of *a priori* scepticism and dogmatism which is to be

---

[1] *Christianity and Agnosticism*, p. 43. The essay in question appeared originally under the title of *Agnosticism*, in the *Nineteenth Century*, Feb., 1889. Flint, in *Agnosticism*, pp. 3–8, discusses the word "Agnostic." Its etymology is open to criticism. There is no corresponding Greek ἀγνώστικος.

[2] *Thoughts on Religion*, pp. 113, 114.

seen in Spencer's position; but, so far as his attitude
is distinctive — one of waiting for purely rational
demonstration — it is a form of rationalism, of which
we have treated in our *Introduction to Dogmatic Theology*.[1] It is also closely related to modern doubt, of
which we shall treat briefly in a subsequent chapter.
It is the agnosticism of Herbert Spencer which demands consideration at this point[2]

§ 2. Spencerian agnosticism was not created by
Herbert Spencer, but has a long history.[3] It was
partly anticipated in ancient scepticism, and its modern history may be said to begin with Descartes and
Locke. *Descartes* (1596–1650 A.D.) adopted the principle of accepting nothing as true which is not evidently known to be true, all doubt being excluded.
All presuppositions, he urged, must be excluded, and
we must prove all things with mathematical certainty. Inasmuch as the bulk of human knowledge
is incapable of being thus established, his position

[1] Ch. iv. § 3.

[2] Theological agnosticism, as maintained by Spencer, is negatively dogmatic, and denies the possibility of acquiring knowledge
of God. Religious doubt, on the other hand, is undogmatic, and is
a state of uncertainty as to the truth of theistic and religious doctrines. On doubt, see below, ch. iii. § 9.

[3] For the history of philosophical scepticism and agnosticism,
consult Flint, *Agnosticism*, chh. iii, iv, xi; Spalding, *Religion, Agnosticism and Education*, pp. 58–78; *Church Quarterly Review*, July,
1897, Art. I. Also the standard Histories of Philosophy; and A. S.
Farrar, *Hist. of Free Thought;* Hurst, *Hist. of Rationalism;* Armstrong, *Agnosticism and Theism in the Nineteenth Century;* Baldwin,
Dic. of Philos., s. v. "Epistemology."

3

lent itself to scepticism and modern doubt. He was also responsible for endeavouring to exclude the will from all cognitive processes — an endeavour which psychology does not justify." [1]

John Locke (1632–1704 A.D.) erred in a similar way when he initiated a modern practice of investigating the cognitive processes in mutual isolation. Inasmuch as the mind always operates as a whole, and in a complex unity, this method is unscientific, and has in fact tended to obscure the validity of the higher mental operations. Locke himself thought that the formation of general notions or concepts was involved in difficulty. A general notion, he urged, must represent all the members of the class of things considered. In order to do this, he thought that we must form a mental image which at once agrees with each individual member of the class and merges these many individuals into an individual image. [2]

Bishop Berkeley (1685–1753 A.D.) based upon Locke's position a denial of the possibility of forming valid general notions. No mental picture which we can frame, he urged, can truly represent all the individuals of a class. [3]

---

[1] On Descartes' position, see Ueberweg, *Hist. of Philos.*, Vol. II. pp. 41–55; Bowen, *Modern Philos.*, chh. ii, iii; Ladd, *Philos. of Knowledge*, pp. 57–60.

[2] See his *Essay on the Human Understanding*, Bk. III. ch. iii. § 11 and Bk. IV. ch. vii. § 9. On his position see *Introd. to Dog. Theol.*, ch. v. § 6; *Church Quarterly Review*, July, 1897, pp. 268–270. Locke's theory of knowledge is the parent of modern empiricism. See on this subject, Baldwin, *Dic. of Philos.*, *s. v.* "Empiricism."

[3] See his *Prins. of Human Knowledge*, Introd. Berkeley's posi-

The logical conclusion of such reasoning is a denial of the validity of generalized knowledge — that is, of the higher knowledge which is gained by reflection upon the sensible data of experience. Knowledge is practically limited to individual sense perceptions and to the products of memory and imagination based upon them. A mistaken assumption vitiates the position of both Locke and Berkeley — that a general notion is a mental image. An image is necessarily individual in its characteristics, and can only represent an individual. A concept is not an image, but a generalization of the attributes common to the members of a class. It represents individuals only in these common attributes. It is similar to a law in science, and is the symbol of generalized *knowledge* of things rather than of the things themselves in their several totalities. Their function is not to merge individuals into one, but to facilitate thought concerning what the individuals considered possess in common. A concept brings many individuals into unity of *thought* — not into unity of an *image*.[1]

Having eliminated all generalized knowledge, Berkeley proceeded, with rare persuasiveness, to deny the substantiality of the outer world, on the ground that

tion is discussed in the *Church Quarterly Review*, July, 1897, referred to in the previous note. Cf. Bowen, *Modern Philos.*, ch. ix.

[1] Cf. *Introd. to Dog. Theol.*, p. 121; Porter, *Human Intellect*, p. 392; Mansel, *Prolegom. Logica.*, pp, 77, 78. The importance for theism of distinguishing images and concepts appears in Calderwood's *Philos. of the Infinite*, pp. 25–27; and Porter's *Human Intellect*, §§ 369, 370.

substance is a purely subjective illusion which cannot be represented by an image. All that can thus be represented consists of sensible impressions.[1]

David Hume (1711–1776 A.D.) applied the logic of Locke and Berkeley inwardly, and denied that we can know the soul, as distinguished from the stream of subjective processes which we really perceive. The soul also is incapable of being represented by any image.[2] By the same logic he arrived at a denial of any knowledge of the principle of causation,[3] and formulated a sceptical philosophy wherein the subject-matter of human knowledge was limited to disconnected sensible impressions and their pale copies in memory and imagination. Human knowledge is thus treated as an uninterpretable stream of particulars.

§ 3. *Immanuel Kant* (1724–1804 A.D.) was moved

[1] Cf. *Introd. to Dog. Theol.*, ch. v. § 7. He first set forth his view in *New Theory of Vision*, 1709. He succeeded in establishing once for all the fact that sense perception is largely an acquired faculty. His idealism is combated with rare clearness of argument by Jevons, *Evolution*, chh. iv, v. A. K. Rogers, *Religious Conception of the World*, pp. 151–175, follows Berkeley in regarding the world as exhibiting the working of God's mind upon our intelligence. His theistic argument is based throughout upon Berkeley, who cannot be charged with a sceptical purpose. Cf. Bowen, *Modern Philos.*, pp. 141–153.

[2] His principles are discussed by Ladd, *Philos. of Knowl.*, pp. 65–69; and Flint, *Agnosticism*, pp. 136–168, 300–309. His attitude towards theism is considered in Caldecott, *Philos. of Relig.*, pp. 374–377; and Pfleiderer, *Philos. of Relig.*, Vol. I, pp. 127–133. Touching his denial of knowledge of the soul, see Flint, *op. cit.*, 144–146.

[3] Cf. Flint, *op. cit.*, pp. 152–154. Hume's view of causation is discussed in relation to theistic argument in ch. v. § 4, below.

by the scepticism of Hume to undertake a thorough investigation of the cognitive faculties.[1] The analysis which he undertook has thrown much light upon psychological problems; but his epistemology is not in accord with the testimony of consciousness. In some respects Kant was successful in showing the fallacies of Hume's position, but he originated a new form of scepticism — one which has proved far more insidious and dangerous than that of Hume.

Proceeding from an *a priori* standpoint, he distinguished in sense perception the *phenomenon*, or sense impression, and the *noumenon*, or thing in itself, to which the phenomenon is referred by the perceiving mind.[2] In the phenomenon, again, he distinguished the *matter*, which corresponds to the sensation in its indeterminate aspect, and the *form*, which corresponds to the relations under which we perceive the phenomenon. All phenomena are perceived as under the forms of space and time, which are called the forms of intuition. Considered simply as an *a priori* analysis of the inseparable aspects of sense intuition, this is suggestive and unobjectionable. His mistake con-

[1] In his *Critique of Pure Reason*, which is translated by Meiklejohn (Bohn Lib.) and by Max Müller. Cf. Jno. Watson, *Philos. of Kant as Contained in Extracts;* Baldwin, *Dic. of Philos., s. vv.* "Kantianism" and "Kant's Terminology"; Bowen, *Modern Philos.,* chh. x–xiv. Criticisms are innumerable. Cf. Flint, *Agnosticism,* pp. 168–238; Martineau, *Religion,* Bk. I. chh. i, ii; Pfleiderer, *Philos. of Relig.,* Vol. I. pp. 147–195; Ladd, *Philos. of Knowl.,* pp. 73–89; and our own *Introd. to Dog. Theol.,* ch. v. § 9.

[2] Cf. Baldwin, *Dic. of Philos., s. vv.* "Noumenon," "Phenomenon," and "Thing."

sisted in regarding the phenomenon and noumenon, on the one hand, and the matter and form of phenomena, on the other, as separable. He maintained that we never perceive noumena, or things in themselves, but phenomena only, or subjective sensations. The forms of intuition he considered to be purely subjective. We perceive phenomena as spatial and temporal simply because our minds are so constituted that they mould the sensations which they receive into such forms. That consciousness testifies to our perception of objects which are in their own nature spatial and temporal is certain, but Kant maintained that this testimony is erroneous, that we do not at all perceive objective things in themselves, and that the forms under which we perceive phenomena are purely subjective and illusory. Such a position is obviously based upon *a priori* grounds, and upon a sceptical treatment of the testimony of consciousness.

Kant deals in the same *a priori* and arbitrary way with the understanding, or interpretive judgment. Mistakenly assuming that the understanding acts separately from and subsequently to sense intuition — its activity is in fact an essential element of sense intuition — he teaches that the understanding imposes certain *a priori* relations upon the results of sense intuition in order to make them intelligible. The judgments of the understanding which are thus arrived at are reduced to certain ultimate categories of the understanding. These consist of four species, viz., quantity, quality, relation and modality; and each of these species is divided into three sub-species. Like the forms of intuition, these categories are subjective, and afford no warrant, he maintains, for asserting any knowledge of things in themselves.

He proceeds to theorize concerning the reason; by which he means the faculty by use of which the mind endeavours to transcend the data of experience. Its results are conclusions which are regulated, he says, by three transcendental ideas, derived on *a priori* grounds from the three forms of the syllogism. These ideas are the soul, the world, and God. They are assumptions merely; and, although unavoidable, are not to be regarded as having objective or cognitive validity. They are not discoverable in experience, but are subjective postulates imposed by the mind as regulative principles of thought.[1] Thus Kant falls into the fallacy of treating the very equipment of the mind for knowing as a limitation, and as a reason for considering its highest activities to be grounded in sophism.

Kant does not remove the sceptical effect of his theory by his doctrine of the practical reason,[2] wherein he bases theistic certainty upon moral imperatives. A basis of belief that is denied validity in the sphere of rational cognition affords no refuge from scepticism; and would not have been thought to do so, if Kant

[1] As if human thought could be trusted if its regulative principles were without cognitive value! Hamilton saw that Kant was inconsistent here, *Discussions on Philos.*, p. 91, note.

[2] Given chiefly in his *Critique of Practical Reason.*

had not regarded the mind as broken up into more
or less separate and independent compartments. The
so-called "pure reason" and "practical reason" are
but aspects and elements of one mind, and cannot
be correctly criticised except as interiorly related,
and as conditioned for their validity by the harmonious
exercise of every psychical faculty. The faculties
are not separate organs but mutually related elements
in every form of psychical activity.[1]

§ 4. In Scotland *Thomas Reid* (1710–1796 A.D.)
had undertaken to meet the scepticism of Hume by
vindicating the validity of "common sense".[2] By
this he meant, on the one hand, the knowledge possessed, or thought to be possessed, by men in general,
and by which ordinary human life is controlled; and,
on the other hand, the universal capacity of men to
arrive at certain original and intuitive judgments
which are generally employed as the basis of deduction. In accepting the validity of these judgments
he pointed out the true refuge from scepticism. But
his language was not always clear or consistent, and
the influence of Kant robbed his work of effect upon
his successors.

This appears in the position of *Sir William Hamilton* (1788–1856 A.D.), the most eminent and learned
thinker of his day. He made use of much of Reid's

[1] Cf. *Introd. to Dog. Theol.*, ch. iv. §§ 4, 5; and the references there
given.

[2] His chief works are *Inquiry into the Human Mind on the Principles of Common Sense*, 1763; *On the Intellectual Powers of Man*,
1785; *On the Active Powers of Man*, 1788.

terminology, but succumbed to Kant's influence in just those points wherein that influence is productive of scepticism.[1] Accepting Kant's divorce between the pure and the practical reason, he sharpened the antithesis between faith and knowledge.[2] All knowledge is relative, which means that we know nothing except as it is related to our consciousness. This, he urged, involves the conclusion that in order to know we must conceive in finite terms. We cannot conceive of or know the infinite and unconditioned, for to think is to condition. But, he adds, although we cannot know the Infinite, it is, must, and ought to be believed by us.[3] The notion of the Infinite which he employs

---

[1] His *Discussions on Philosophy* and *Lecs. on Metaphysics* are of chief importance. His position is criticised in Flint, *Agnosticism*, pp. 604–621; *Church Quarterly Review*, July, 1897, pp. 281-284; J. S. Mill, *Exam. of Sir Wm. Hamilton's Philos.;* Calderwood, *Philos. of the Infinite.*

[2] Cf. *Introd. to Dog. Theol.*, ch. v. § 10. Also S. Harris, *Self-Revelation of God*, pp. 97–99. The attitude of the Roman Catholic Church on the relations between faith and knowledge is expounded in Wilhelm and Scannell, *Manual*, Vol. I. pp. 138–141. Cf. Fairbairn, *Philos. of the Christian Religion*, pp. 201, 202. St. Anselm's famous principle, that we believe in order to know, is worthy of note, *Proslog.*, ch. i. *fin.*

[3] Knowledge is both the presupposition and goal of belief. A belief which cannot be thought to be warranted by existing knowledge soon dies; and men do not persist in belief when its verification is seen to be impossible even in the life to come. Thus belief is in line with knowledge, and is estimated as to its validity from the standpoint of knowledge. This appears in the fact that when knowledge and belief conflict, belief conforms to knowledge; and what is seen ultimately to be unknowable is not a proper subject-matter of either belief or unbelief, but of unconcern. Cf. Baldwin,

is of an abstract infinite — the unlimited. As Henry Calderwood pointed out, this is not the Infinite with which theology is concerned, but unreal.[1] To conceive is not to condition the object of conception. To say so is to confuse the limitations of our conception with the limitations of their objects. There is such a thing as a conception which is at once true and inadequate to its object. There can be a finite conception of the Infinite.

Henry L. Mansel (1820–1871 A.D.) followed in Hamilton's wake, and limited all knowledge to conditioned or finite things. In his *Bampton Lectures*[2] he exhibited a formidable array of contradictions of thought and language, which he considered to be involved in endeavouring to conceive of the Infinite. Our conception of the Infinite is in reality, he urged, a negation of every positive object of thought. In short, he was handicapped by a false notion of the Infinite as the absolutely unlimited. The Infinite of Christian belief is not the unlimited. If it were it would be equivalent to the unreal. It is the Being whose limitations and determinations are wholly

Dic. of Philos., *s.v.* "Faith and Knowledge," by R. M. Wenley; Flint, *Agnosticism*, pp. 616–618.

[1] *Philos. of the Infinite*, pp. 76–98. Cf. S. Harris, *Self-Revel. of God*, pp. 210, 211; Pfleiderer, *Philos. of Relig.*, Vol. III. pp. 278–280; Martineau, *Religion*, Vol. I. pp. xii, xiii. Cf. also § 7, below.

[2] *The Limits of Religious Thought*. Expositions and criticisms of his position are to be found in Caldecott, *Philos. of Relig.*, pp. 405–410; Flint, *Agnosticism*, pp. 621–629; Boedder, *Natural Theol.*, pp. 214–232.

within His own essence. He is non-finite indeed, but this means that His limitations are not external. He is not dependent upon or conditioned by anything else than Himself to be what He is.[1]

Herbert Spencer (1820–1904 A.D.) found Mansel's philosophy convenient, and took over whole pages of his language *verbatim*. We need not repeat our description of his position.[2] It is enough at this point to say that in his hands the agnostic theory was employed as a means to harmonize theology and natural science by reducing the former to nullity. Theology, in his judgment, represents an effort to describe the unknowable — an effort which is none the less futile because instinctive and inevitable.

In the meantime other developments have tended to give agnosticism a strong hold on current thought. The empiricism of Hume has been accepted by many, and the view which limits knowledge to sensible phenomena is somewhat wide-spread. The marvelous success of the sciences which derive their data from such sources has increased the influence of empiricism.[3]

[1] See ch. x. § 5, below.

[2] See § 1 of this chapter. His position is criticised by Pfleiderer, *Philos. of Relig.*, Vol. I. pp. 157–160; Flint, *Agnosticism*, pp. 629–639; *Theism*, pp. 288-301; S. Harris, *Self-Revel. of God*, pp. 172–182; *Catholic Encyc.*, *s. v.* "Agnosticism," V; Martineau, *Religion*, Vol. I. pp. 124, 125; Caldecott, *Philos. of Relig.*, pp. 387–391. It has frequently been noted that Spencer's inconsistency in treating a Being whom nature *manifests* to us as unknowable is *naïve*. Spencer was a theist who failed to discover the fact, although his theism was abstract and inadequate. Cf. S. Harris, *Self-Revel. of God*, pp. 177–181.

[3] Physical sciences are concerned with the mechanical aspects of

The scientific claim of theology has been discredited among many by partisan and sectarian conflicts, and by the identification in popular estimation of the most fundamental theological dogmas with speculative theories and exploded shibboleths. The very rapid enlargement of the knowledge of nature which is now occurring has for the moment thrown theological propositions out of perspective; and many are mistaking this phenomenon for a demonstration that theology is not a department of knowledge, but a bundle of unverifiable conjectures concerning the unknown and unknowable.[1]

II. *Its Arguments*

§ 5. The arguments advanced in support of theological agnosticism are chiefly three: the relativity of all human knowledge; the anthropomorphic nature of our conceptions of God; and certain contradictions which are alleged to be involved in our notion of the Infinite and Absolute.

nature, and do not depend for their advance upon any conscious reckoning with theistic doctrine. They do indeed raise questions which theism alone can answer; but such answers belong to philosophy rather than to physical science. To one who acquires the habit of reducing the universe to order under mechanical generalizations, a theocentric philosophy may easily seem remote and even incredible. See Illingworth, *Reason and Relig.*, pp. 143–147; Tennant, in *Cambridge Theol. Essays*, pp. 57–99; Whetham, *Recent Devel. of Phys. Science*, pp. 15–20. Cf. p. 113, note 2, below.

[1] Ritschlianism, with its reduction of religious beliefs to the level of value-judgments (cf. *Introd. to Dog. Theol.*, pp. 23, 24, 37, 103), and Pragmatism, which identifies truth with practical value (cf. Prof. James, *Pragmatism*), illustrate powerful tendencies of the day.

(a) Hamilton asserts the relativity of human knowledge with reference respectively to things in themselves, to our consciousness, and to the objects of our knowledge.[1] Things in themselves, he maintains, cannot be known by us in the abstract, out of relation to other things, or independently of internal distinctions and external manifestations. This is obviously true. We know things only by virtue of the relations which they exhibit, and we are utterly unable to perceive anything or conceive of anything as wholly unrelated. But no agnostic inference is involved in such a contention. God is not, according to Christian conceptions, an unrelated or distinctionless being, nor do we profess to know Him otherwise than as manifesting Himself through His handiwork and as possessing attributes and internal distinctions which can be apprehended by us, although they transcend our capacity adequately to comprehend them.

Hamilton goes on to maintain that we can know nothing except, and so far, as it comes into relation to our perceiving minds. Things in themselves, therefore, considered apart from their relations to our consciousness, are utterly unknown.[2] This also is undeniable, when rightly understood, but it affords no basis for theological agnosticism. To assert knowl-

---

[1] See his *Lecs. on Metaph.*, Vol. I. pp. 61, 137–148. Flint, *Agnosticism*, pp. 607–610, thus distinguishes his various uses of the phrase "relativity of knowledge." Cf. Martineau, *Religion*, Bk. I. ch. iv; Baldwin, *Dic. of Philos.*, *s. v.* "Relativity of Knowledge."

[2] So also Mansel, whose language is accepted by Spencer, *First Prins.*, pp. 64, 65.

edge of anything is equivalent to asserting that it has come into a relation to our consciousness which may be described, on the one hand, as manifestation and, on the other, as cognition.[1] We know things as they are thus related to our consciousness, and things in themselves are not other than the things which we know in their relations to our minds. It is true that they are more than we know concerning them, but in discerning the relations of things to our own minds we discern the things themselves to the extent of these relations. We at least know them to be such things as are capable of being thus related to our consciousness — very important knowledge indeed.[2]

Finally, Hamilton asserts that our knowledge is

[1] It is a commonplace of theology that the knowledge of God is conditioned by His self-revelation to us, Rom. i. 19, 20. Knight shows, *Aspects of Theism*, pp. 142, 143, that to deny the knowability of God is to deny His capacity to reveal Himself as well as our ability to know Him. Gwatkin points out that revelation and discovery are correlative aspects of the process of manifestation, *Knowledge of God*, Vol. I. pp. 155–161.

[2] It was Kant who invented the conception of a *ding an sich*, wholly unrelated to our consciousness. See Baldwin, *Dic. of Philos.*, s. vv. "Thing" and "Noumenon." Things wholy unrelated to our consciousness cannot even be known to exist. The only things of which we can say anything, whether positively or negatively, are such as come in some manner into relation to our consciousness. Others may indeed know more about things than we know, but if we know them at all we know the same things that they know — things in themselves. The only conceivable basis for speaking of things in themselves is our possession of *some* knowledge of them. See Martineau, *Religion*, Vol. I. pp. 107–117; S. Harris, *Self-Revel. of God*, p. 80; Fisher, *Grounds of Belief*, pp. 82, 83.

relative in the sense that it is wholly phenomenal.[1]
This assertion is quite contrary to the data of experience, and cannot be maintained, except from an *a
priori* standpoint which reduces psychological data
to subjective illusion, and involves a thorough-going
scepticism which Hamilton himself repudiated. A
true psychology teaches us that phenomena constitute
the invariable conditions and the starting-point of
thought and cognition. But the very nature of phenomena, as intuitively perceived by the mind, is this,
that they are manifestations to us of objective realities.
They cannot be contemplated as having any reality
of their own except as implying more than mere phenomena, and as enabling and even compelling the mind
to transcend them. Phenomena in the abstract, that
is, phenomena which manifest no objects to us and
imply nothing but themselves, are never experienced.
They constitute the baseless fabric of a dream.[2]

The conclusion of the matter is that the relativity
of human knowledge cannot be employed with truth
or sound logic to support agnosticism. The precise
contrary is true. If human knowledge is necessarily
characterized by relativity, then this relativity, so far
from being an evidence of subjective illusion, is a

[1] In this he follows Kant. See Baldwin, *Dic. of Philos.*, *s. vv.*
"Noumenon" and "Phenomenon." Spencer urges the same view,
First Prins., pp. 57, 78.

[2] That in perceiving phenomena we know that something exists
which *appears* is conceded in effect by Spencer, *First Principles*, pp.
73, 74, 82, 83. Cf. Martineau, *Religion*, Vol. I. pp. 117–128; S.
Harris, *Self-Revel. of God*, pp. 75–77; Flint, *Agnosticism*, pp. 609, 610.

condition and criterion of the reality of such knowledge. To employ relativity in support of agnosticism
involves logically a repudiation of all human knowledge, that is, absolute scepticism; and this means the
nullification not only of theological knowledge, but
also of such knowledge as is required to give validity
to agnostic arguments.[1]

§ 6. (b) The second argument for theological agnosticism is that all human knowledge, in so far as it is
human, is necessarily anthropomorphic. What this
means is that the human mind is unable to frame
notions of anything except in the forms of its own
thinking; and that it can describe nothing except in
human terms. These forms of thought and these
terms are necessarily finite, and cannot transcend
human analogies or the contents of finite experience.
God must be conceived under such limitations; and,
however great we may believe God to be, we are
under the necessity, it is said, of conceiving Him as
an enlarged finite being. The element of finiteness
remains, so that what we think ourselves to know is
not the Infinite, but a finite image which we have mistakenly identified with the Infinite — a mere symbol
of what we can neither know nor imagine.[2]

That all our conceptions are anthropomorphic
cannot, of course, be intelligently gainsaid. As human
beings we must think, conceive and imagine human-

---

[1] See Martineau, *Religion*, Vol. I. pp. 126–128.

[2] Hume, *Dial. on Natural Relig.*, Pts. IV, V; Tyndal, *Fragments
of Science*, p. 523; Sir W. Hamilton, *Discussions on Philos.*, p. 14.

wise; and we can contemplate no reality whatever except through the windows of human forms of thought, forms of thought which are essentially finite and are conditioned by finite experience.[1] But two mistaken assumptions are involved in the agnostic inference, viz., that our conceptions are limited by the capacity of imagination; and that the finiteness of our conceptions reduces every reality of which we conceive to the same finite level.

We have already pointed out the fallacy of confusing conceiving with imagining.[2] Herbert Spencer makes this mistake when he urges that we cannot conceive of the universe as a totality because our imagination is unable to embrace in one mental picture the manifold attributes and contents of the cosmos.[3] The truth is that we conceive the universe not by

[1] Illingworth, *Personality*, Lec. i. note 2, pp. 219–222; Gwatkin, *Knowledge of God*, Vol. I. p. 45; Knight, *Aspects of Theism*, pp. 128–130. Knight calls attention to the need of preferring a higher rather than a lower anthropomorphism. Spencer violates this principle when he chooses to describe God in terms of power rather than of personality: See *Catholic Encyc.*, *s. v.* "Anthropomorphism." Some writers choose to call God "supra-personal." As Illingworth says, *Divine Immanence*, pp. 188, 189, this would be unobjectionable if it did not imply an exclusion of personality. The impersonal is inferior to the personal. Calling God supra-personal is equivalent to calling Him supra-highest. We call Him personal because we can in no other way avoid implying that He is inferior to ourselves. Cf. Martineau's distinction between *anthropo*morphism, *bio*morphism and *hylo*morphism, *Religion*, Vol. I. pp. 316, 317.

[2] See p. 19, above.

[3] *First Prins.*, ch. ii. We have discussed the difficulty in *Introd. to Dog. Theol.*, ch. v. § 6.

stretching our imagination but by bringing into unity of thought such attributes as experience and our reflection thereon show to be characteristic of the universe considered as a whole. The fact that we cannot frame a satisfactory mental picture of the universe, while it establishes the unimaginable vastness and complexity of the universe, does not nullify our knowledge that it possesses certain attributes, or our ability to form a true, although limited, conception of them. So it is with the Infinite. God cannot be imagined; and this is not, as in the case of the universe, because He is too vast for us to picture the whole of Him, but because the infinite Spirit has no figure, and therefore cannot be imaged. To conceive correctly in this case is to exclude every image. It is to think of God as possessed of certain attributes, but to think of these attributes as free from external limitations.[1] The Infinite is not the abstract unlimited of agnostic definition, but the non-finite, or that which is limited only by itself. Nor is the God of Christian theology an expanded image of the finite, but a Being of whom we think as possessing attributes which transcend all quantitative symbols. These symbols are, indeed, necessary windows through which to contemplate the Infinite, but we have no difficulty in distinguishing the reality which we conceive from the human forms of thought and description which we employ.[2]

[1] Cf. ch. x. § 5, below.

[2] That men have often failed to do this is true, but no such charge

The other fallacy appeared in Hamilton's proposition that "to think is to condition." It is true that human thinking is externally conditioned, and cannot result in conceptions that are adequate to or exhaustive of the external realities with which they are concerned. If their validity for knowledge depended upon their adequacy we should be unable to conceive of any object whatever, for no object can be conceived in its entirety. The mind is under no delusion here. We are conscious of the partial nature of all our conceptions, and this consciousness is part of the knowledge which is symbolized in our conceptions. Our knowledge, in brief, embraces not only the attributes and relations of things which are included in our conceptions of them, but also the truth that our knowledge even of what is most familiar to us is relative, limited, and inadequate to reality. And when we treat

can be made good against Christian theologians in general. The ancient *anthropomorphitae* constituted exceptions among Christian believers, and their position was regarded as heretical. See Smith and Wace, *Dic. of Christian Biog.*, *s. v.* "Anthropomorphitae." The fact is that Christian apologists were frequently engaged in criticising adversely the anthropomorphism of the pagans. See Martineau, *Religion*, Vol. I. pp. 313, 314. God is described anthropomorphically in many passages of Scripture, especially in the Old Testament. See Davidson, in Hastings' *Dic. of the Bible*, *s. v.* "God (in O T)," ii. But, as Sanday shows in the same work, *s. v.* "God (in N T)," a growing emphasis on divine transcendence led to the removal of anthropomorphic conceptions.

The term *anthropomorphism* originally meant attributing human shape to God. It has come misleadingly to include *anthropopathism* or attributing men's intellectual and moral attributes to Him. See Schurman, *Belief in God*, pp. 63, 64.

our conceptions as adequate measures of realities, we go contrary to the data supplied by our own consciousness. It is, therefore, utterly erroneous to maintain that nothing can be known which cannot be fully comprehended within our conceptions. No object of human knowledge is thus comprehended. All realities are known incipiently, but none the less truly; and there is no contradiction between what is comprehended in our conceptions and the larger content of the realities to which they refer. If human conceptions are symbolic — and they are all of such nature, — they are not for that reason inconsistent with anything in the realities which they describe, but, when rightly framed, constitute true knowledge so far as they go.[1]

§ 7. (c) This brings us to the third objection. Granting that we are able to know finite things in spite of the non-exhaustiveness of our conceptions of them, the agnostic contends that this is because they are finite. It is their finiteness which makes it possible for finite conceptions of them to be free from inherent contradiction. The case is different, it is urged, when

[1] On this objection see Flint, *Agnosticism*, pp. 610–613. Ladd says, *Philos. of Religion*, Vol. I. p. 314, "The fundamental error . . . of dogmatic or sceptical agnosticism is the assumption that the so-called categories, or constitutional forms of human cognition, are inescapable limitations, if not the fruitful source of illusion, for all attempts at knowledge." Cf. our treatment of divine inscrutability, ch. x. §§ 4, 7, below; and the references there given, which establish the contention that catholic theologians are fully aware of the inadequacy of our idea of God.

we try to conceive of the Infinite and Absolute. All human conceptions postulate limitations and relations. Their very nature is such that the attributes which they comprehend constitute so many limitations and relations which are hypothecated as inhering in the things conceived. Things are, therefore, invariably conceived as finite and related. To conceive the Infinite and Absolute is a self-contradictory and obviously unthinkable process.[1]

The reply to this is not far to seek. We only have to remember that we are concerned with the knowability of a real Being, the living God, to perceive that we are under no necessity of proving that we can know the abstract unlimited and unrelated. In brief, agnostics — who profess to know nothing of God — postulate a very dogmatic proposition about Him which is true neither to reality, nor to the conceptions of Him, the validity of which is being considered. A thing that is wholly unlimited or wholly unrelated is, of course, wholly unknown and also wholly unreal. Such a conception is not only pure negation, but pure nonsense. The doctrine that God is infinite and absolute has never signified in theology any such vacancy of thought. The Infinite and Absoute to whom theistic evidence points, and whom Christians claim to know, is not the abstract unlimited and unrelated, but the self-limited or self-existent and self-sufficient Being. The term infinite is not the negative

---

[1] Herbert Spencer, *First Prins.*, § 26, who echoes Sir W. Hamilton and Hy. Mansel.

of *every* limitation, but of the limitations which characterize finite things — of *external* limitations. Similarly, the term absolute does not signify the negation of relations, but perfection and the freedom of God from dependence upon relations *to other beings* in being what He is. External relations are not a part of His essence, but arise from His voluntary operation in creating the universe. Nothing else can exist which is not dependent upon Him; and, therefore, if a universe exists at all, the relations existing between God and the cosmos become necessary. But this necessity does not arise simply from the nature of God. It is also a result of His will. He is, therefore, in His own essence, absolute.[1]

It can be seen that the Infinite and Absolute, when defined in accordance with the accepted doctrine of God, are not self-contradictory notions, but readily conceived by all who make reasonable efforts to learn what they signify. If we can form an intelligible

[1] See Calderwood, *Philos. of the Infinite*, pp. 76–98; Dorner, *Christian Doctrine*, Vol. I. pp. 198–200; Pfleiderer, *Philos. of Relig.*, Vol. III. pp. 278–280; Max Müller, *Origin of Relig.*, pp. 26–28; S. Harris, *Self-Revel. of God*, pp. 172–174, 210–212. Bishop Gore says, *The New Theol. and the Old Religion*, p. 57, that "the universe does not exhaust Him [God] or limit Him. Beyond the universe and independent of it, He is in Himself, limited by nothing outside Himself, in the eternal fellowship of His own being." He adds in a footnote, "It is often said, and may be truly said, that God is infinite, or 'unlimited.' But it is more exact to say that God is self-limited: limited by nothing except the eternal law and character of His own being." We return to this in connection with the subject of divine attributes, in ch. x. § 5, below.

conception of the finite, we can with equal facility
conceive of the Infinite. These terms are correlatives,
and their meaning consists in their mutual distinction.
We conceive of neither except from the point of view
of our conception of the other. And our conception
is as truly relative and partial in the one case as in
the other. In other words we do not conceive of
either in its full reality, but of both in so far as their
attributes are comprehended in our conceptions. The
same is true of the Absolute and the conditioned. Each
is known as distinguished from the other, and to
distinguish two correlatives is to know somewhat of
both.[1] The problem, if there be one, is not how to
conceive of the Infinite and Absolute, but how to
vindicate our alleged knowledge that a Being *exists*
whose nature is rightly described by such terms.
This is the task of theism. It signifies much for
the success of theism that Spencer, the modern
apostle of agnosticism, acknowledges the necessity
of postulating a Power from which all things proceed.[2]

Much has been said as to the impossibility of conceiving of the Infinite as personal without hypothecating the existence of a limiting non-ego. We shall

[1] See Max Müller, *Origin of Relig.*, pp. 33–48; Knight, *Aspects of
Theism*, pp. 135–141; Flint, *Agnosticism*, pp. 614–616; Baldwin,
Dic. of Philos. s. vv. "Infinite (the) and the Finite"; "Finite";
"Relative (and Absolute)"; *Catholic Encyc., s. v.* "Absolute";
Royce, *Conception of God*, pp. 48, 49.

[2] Cf. S. Harris, *Self-Revel. of God*, pp. 177–181; Martineau, *Religion*, p. 124.

consider this objection in its appropriate place when we treat of divine personality.[1]

III. *Its Fallacies*

§ 8. The fallacies of agnosticism have been indicated to some extent in summarizing its history. But it is desirable to exhibit them systematically.

(*a*) First of all, agnostic arguments are largely of an *a priori* nature. No serious effort is made to discover what human knowledge is in the concrete, or what in practice has to be treated as knowledge in order to get on in life, and in order to pursue scientific investigation.[2] Knowledge is conceived as requiring for its validity certain conditions which in fact are never present in human experience. It is forgotten that knowledge consists of the data of experience and cannot be described correctly except in the terms of experience. We discover what knowledge is by actual knowing, and there is nothing within our experience with which to compare it, except itself. We have to start with the fact that we know, and a sound philosophy of knowledge assumes that the knowledge which we actually experience, and which all men experience in the same manner, is knowledge.[3] The alternative is

[1] See ch. x. § 8, below.

[2] Kant's separation between the pure and the practical reason has had much to do with this.

[3] Porter, *Human Intellect*, § 46; Flint, *Agnosticism*, pp. 34, 35, 336–348; Schurman, *Belief in God*, pp. 27, 28; Newman, *Grammar of Assent*, pp. 331, 332. Even Hamilton says, *Lecs. on Metaph.*, Vol. II. p. 122, "We know and can know nothing *a priori* of what is possible

complete scepticism. If the kind of knowledge which we are conscious of possessing is not real knowledge, we have no knowledge whatever—not even the knowledge that would enable us to affirm an agnostic position.

There is, of course, such a thing as human error. Experience teaches us that we sometimes think that we know when we do not. It is inevitable, therefore, that we should seek for some subjective criterion by which to distinguish between knowledge and illusion. But the criterion is not abstract or *a priori*, — not the fulfilment of conditions evolved by *a priori* speculation, — but concrete and empirical. It is the agreement of alleged knowledge in given instances with what has been ascertained to be the normal methods of knowledge in general.

To give one illustration. If certain knowledge is found to be relative, partial, and symbolic, it is not thereby proved to be spurious; for we find that all human knowledge is of that nature. If knowledge which is relative and symbolic is not knowledge, human knowledge has never been experienced, and the deepest convictions of the human mind are the purest illusion.

or impossible to mind, and it is only by observation and generalization *a posteriori* that we can ever hope to attain insight into the question."

All knowledge begins with undemonstrated assumptions; but, as Martineau says, *Religion*, p. 128, "To demand *a reason* for assent to a primary belief is to insist that it shall not be primary, but secondary: and the absence of this self-contradictory condition can disturb no rational mind with idealistic doubt." Cf. our *Introd. to Dog. Theol.*, ch. v. Pt. I.

There is also an objective criterion of knowledge. It is the practical or working value of what we think ourselves to know, when treated as a basis of investigation and practice.[1] The point to be emphasized is that whether the criterion employed is subjective or objective, it is not derived from *a priori* speculation, but from the data of knowledge itself, the testimony of consciousness.

§ 9. (*b*) This brings us to the second fallacy; which is the inconsistency involved in making dogmatic assertions upon a sceptical basis. It is an evidence of the futility of scepticism that it cannot escape inconsistency in any form. If it impugns the validity of the normal testimony of consciousness at one point, it is deprived of reasonable warrant for accepting such testimony at other points. In brief, partial agnosticism, in order to be logical, must issue in complete scepticism. But complete scepticism is self-destructive, for it invalidates all affirmations and denials whatsoever. If human knowledge cannot be asserted, then such knowledge as enables one to assert the sceptical position is illusory. The sceptic has sawed off the branch upon which he sits.[2]

---

[1] Ladd says, *Philos. of Relig.*, p. 600, "The most nearly final test which man can have, or which he can ever conceive, is essentially the same as the corresponding test in any other [than religious] realm of truth. It is the completeness and self-consistency of the answer which the conception of Reality gives to the total experience of the subject." Cf. our *Introd. to Dog. Theol.*, p. 109; and *Authority, Eccles. and Biblical*, ch. i. §§ 18, 19.

[2] Cf. Jevons, *Evolution*, p. 173; Flint, *Agnosticism*, pp. 254–295;

The application of what we have said is not difficult. Human experience in general assures us that
sense intuitions involve consciousness of perceiving
and knowing external realities. It also assures us
that the same consciousness of knowledge is present,
and ineradicable, in necessary and normal judgments
of the understanding and in rational perception of
the necessary implicates and postulates of experience
and thought. These experiences are organically related, and their validity as cognitions is known by us
upon one and the same basis — the testimony of
consciousness. If that testimony is illusory in any
one of these fundamental particulars, it is trustworthy
in none. *A priori* distinctions, such as Kant was so
skilful in formulating, cannot nullify such testimony,
except upon the basis of a scepticism that is as fatal
to his position as it is to our own.[1]

§ 10. (*c*) The mistake of Kant, one that is by no
means confined to him, is his attempt to criticise the
cognitive faculties apart from other psychical faculties
and in mutual isolation. He treats them as if they
were so many separate and self-sufficient organs of
the soul, as if sense intuition, the understanding, and

Knight, *Aspects of Theism*, pp. 138, 139; Royce, *Conception of God*,
pp. 18–22; Schurman, *Belief in God*, p. 32; Martineau, *Religion*, Vol.
I. pp. 71, 128.   Royce says, *Conception of God*, p. 46, "People think
it very modest to say: We cannot know what Absolute Reality is.
They forget that to make this assertion implies — unless one is using
idle words without sense — that one knows what the term 'Absolute
Reality' means."

[1] Cf. Calderwood, *Philos. of the Infin.*, pp. 22–24.

the pure reason were what they are independently of each other. This is to treat them as something else than what we are conscious of their being. Our experience of them teaches that they are aspects of one indivisible mind — distinguishable indeed, but never observed as exercised independently or self-sufficiently. Sense intuition is an act of a judging and rationalizing intelligence; and judgments of the understanding and postulates of the reason are both invariably involved. Every judgment of the understanding is conditioned by sense intuitions, whether immediate or represented by memory and imagination; and is regulated by the postulates of higher reason. These postulates, in turn, are the validating conditions and invariable implicates of intuition and judgment.[1]

Nor is this all. The human intelligence is but one aspect of psychical functioning, in which feelings and volitions are necessarily involved as inseparable conditions and aspects. We cognize after the manner of agents who will and feel in the very act of cognition. Pure intellect is a fiction, and when cognitive processes are criticised as if independent of feeling and will, they are criticised under misapprehension. They are treated for what they are not. The subjective criterion of knowledge is not the self-sufficiency of the intellect considered in isolation, but the normal

[1] Martineau, *Religion*, Vol. I. pp. 117–123; Pfleiderer, *Philos. of Relig.*, Vol. I. p. 171; Flint, *Agnosticism*, pp. 190, 191, 193, 194, 197, 231, 232, 234, 235.

working of a feeling, willing, and cognizing soul considered in relation to knowledge.[1]

§ 11. (d) Finally, agnostics err seriously in treating the characteristics of the mind which constitute
its equipment for knowledge as so many reasons for
suspecting its capacity to know. It is obvious, of
course, that, whatever may be the equipment of a
finite mind for knowledge, such equipment will constitute a limiting condition of knowledge. If we are
to know anything we must know in manners and
under conditions which are determined by our mental
equipment. But it is clearly fallacious to transfer
the conditions of our knowing to the objects of our
knowledge, and to infer that because we know only
under certain conditions, therefore, we know only
those things which are similarly conditioned in themselves. We know under conditions, but this does not

[1] Psychologists now show a tendency to repudiate the psychological distinction between faculties. V. F. Storr says, *Devel. and Divine
Purpose*, p. 277, "The days of a facultative or departmental psychology are numbered." His meaning is less radical than such a
proposition appears to imply. It is neither necessary nor desirable
to repudiate the term "faculty," so long as we remember that it does
not signify a separate or independent organ or function. That the
capacities of the soul in knowing, feeling, and willing are distinct is
as certain as that they are never exercised in mutual isolation or
independence: Cf. *Introd. to Dog. Theol.*, ch. iv. §§ 4, 5. See also, on
the indissoluble unity of all psychical activities, R. C. Moberly, *Reason and Relig.*, pp. 91–93; Illingworth, *Divine Immanence*, pp. 59–73;
Reason and Revel., pp. 44–54; Romanes, *Thoughts on Relig.*, pp.
140–147; Ladd, *Philos. of Relig.*, ch. x; Flint, *Theism*, pp. 68–71;
Caldecott, in *Cambridge Theol. Essays*, p. 105 (cf. pp. 110–123). Cf.
pp. 69, 70, below.

mean that we know things as subject in themselves
to such conditions. We know things as transcending
the conditions under which we know them. What
is conditioned is the relation in which, and the extent
to which, we can know them. The sum of the matter
is that subjective limitation in knowledge, when seen
to inhere in all human knowledge, cannot be interpreted as meaning subjective illusion without neces-
sitating logically the acceptance of a complete and
self-destructive scepticism.[1]

§ 12. We now proceed to sum up the position to
which Christian theologians are committed, as against
theological agnosticism and every type of destructive
scepticism.

(a) First of all, the knowledge of God is spiritual.
The natural man, St. Paul says, "receiveth not the
things of the Spirit of God: for they are foolishness
unto him; and he cannot know them, because they
are spiritually examined." [2] "Spiritually" means, of
course, by the aid of divine grace, and with a right
ordering of the affections and the will in relation to
the object of knowledge.[3] The attitude of the soul
has scientific value.

(b) But, while men cannot attain to the knowledge
of God without divine assistance, it is not to be for-

[1] Martineau, *Religion*, p. 116; S. Harris, *Self-Revel. of God*, pp.
77-80; V. F. Storr, *Devel. and Divine Purpose*, p. 206. Cf. our
Introd. to Dog. Theol., pp. 127, 128.

[2] 1 Cor. ii. 14. Cf. *Introd. to Dog. Theol.*, ch. v. §§ 12, 13.

[3] Jerem. xxix. 13, "Ye shall seek Me, and find Me, when ye shall
search for Me with all your heart."

gotten that such assistance is available for all, and that the knowledge of God thus made possible is human. It is knowledge that is gained by the faculties which we employ in acquiring other knowledge, and is acquired in manners that conform to the laws of all human cognition. When we use a glass to perceive objects that are invisible to the naked eye we do not abandon or subvert the use of our eyes. Similarly the light from above that enlightens our minds to examine spiritual things does not displace or alter the operation of our natural reason. The laws of natural reason retain their validity in the knowledge of God.[1]

(c) The knowledge of God is relative and conditioned. We cannot know God unless He manifests Himself to us, and this relativity inheres in all human knowledge. Our knowledge of God is also limited by the necessity of conceiving and describing Him in human forms of thought and human terms. It is symbolic. But it is not merely symbolic, and we are not misled into regarding our conceptions as adequate to divine infinitude. The symbols are windows through which we apprehend a reality which transcends, and is seen to transcend, our conceptions. And the symbols are true so far as they go.[2] The Infinite is not a contradiction of our conceptions, but their necessary postulate. We conceive of divine attributes in human

---

[1] Cf. *Introd. to Dog. Theol.*, ch. iv. §§ 2, 3.

[2] The symbolical and inadequate nature of our conception of God is considered below, ch. x. § 4. Cf. also p. 15, note 2, above.

terms, but none the less as infinite; that is, as the attributes of a Being who is self-existent, self-sufficient, and the ultimate ground of all reality.

(d) The validity of our knowledge of God and of divine things is an essential postulate of morality and of human responsibility. If I have no proper knowledge whatsoever of spiritual things, I cannot justly be held accountable in the sphere of spiritual things. If there are truths by which I ought to live, then there ought to be ways by which I can bring these truths within my knowledge. Invincible ignorance can never be a legitimate basis of morality or of religion.[1]

(e) The knowledge of God is the least adequate to reality, no doubt, of all human knowledge; and it is indirect — mediated through the data of finite experience. But mediated knowledge may be very real and very abundant. What is perceived to be a necessary implicate of experience is as truly known as are the immediate contents of experience. God manifests Himself through all our experience, and the avenues of His self-manifestation to us are more manifold than are the avenues of manifestation of any other realities. The fact is that, if our knowledge of God is the least adequate to reality, it is none the

[1] Spencer attempted to show that the basis of reconciliation between religion and science is the unknowable: *First Prins.*, introd. chapters. See, on the necessity of some knowledge of God for religion and morality, Flint, *Theism*, pp. 2–12; Liddon, *Some Elements*, Lec. i. Schleiermacher and, more recently, the Ritschlians, with their judgments of worth, fail to do justice to this principle.

less truly the most abundant and significant of all human knowledge. It is so abundant and so significant that only the fool can persuade himself that there is no God.[1]

[1] Psa. liii. 3. Cf. Rom. i. 20–23. Schlegel, *Philos. of Life*, Lec. iv., says that God is more knowable than all else; although, by reason of His greatness, *less completely* known. Our knowledge of God is progressive, and requires for its fuller development the co-operation of multitudes. No isolated individual and no age can survey all the aspects under which the Infinite manifests Himself to us. Cf. Knight, *Aspects of Theism*, pp. 114–118.

We shall treat theologically of our knowledge of God in ch. **x.** Pt. I, below.

CHAPTER III

CHRISTIAN THEISM

I. *Its task*

§ 1. The task of Christian theism is twofold: to confirm Christian belief in God by the evidence which natural experience affords; and to investigate and exhibit the implications of this evidence as to the nature and attributes of God.[1]

[1] The literature of theism is very extensive indeed. An exhaustive bibliography is given in Baldwin's *Dic. of Philos.*, Vol. III. pp. 745–811. We subjoin a selection only.

The arguments of patristic and mediæval writers are summarized in various Histories of Christian Doctrine, *e.g.* Hagenbach, §§ 35, 123, 163; and in Histories of Philosophy, *e.g.* Ueberweg, §§ 76–106, *passim*. Also in the *Theol. Dogmata* of Petavius, and of Thomassinus. L. T. Cole's *Basis of Early Christian Theism* (paper, N. Y., Macmillan's, 1898) gives a valuable survey of patristic arguments. Cicero's *De Natura Deorum* is the fullest pagan treatise, and Aristotle's *Metaphysics* should not be overlooked (as a source of mediæval argument). To these should be added St. Augustine, *Contra Academicos;* and *De Civitate Dei;* St. Anselm, *Monologium;* and *Proslogium*; and St. Thomas Aquinas, *Summa Theologica*, Pt. I. Q. ii.

Modern arguments are summarized in Pfleiderer, *Philos. of Relig.*, Vols. I, II; Ueberweg, *Hist. of Philos.*, Vol. II, *passim;* Bowen, *Modern Philos.*, *passim;* and Caldecott, *Philos. of Religion.*

Among serviceable modern treatments may be mentioned, R. Flint, *Theism; Anti-Theistic Theories;* and *Agnosticism;* Geo. Fisher, *Grounds of Theistic and Christian Belief*, chh. i–iii; Illing-

Christian theism starts with the Christian idea of God — an idea which derives its fulness and definiteness from supernatural revelation, as assimilated with the assistance of grace, and as defined in the ecumenical creeds. Its task, therefore, is not to find out God, but to confirm the truth of Christian doctrine concerning Him by an examination of His self-manifestation in the natural order.

It is presupposed that, if the Christian idea of God is in accordance with truth, its truth will receive some confirmation from an enlightened examination of natural phenomena. These phenomena are so many manifestations to us of divine operations. The realities of the natural order constitute the handiwork of God; and, as such, must inevitably imply somewhat as to the nature and methods of operation of their

worth, *Personality*, Lec. iv; Liddon, *Some Elements of Religion*; S. Harris, *Self-Revelation of God;* A. C. Fraser, *Philos. of Religion;* O. Pfleiderer, *Philos. of Religion*, Vol. III. Sect. II. ch. i; Jas. Martineau, *Study of Religion*, Bks. II, III; Jno. Caird, *Philos. of Religion*, esp. ch. v; W. L. Davidson, *Theism and Human Nature;* Schurman, *Belief in God;* Jas. Iverach, *Theism;* Jas. Orr, *Christian View of God*, Lec. iii; F. J. Hall, *Doctrine of God*, chh. iv, v; B. Boedder, *Natural Theology;* J. T. Driscoll, *God;* W. G. Ward, *Philos. of Theism*. These last three are Roman Catholic writers. Paley's *Natural Theology* has historical value.

Among the classic adverse criticisms of theistic arguments are Hume, *Dialogues Concerning Natural Theology;* Kant, *Critique of Pure Reason; Critique of Practical Reason;* and *Critique of Judgment* (the pertinent sections of which are gathered together and translated in Caldecott and Mackintosh, *Selections from the Literature of Theism*, pp. 183 *et seq.* — an indispensable work); J. S. Mill, *Theism* (in *Three Essays on Religion*); G. J. Romanes, *Candid Examination of Theism* (by "Physicus").

immanent and transcendent Creator and Governor. "The heavens declare the glory of God, and the firmament showeth His handiwork. Day unto day uttereth speech, and night unto night sheweth knowledge. There is no speech nor language where their voice is not heard. Their line is gone out through all the earth, and their words unto the end of the world." [1]

§ 2. The data of theism are found in the natural order, by which is meant the visible universe, including man, its observed working, and its resident forces. These data are perceived partly by the external senses and partly by subjective introspection; and theistic argument is based upon the assumption that whatever is seen to be a necessary implicate of experience and thought is truly known.[2] It is this assumption that warrants our acceptance of St. Paul's teaching that God has manifested Himself to all men. "For the invisible things of Him since the creation of the world are clearly seen, being perceived through the things that are made, even His everlasting power and Divinity." [3]

The data of theism are open to the contemplation

---

[1] Psa. xix. 1–4. Cf. Job. xii. 9–13; Psa. xciv. 8–10; Wisd. of Solomon, xiii. 1–5; Acts xiv. 15–17; xvii. 22–29; Rom. 1. 18–25. The Scriptures nowhere undertake the task of proving God's existence. It is presupposed as so evident that only the fool can say in his heart, "there is no God," Psa. liii. 1. See A. B. Davidson, in Hastings' *Dic. of the Bible, s. v.* "God (in O T)." Also his *Theol. of the O. Test.*, pp. 78–80.

[2] The *a priori* argument of St. Anselm and his successors is to be estimated from this standpoint. See ch. viii. §§ 4 (*e*), 5.

[3] Rom. i. 18–20.

of all men, and scientific culture is not necessary in order that their theistic bearing should be sufficiently apparent to those who are rightly disposed toward God and the knowledge of Him. Yet the sciences are obviously necessary handmaids to theism, since they co-ordinate its data, and enable us to interpret them intelligently, accurately, and securely.[1]

§ 3. Theism has the limitations which inhere in all the sciences that have to do with religion. It serves the purpose of making faith more intelligent, and our knowledge of God more rational and coherent; but it is not the primary basis of Christian conviction or of spiritual knowledge. Its arguments are rational and amply sufficient for their purpose, that is, when considered by spiritual minds. Their validity cannot be impugned successfully; nor do men attempt to impugn them except on purely formal grounds and with neglect of the principles of reason and knowledge which govern the ordinary thinking and actions of men. In brief, theism articulates and interprets the obvious implications of all human knowledge, and cannot be refuted on any basis which is not fatal to practical reason. This is the key-note of our whole argument.

But the knowledge of God is impossible for such as are unwilling to acquire such knowledge spiritually, and to do this involves humble-mindedness and dependence upon the Spirit of grace. Every subject of knowledge is to be investigated according to its nature and in its own manner. Just as beauty can-

[1] Cf. *Introd. to Dog. Theol.*, ch. i. Pt. VI.; ch. iii. Pt. I.

not be understood, or even be believed in, by the methods of chemistry, so a person cannot be known by one in whom the personal equation [1] is wanting. The personal God is known only by persons in whom the divine likeness has not been subverted, and who cultivate that personal character and disposition which is required in order that the being and nature of God should appear to possess the verisimilitude of truth.[2]

What theism can achieve is limited in another direction. Although the self-manifestation of God through physical and human nature is real, and sufficient to put all men to a probation and to make them responsible for rejecting Him, it is not complete or articulate. It needs to be supplemented and defined by supernatural revelation. And it is only since the revelation of God-Incarnate that theism has become truly scientific, and able to obtain a significant place in human philosophy.

To put this in another way, the contents of supernatural revelation alone enable us to discern the full significance of natural revelation, and theism is but

[1] The phrase "personal equation," in its original use, signifies "an error made by a person in a measurement or exact observation of any kind, which is peculiar to himself, and which must be allowed for when the precise result of the observation or measurement is to be derived": Baldwin, *Dic. of Philos*, *s. v.* "Personal Equation." Recent writers have employed it, however, to signify a suitable personal capacity for, and attitude towards, questions a successful investigation of which requires such capacity and attitude. So here.

[2] Cf. *Introd. to Dog. Theol.*, ch. ix. Pt. III.

a pale shadow of itself until it becomes Christian. This is not to disparage the validity and important significance of nature's theistic teaching. Rather it is to indicate the point of view from which alone its validity and significance can be appreciated and vindicated to thinking men. As is elsewhere shown,[1] the doctrine of the Trinity affords indispensable light for adequately investigating the indications of God's self-manifestation in nature.[2]

II. *Its Logic*

§ 4. It should be emphasized that theism has no other logic than that which all men employ in other departments of reason. Subjectively and formally considered, the grounds of certainty which determine men's convictions are the same for all, and under all circumstances. The laws that are seen to govern human reason in ordinary thinking are the laws which govern true theological thought; and, if conformity

---

[1] *E.g.* in ch. x. § 8, below. Cf. Orr, *Christian View of God*, pp. 75-79.

[2] The teaching of nature comes first, and affords what are called *praeambula fidei*. But these *praeambula* are but beginnings of the knowledge to which they introduce us. See Boedder, *Natural Theol.*, pp. 3, 4; Hastings, *Encyc. of Relig.*, *s. v.* "Aquinas," p. 657; Flint, *Theism*, Lec. x; St. Thos., *Summa Theol.* I. i. 1; Hooker, *Eccles. Polity*, I. xi. Cf. our *Introd. to Dog. Theol.*, ch. ii. §§ 8, 9. This thought is ancient. Tertullian, *Adv. Marc.*, i. 18, maintains that God must be known first through nature, this knowledge being authenticated by supernatural revelation. Novatian, *De Trin.*, iii, says that, as God is invisible, we must learn about him from His works.

to these laws gives validity to other human arguments, it also gives validity to theistic arguments. The logic of theism is a logic which every intelligent person is accustomed to employ, and which he cannot consistently impugn in any domain of thought. It is true that the things with which theistic doctrine is concerned are spiritually investigated; and that in theistic argument we depend upon the aid of supernatural enlightenment and upon moral predisposition to believe. But, as shown elsewhere, these conditions neither alter the logic which we employ nor weaken its intrinsic force.[1]

Summarizing particulars which are to be elaborated in the following sections, we maintain that theistic arguments are to some extent *a priori*, but more largely *a posteriori;* and they enlist processes of induction more freely than of deduction. As is the case with much other human reasoning, the value of theistic proofs is moral, or probable, and cumulative, rather than demonstrative in the strict sense of that term. The certainty which they are calculated to produce is moral, rather than mathematical, but none the less sufficient and valid as a preliminary and introduction to knowledge. Finally, as is the case with other human cognition, the act of knowing God, although made possible by logical processes, itself transcends such processes, and possesses a certain intuitive and self-evidencing quality.

[1] See *Introd. to Dog. Theol.*, ch. iv, v, *passim.* Cf. Max Müller, *Origin of Religion*, pp. 20, 21.

§ 5. In earlier terminology *a priori* reasoning meant to proceed from causes to effects, while *a posteriori* reasoning signified the opposite method of arguing from effects to causes.[1] Since the time of Kant, however, to proceed *a priori* has meant to start with premises which are seen to be true independently of and prior to experience.[2] These premises constitute universal postulates of experience rather than observed contents thereof, and are discovered by reflection upon experience and its fundamental implicates. Experience affords the necessary condition and occasion of their discovery, but is not the source from which we derive them.

So far as *a priori* reasoning implies that the premises of argument are essentially prior to the conclusion, such reasoning cannot logically establish the being of God, for God is the fundamental postulate of all reason, and there is no prior truth from which His being can be deduced. But inasmuch as the validity of experience itself is based upon the truth of *a priori* principles, it will be found that the *a priori* element cannot wholly be excluded from theistic argument. As the same condition attends all human reasoning, this fact ought not to cause difficulty.[3]

---

[1] So St. Thomas, *Summa Theol.*, I. ii. 2; who follows Aristotle. Cf. Signoriellus, *Lexicon Peripateticum*, *s. v.* "Argumentari a priori — a post."

[2] See Baldwin, *Dic. of Philos.*, *s. v.* "A priori and a posteriori." Cf. Flint, *Theism*, note xxxvii, pp. 424, 425; Hastings, *Encyc. of Relig.*, *s. v.* "A priori," by Paul Kalweit.

[3] Cf. Flint, *Theism*, pp. 267–269; Ladd, *Philos. of Relig.*, Vol. I.

Formally speaking, however, theistic arguments are chiefly *a posteriori*. That is, they are based upon premises derived from experience, and depend for their validity upon *a priori* considerations only so far as such considerations have to be presupposed and postulated in interpreting the data of experience. The experience from which these data are derived is human experience in its totality,[1] that is, both external and internal experience.

§ 6. The reason which gives *a posteriori* arguments the larger place in theism, also causes induction to be depended upon more obviously and more generally than deduction. In deduction we start with general propositions already accepted, and by analysis and comparison of notions arrive at particular conclusions implicitly contained in them. The premises are more fundamental and basic in their significance than the conclusion. They are prior in the sequence of ideas.[2] The being of God, however, is the most fundamental of propositions, and is, in the estimation of intelligent theists, the implicit postulate of all deductive reasoning. It cannot become the conclusion of a syllogism unless we premise what we seek to prove, and this is not logically permissible in deduction.[3]

pp. 309, 310. Truths which are discovered by *a priori* thought can be treated as data of the inductive method of argument. In this case, the fallacy of treating the being of God as a secondary truth is avoided.

[1] Cf. on this point, Ladd, *Philos. of Relig.*, Vol. II. pp. 38–40, 44; Conder, *Basis of Faith*, Lec. iii.

[2] See Baldwin, *Dic. of Philos.*, *s. v.* "Deduction."

[3] Thus, when we base an argument for God upon the law of

Yet deduction is not wholly invalid in theistic argument, for the validity of any proposition can be tested logically, and without fallacy, by using it as the premise of deduction in order to determine whether the particular conclusions that follow are in accordance with the facts of experience. To put this in another way, the being of God may be treated as an accepted hypothesis and tested by its working value, or by the agreement of its logical implications with the particulars of human knowledge.[1]

But the formal method of theistic argument is primarily inductive. The particulars of experience

causality we start with a premise which is equivalent to the theistic doctrine that an uncaused cause exists; for no other cause satisfies the idea of a cause, and the only uncaused cause that can rationally be hypothecated is the very God whose existence we seek to prove. Cf. Conder, *Basis of Faith*, pp. 97, 98.

[1] A good illustration is to be seen in the evolutionary hypothesis. It was not arrived at by deduction, but has become the premise of many scientific deductions; and the agreement of the conclusions thus obtained with relevant facts of scientific observation is regarded as a verification of the evolutionary hypothesis. Whether the verification in this case is sufficiently extensive to establish the hypothesis beyond possibility of dispute we are not obliged to determine. In any case the *method of procedure* is generally acknowledged to be valid, and its validity cannot be consistently denied in theistic argument. A verifiable hypothesis, according to Baldwin's *Dic. of Philos.*, s. v. "Verification," is "one which presents an abundance of necessary consequences open to experimental test." Surely the theistic hypothesis meets such a requirement. The transcendental method of proof is substantially this: Caldecott, in *Camb. Theol. Essays*, pp. 126 *et seq.* Cf. Gwatkin, *Knowl. of God*, Vol. I. p. 11; Davis, *Elem. of Ethics*, pp. 20–23; Schurman, *Belief in God*, pp. 41–48; Calderwood, *Moral Philos.*, pp. 229, 230.

are generalized, and their necessary implications are made the basis of theistic inference.[1] We say that the method is *primarily* inductive, but deduction cannot be wholly excluded from theistic induction or from any line of inductive reasoning. All induction is based to some extent upon interpretations of particulars, and these interpretations are the result of deductions from the fundamental postulates of reason.

It is not logical to impugn theistic argument because it is based upon such postulates, for all argument is thus conditioned. But there is another difficulty which requires attention. The particulars of experience are not adequate to a theistic conclusion. The being of God is a larger proposition than is contained within the range of such data, however full, relatively speaking, our experience may become. The mind has to transcend the data of experience in order to arrive at the conclusion that the Infinite in whom we believe exists. If we ignore the laws that govern human reason in practice, and seek to overcome this difficulty by abstract considerations only, we shall find that it is insuperable. In brief, we cannot justify on exclusively *a priori* grounds the acceptance of a proposition when its truth cannot rightly be regarded as at least implicitly embraced within the contents of experience and practically involved in them. Empiricism must triumph, if we depend upon formal demonstration to justify the claim that human reason

[1] On induction, see Baldwin, *Dic. of Philos.*, *s. v.* "Induction"; and any standard logical treatise.

can transcend experience and is to be trusted in doing so.[1]

But, if we once accept the premise that human reason is trustworthy in its fundamental and necessary processes, the difficulty is not insuperable. Unless we do accept this premise, we are without rational basis for accepting reason at all. Human reason is conditioned in every form, and at every stage, by the acceptance of transcendental ideas. Kant has made this perfectly clear. We cannot demonstrate the truth of any of these ideas on grounds that are independently valid. If they may not be accepted as rationally acquired and as objects of human knowledge, then we can know nothing, for the validity of these ideas for cognition is the presupposition of all reason and, therefore, of all rational knowledge.

Our conclusion is a practical one. The human reason is found in fact to transcend experience continually, and this fact is the condition *sine qua non* of empirical knowledge. If we cannot attain to any knowledge which is not derived wholly from experience, we cannot attain even to knowledge which is thus derived.

The truth is that all generalized knowledge, and all scientific views of nature, transcend the data of experience. The peculiar value of induction lies in the fact that it enables the mind to arrive at knowledge

[1] We have in view the Kantian denial of validity for knowledge to the transcendental postulates of reason. The subject has been discussed in ch. ii. §§ 3 *fin.*, 8.

which is wider in range, and more significant, than the data of the most abundant experience.[1] The validity of this larger and higher knowledge is practically verified by its working value; and the impossibility of otherwise demonstrating its truth troubles no competent scientist. It is inconsistent, therefore, for those who trust human reason in its normal operations, to deny the validity of theistic inductions merely on the plea that they imply an ability of our minds to transcend the data of experience.

§ 7. Theism employs moral proof rather than demonstration, strictly so called. The difference between moral and demonstrative proof is due to the purely probable nature of the evidence employed in the former,[2] and it appears when we consider the kind of certainty which each method of proof is able to produce. The conclusions of moral proof are credible in various degrees, and when the evidence is discovered to be overwhelming for one conclusion the

[1] Every intellectual process by means of which we interpret the meaning of experience obviously and necessarily requires that we should transcend what we interpret.

[2] Much confusion will be avoided by remembering that many writers employ the word demonstration for both kinds of proof: Cf. St. Thomas, *Summa Theol.*, I. ii. 2; and that patristic writers who deny that the existence of God can be proved have deduction in mind and what is here called demonstration: Cf. Clement Alex., *Strom.*, v. 12; viii. 3; Justin M., *Fragm. Resurrec.*, 1. Baldwin, *Dic. of Philos.*, *s. v.* "Proof," distinguishes (a) demonstration; (b) highly probable deduction; (c) induction. In our division (b) and (c) fall under moral proof. If induction were exhaustive, it might become demonstrative, of course.

opposite conclusion becomes incredible, and moral certainty results.[1] But moral certainty does not imply metaphysical necessity. That is, it does not exclude the *abstract possibility* that an opposite conclusion may be true. The consequence is that conviction which is produced by moral proof is dependent upon disposition to believe and willingness to give adequate attention to the considerations which make for the conclusions in question.[2] This fact accounts the name "moral proof"; and it is to such proof that the saying applies, "A man convinced against his will is of the same opinion still."

Demonstrative proof, on the other hand, when its particulars are attended to and understood by a sane mind, produces a certainty which cannot be evaded. The contradictories of its conclusions are not only incredible, but are seen to be absurd, impossible, and necessarily false. Moral elements are indeed involved, but they are less obtrusive and are related exclusively to willingness and effort to attend to the particulars of argument. Wholly to banish the moral conditions

[1] Moral proof might be defined as proof which makes its conclusion credible, whatever may be the degree of credibility which is established.

[2] Such disposition and willingness is often so easily and naturally attained as to blind many to its moral nature. But differences in the ease, or in the difficulty, with which we are disposed to believe, or willing to attend, do not of themselves determine the objective value of moral proof. Some truths are less welcome than others, but that fact, while it will often reduce our readiness to be convinced, does not in the least reduce the validity of the moral proof upon which conviction depends.

from persuasion is as impossible as to exclude the reason itself. But if demonstrative proof is once understood, doubt or honest denial is impossible for sane thinkers.[1] Demonstrative proof is confined to the sphere of universal or exhaustive induction, and of deduction from premises which are previously accepted as necessarily true — that is, if human reason is to be trusted in its fundamental postulates and intuitions. Scepticism as to this point makes proof impossible. All proofs and convictions are based ultimately upon trust — a trust which is instinctive, and is found to be essential to a rationally ordered life.[2]

Probable proof may result in different degrees of subjective conviction — degrees ranging all the way from the most precarious opinion as to likelihood, to a certainty which is free from doubt. Certainty means, strictly speaking, freedom from doubt, and it does not admit of degrees. To speak of being more certain is to use language inaccurately. We should speak of being more fully convinced. Certainty is not real if any doubt remains. The difference between moral and demonstrative certainty is not of degree but of stability, or of possibility of being destroyed. Demonstrative certainty cannot be destroyed by sound logic,

[1] Mathematical science affords the most numerous examples. No one who attends to the proof that the sum of the angles of any triangle is equal to the sum of two right angles, and understands it, can honestly deny that proposition.

[2] This has been emphasized at various points in the previous chapter.

but moral certainty can often be undermined by contrary proofs and arguments. To put this in another way, in demonstrative certainty doubt is not only excluded in fact but is made logically impossible; whereas in moral certainty, although doubt has been banished, its return is possible.[1]

The fact that moral certainty can sometimes be nullified by additional arguments does not prove that such certainty in a given case is invalid. Any certainty which appears to be warranted by existing knowledge, or by the state of the question, is at least logically valid until the state of the question is changed. The logical validity of a conclusion depends not upon demonstration, but upon sound judgment as to the bearing and force of available evidence. It is irrational to deny a conclusion which appears to be warranted by such evidence as is available for consideration; and not less so because it is possible that the conclusion may be overthrown by fuller evidence, or because complete demonstration is wanting. Such a course is especially irrational when, as is sometimes the case, we have reason to think that additional contrary evidence is from the nature of the question beyond human capacity to discover. This is so with theistic argument. It seems clear that no new line

[1] Thus I am utterly free from doubt as to the reality of the death of Jesus Christ under Pontius Pilate. Yet the abstract possibility remains that evidence, whether true or false, might be produced which would destroy my certainty; and this possibility would become likelihood if I became desirous to be convinced that my existing certainty was unwarranted.

of evidence, contrary to theistic doctrine, will ever
be available. The mystery of evil, already known
and allowed for, sums up apparently all that can ever
be urged as constituting anti-theistic evidence in the
proper sense of that term.

§ 8. We have said that the logical validity of a
conclusion depends upon "sound judgment as to the
bearing and force of available evidence." But the
human mind is too resourceful to have its inferential
judgments regarded as mere registers of the results
of formal argumentation. The mind can transcend
mere logic, and can arrive at conclusions which are
not less normal, rational, and credible because their
grounds cannot be fully exhibited in the manner of
formal logic. In brief, the rational validity of a conclusion does not always wholly depend upon its logical
validity—that is, upon the *adequacy* of its logical basis.[1]
Formal argumentation itself depends for validity upon
the fundamental postulates of reason; and these have
to be accepted without logical proof, because, if they
are not accepted, no sound argument is possible and
no conclusions are valid.

But formal logic is also transcended constantly
in judging concerning concrete matters.[2] A good

[1] A conclusion is *logically* valid in so far as the inferential process
agrees in method with the laws of formal logic. It is *rationally* valid
in so far as the inferential method is normal to human reason. The
normal methods of human inference are formal and informal, and
informal inference cannot be described adequately by the terms of
logical science.

[2] We are much indebted in this section to J. H. Newman's *Gram-*

illustration of this is to be found in the use of circumstantial evidence — evidence which points to a conclusion without proving it in the proper and logical
sense of that term. Many a man has been justly
condemned to death on circumstantial evidence, when
formal proof of guilt has been either inadequate or
wanting. And a large proportion of men's opinions
are incapable of formal proof.

It is the function of logical argument to point out
the road to truth.[1] But the mind, while depending
upon the aid of argument, does its own judging;
and is able both to bridge gaps in the argument,
and, out-stripping logic, to leap to its conclusion with
a facility and swiftness resembling intuition. This is
illustrated by the inferential reasoning employed by
generals in war, by statesmen in public policy, and by
all men in the management of practical concerns. If
logic were waited for in all inference, life would come
to a standstill.

The point is that men possess what Newman calls

mar of Assent, esp. chh. viii, ix. That writer did not do full justice
to the part and function of the intellect in attaining theistic belief;
but his contention that the mind is able to transcend logic in making
inferences concerning concrete matters, and that in doing so it acts
normally and therefore rationally, is sound and is admirably expounded. He calls the "power of judging about truth and error in
concrete matters" the "illative sense" and the "illative faculty."
Cf. our *Introd. to Dog. Theol.*, ch. v. §§ 4, 5.

[1] Newman says, "If language is an inestimable gift to man, the
logical faculty prepares it for our use. Though it does not go so far
as to ascertain truth, still it teaches us the direction in which truth
lies, and how propositions lie towards each other." *Op. cit.*, p. 274.

an "illative sense," or "illative faculty," which enables them to arrive at rationally valid conclusions touching problems that cannot be fully solved by mere logic. This faculty, and the inferences which we make by means of it, are normal to human reason, and therefore cannot be impugned merely because formal logic is transcended.[1] This does not mean that logic can be violated by sound reason, but that it can be transcended. To transcend logic is not necessarily to be illogical; nor does it require that we should neglect the assistance of logic so far as it is available. The fact is that logical argumentation — often implicit, or too rapid for analysis — constitutes the starting-point of inference, and gives proper direction to the mind. But human inferences involve mental operations which lie, partly at least, beneath the threshold of consciousness; and they cannot be fully described by the terms under which writers generalize their conscious elements in logical treatises.[2] Moreover,

[1] Newman says, *Op. cit.*, p. 331, "Earnestly maintaining, as I would, . . . the certainty of knowledge, I think it enough to appeal to the common voice of mankind in proof of it. That is to be accounted a normal faculty of our nature, which men in general do actually exercise. That is a law of our minds, which is exemplified in action on a large scale, whether *a priori* it ought to be a law or no . . . Our possession of certitude is a proof that it is not a weakness or absurdity to be certain." Cf. our *Introd. to Dog. Theol.*, pp 109–111; Schurman, *Belief in God*, pp. 27, 28.

[2] On subconscious operations of the mind, see Baldwin, *Dic. of Philos.*, *s. vv.* "Sub-conscious" and "Herbartianism." Cf. *Introd. to Dog. Theol.*, p. 116, note 2; and Gwatkin, *Knowledge of God*, Vol. I. pp. 163–167.

the particulars of experience from which inferences are made — and rightly made — are, in countless instances, quite too diverse and complicated to be formulated by, or comprehended within, the terms of premises of formal argument.

What has been said does not cease to be true when theistic inference is considered. The particulars with which theistic inference begins are world-wide, and are quite too diverse and complex to be embraced within formal premises of argument. The being of God is not susceptible of strictly formal proof, but the certainty of His existence and fundamental attributes is attained, so far as it is attained by inference, by transcending formal logic. This does not mean that theistic proofs, so called, are either invalid or useless, but that their function in theistic inference is limited. They do enable the mind to transcend them and to attain to theistic certainty in a manner that is strictly rational and in accord with the normal operations of the mind in other spheres of its exercise.[1]

It is not to be forgotten that we have been speaking of theistic certainty in its intellectual aspects. As

[1] W. R. Sorley says, in the *Critical Review*, Jan., 1900, p. 21, "From a world of spirits to a Supreme Spirit is a possible step. The difficulty is not to take the step, but to describe and understand the way." St. Gregory Naz. says that God is beyond our logic, because He manifests Himself in such wise as to escape our logic: *Orat.*, xxxi. 8. Cf. Calderwood, *Philos. of the Infinite*, pp. 48–51; Flint, *Theism*, pp. 60, 61. Sorley's distinction between taking the step to theistic inference and being able to describe the method in formal terms helps us to understand why unscientific minds are often more successful than scientific experts in theistic inference.

has been said already, the mind cannot cognize except under conditions of feeling and will. It is a feeling and willing person who knows, and the personal equation cannot be escaped from in any operation of the mind.[1] Nor is this all. Our feelings and volitions themselves are experiences which afford important and necessary data of thought and knowledge.

Once more, our contention that theistic certainty, and the knowledge of God generally, is strictly rational — that is, is the certainty and knowledge of the human mind in its proper and normal functioning — is quite consistent with the position, elsewhere maintained, that the human mind cannot know God without the aid of grace.[2] This grace is not a substitute for reason, but a cause of its enlightenment. The effect of grace is to enlarge the capacity of reason, and to enable it to assert itself in its own proper manner and to its fullest capacity. So far from violating or changing its laws, grace fortifies reason against subverting influences, and increases both the facility and the trustworthiness of its processes and cognitions.[3]

---

[1] Ch. ii. § 10, esp. pp. 44, 45, above. Further references are there given. Cf. Fisher, *Faith and Rationalism*, pp. 45–50. Theophilus says, *Ad Autol.*, i. ch. 2, "If thou sayest, show me thy God, I answer, show me first thy man, and I will show thee my God. Show me first whether the eyes of thy soul see, and the ears of thy heart hear." The passage is given more fully by Flint, *Theism*, p. 353. Cf. that treatise, pp. 76–81, 351–355.

[2] Ch. ii. § 12 (*a*), above. Cf. *Introd. to Dog. Theol.*, ch. v. §§ 12, 13.

[3] Ch. ii. § 12 (*b*), above. Cf. *Introd. to Dog. Theol.*, chh. iv. § 2; v. § 13.

The sum of the matter is that the certainty which theistic argument is intended to subserve is at once in accord with logic, and above logic; humanly rational, and dependent upon divine grace; properly intellectual, and conditioned by a right personal equation and by appropriate exercises of the affections and the will.

§ 9. No one of the so-called proofs of theism is sufficient of itself to prove the existence and supremacy of the Infinite. The logical force of these proofs is cumulative.[1] Moreover their cumulative force is probable rather than demonstrative. They indeed bring the illative faculty into exercise,[2] and constitute rational justifications of its transcendent theistic inference. But in its formal and purely logical aspects theistic proof is moral only, and theistic certainty is dependent upon the personal equation — upon moral and spiritual conditions. These conditions are not present in all individual truth seekers, and many fail to acquire the certainty of faith.[3] The phenomenon of theistic doubt is one of common observation.

[1] See ch. viii. § 6, below.

[2] The inferential faculty described in the last section, which is capable of transcending formal argumentation.

[3] Newman's well-known description of faith, *Univ. Sermons,* xi., illustrates the truth that theistic inference is a more complex act than can be adequately described in the terms of pure logic. He says, "Faith is a process of the Reason, in which so much of the grounds of inference cannot be exhibited, so much lies in the character of the mind itself, in its general view of things, its estimate of the probable and the improbable, its impressions concerning God's will, and its anticipations derived from its own inbred wishes, that it will ever seem to the world irrational and despicable; — till, that is, the event

In its more comprehensive meaning doubt signifies any and every form of lack of certainty. Thus belief, so far as it falls short of absolute certainty, is rightly said to imply some degree of doubt. Like belief doubt admits of degrees, and in its supreme form is an inability to arrive at any opinion. The mind is in a state of suspended judgment, and finds itself unable to rest in any conclusion. This is the stricter meaning of doubt — the meaning in which we now proceed to consider it.[1]

Such doubt cannot rationally justify itself when the doubter is in a position to perceive that the available evidence is logically sufficient to warrant the opinion that the proposition in question is more probably true than false. Yet it is a fact that such conditions do not invariably banish the kind of doubt of which we are speaking.

(a) Doubt has various forms and causes. It may be primarily intellectual, arising from conclusions adopted as to the state of the question. Thus the doubter may consider that there is an entire lack of determinative evidence, or of preponderance of evi-

confirms it. The act of the mind, for instance, by which an unlearned person savingly believes the Gospel, on the word of his teacher, may be analogous to the exercise of sagacity in a great statesman or general, supernatural grace doing for the uncultivated reason what genius does for them."

[1] On doubt, see J. W. Diggle, *Religious Doubt;* Baldwin, *Dic. of Philos.*, *s. v.* "Doubt"; Hastings, *Dic. of Christ, s. vv.* "Doubt," "Thomas," and "Unbelief"; A. W. Robinson's edition of Tennyson, *In Memoriam.*

dence, in either direction. Such doubt cannot be rationally vindicated in relation to theism, for the self-manifestation of God is too manifold and too generally apprehensible to permit of such an attitude of mind, if the reason is properly exercised and trusted.[1]

(b) Doubt, again, may be sceptical. That is, it may be due to a lack of trust in human reason, whether this lack of trust is partial only or complete. It is based upon a mistaken epistemology — an epistemology which is logically fatal not only to theistic certainty but to every form of human certainty and knowledge. The fallacies of scepticism have been discussed in the previous chapter.[2] Theological agnosticism is another name for such doubt in relation to theism.

(c) Finally, doubt may be moral and spiritual. We mean that the judgment may be hindered by absence of the moral and spiritual conditions — the personal equation — which are required for belief in God and for knowledge of Him. And this subjective difficulty is often connected with failure to make full and proper use of divine grace.

---

[1] Bald intellectuality, for instance, is inconsistent with a proper exercise of reason. The state of the question is considered in ch. iv, below. The specious notion that God's existence, if real, ought not to be open to doubt is shown to be false by Davidson, *Theism*, pp 24, 25. Cf. Flint, *Theism*, p. 79.

[2] Diggle, *Relig. Doubt*, pp. 247, 248, calls attention to the fact that a capacity for doubt is evidence of capacity for belief. In ch. v, he shows that the difficulties which attend doubt are more serious than those which attend belief.

This kind of doubt is by no means rare, and its remedy is difficult to apply. We do not mean to imply that it is necessarily due to personal guilt, because of its moral quality. The failure is often due to unfortunate training, and to ignorance of the conditions which have to be fulfilled in order rightly to exercise the reason in spiritual matters. A perverted psychology, or a mistaken epistemology, may coexist with trust in human reason, as the doubter would define its nature and functions, and with the most sincere desire to believe the truth. This very desire may be robbed of its value by the mistaken notion that loyalty to truth demands suspension of judgment until more evidence is discovered than is in fact available.[1]

So far as the doubter's procedure is concerned there

[1] The sensitive loyalty to truth which characterizes many persons tormented with doubt is most praiseworthy. But this very loyalty ought to suggest the necessity of being guided *practically* by the apparent bearing of the evidence actually available. In moral issues involving an immediate determination of conduct, neutrality is in effect evasion of, rather than loyalty to, truth. What seems to be duty cannot be tested by inaction, nor can the absence of conclusive evidence justify refusal to make the venture. Sympathize as we must with honest doubters, we cannot justify the too common glorification of doubt. It is neither the necessary mark of earnest truth-seeking, nor to be regarded as other than something to be thrown off by the grace of God and by courageous *action*.

Our Lord's language to the doubting Thomas contains an implied rebuke. He plainly reserves His praise for those who escape doubt: St. John xx. 29. To suspend judgment when the data available are not sufficient for satisfying proof is not to show loyalty to truth, but is to miss the only available road thereto. Cf. Diggle, *op. cit.*, pp. 177-179.

is but one way out, viz., what is called "the venture of faith"; and this venture is dependent for its success upon humble reliance upon divine grace. By the venture of faith is here meant a brave and self-sacrificing adoption of the rule of conforming one's life to the practical principles which are involved in an acknowledgment of God's existence and moral sovereignty.[1] This is a strictly scientific procedure, for it is the only method by which the working value of theistic doctrine can be tested, and its working value is its objective criterion. In maintaining this we assume, as is shown by our whole theistic argument, that only the unintelligent and sceptical can honestly evade the conclusion that evidences are available for all which suggest and confirm the probability[2] that God exists and is our supreme moral Sovereign.

A principle which is involved in all this is that "probability is a very guide of life";[3] and the rational

[1] Cf. St. John vii. 17: "If any man willeth to do His will, he shall know of the teaching, whether it be of God." Cf. W. L. Robbins, *Essay Toward Faith*, pp. 48, 49. The whole book is permeated with the thought that faith is "the great venture of the soul."

[2] The word "probability" describes the force of theistic evidence in its lowest term. We maintain, however, that sufficient theistic evidence is available to justify unqualified moral certainty.

[3] Bishop Butler's treatment of this subject is classic: *Analogy*, Introd. Cf. Pt. I. ch. vii. 11; Pt. II. ch. vi. 3; and ch. vii. 43. As J. H. Bernard points out, in his edition of Butler, Vol. I. pp. 10, 11, Butler's contention is "in direct conflict with the doctrine of 'probabilism' laid down in Jesuit text-books," according to which probabilities may give way to the authority of individual ecclesiastical doctors. Gladstone treats of the subject in his *Studies*. Richard Hooker, *Eccles. Polity*, II. vii. 5, tells us that men seek the most

validity and imperative moral force of this principle has never been successfully impugned. Its undeniable truth can be recognized when we consider the irrationality of its opposite — that we should be governed in life by improbabilities; — and also when we perceive the impossibility of preserving real neutrality as to truths which can be seen, when once accepted, to modify our conceptions of duty.

No one maintains that it is reasonable or right to be guided in matters in which moral issues are involved by what appears to be probably untrue; but it is not a rare occurrence that men who are otherwise intelligent persuade themselves that entire suspense of judgment is justifiable when the probability that theistic doctrine is true appears to be lower in degree than is thought to be desirable. Even the slightest likelihood that we ought to be guided by belief in God — a belief which, when once adopted by an unbeliever, must bring an enlarged conception of duty — puts one who perceives this likelihood under as *real* a responsibility for service under God as does the most assured conviction of the truth of theistic doctrine.[1] For what is the practical alternative involved in such

assured conclusion possible, in this order: (*a*) intuitive; (*b*) demonstrated; (*c*) the most probable.

[1] The word "real" is emphasized because the *extent* and *degree* of responsibility depends upon the extent and clearness of our knowledge of the indications of duty.

On the obligation involved in the reception of probable evidence, see Chalmers, *Natural Theol.*, Bk. I. chh. i, ii; Pusey, *Responsibility of the Intellect in Matters of Faith;* Newman's *Univ. Sermons, passim.*

a state of the question? It is obviously this: either to practise what appears probably to be one's bounden duty, or to persevere in a manner of life which makes no credible claim upon the conscience, but which appears probably to be contrary to duty. Neutrality is clearly out of question; for one is forced to be guided practically either by theistic doctrine or by what is contrary to such doctrine.[1] We must live and act upon some basis, and no basis for action is thinkable which is not either theistic or anti-theistic in its practical application.[2]

III. *Its History*

§ 10. It has been pointed out that no theism has been, or can be, developed adequately except in the light of the Christian idea of God.[3] Thus it was the task of Greek philosophy to develop forms of thought which theism employs, rather than to impart to these forms a genuine theistic significance. This was an

---

[1] The ideal of life which theism involves is no mere enrichment of lower ideals, but a radical correction of them. The manner of life which seems right to a non-theist is not only *lacking* in vital elements, but *inconsistent* with them. Materialistic, hedonistic or pantheistic ethics can never *evolve* into theistic ethics. They must *give way*. The determinative end of moral conduct, and therefore a multitude of its particulars, are involved.

[2] The moral quality of much contemporary doubt is to be seen in its consequences as well as in its causes. Cf. Diggle, *op. cit.*, ch. vi.

[3] See § 3, above. For a brief list of works useful in studying the history of theism, see p. 50, note 1, paragraphs 2 and 3, above. To which should be added Caldecott and Mackintosh, *Selections from the Literature of Theism*.

important achievement, and has proved to be of the greatest value to Christian theists; but it is a mistake to read a definite theism into the language of ancient philosophy. Its interest was cosmological rather than theistic. Its aim was to discover a principle of unity in the phenomenal universe, and to arrive at a rational and coherent view of the world. It is clear to us that theism affords the only point of view from which such an aim can be adequately fulfilled. But it cannot be shown that ancient philosophers realized this.

The pre-Socratic schools looked for a first principle, an Ἀρχή, something permanent behind universal change. They were dominated by mechanical conceptions, and their hypotheses were offered without any serious attempt to prove them. In particular, the idea of creation was wanting, and the world was looked upon as eternal. The form of the aetiological argument emerged, but without any genuine theistic conclusion.

Socrates formulated a teleological argument for the existence of controlling intelligence behind the world; [1] but there is no evidence that he was emancipated from the polytheistic point of view. [2] Plato employed his well-known dialectic to arrive at universal ideas — the realities which individual things imply.

[1] See Xenophon's *Memorabilia*, i. 4.

[2] Note his dying request that a cock should be sacrificed to Asclepius: Plato's *Phaedo*, *fin.* Cf. L. T. Cole, *Basis of Early Christian Theism*, p. 17, and ch. ii at large, on the limitations generally of Greek thinkers. On Socrates, see also Zeller, *Socrates and the Socratic Schools;* Ueberweg, *Hist. of Philos.*, Vol. I. pp. 80–88.

And these ideas were generalized under a supreme idea — the good, — which is the first principle and end of all things. This is the idealistic form of the onto-logical argument, and its influence is perceptible in St. Augustine and other Christian writers. But Plato's reasoning after all did not issue in any deter-minate theism. The personality of the supreme good was not a part of his hypothesis. His good is divinity in the abstract only.[1]

Aristotle hypothecated a first mover to account for the changing course of nature, and regarded it as itself immovable.[2] This form of the cosmological argument was taken over by scholastic writers. But Aristotle was not a theist. The first mover with him is the immanent principle of a world which is itself eternal. It is nowhere treated as a personal Creator.[3]

The Epicureans gave testimony to the common consent that gods exist, but were polytheistic, and banished their gods from any control or concern with human affairs.[4] The Stoics believed in controlling

[1] On Plato's philosophy, see Zeller, *Plato and the Older Academy;* Ueberweg, *op. cit.*, Vol. I. pp. 98–132. On his theism, see Prof. Patton's *Theism*, Pt. II. pp. 13, 14; Gratry, *Knowl. of God*, ch. ii; L. T. Cole, *op. cit.*, pp. 17–19; Illingworth, *Personality*, pp. 60–64.

[2] See especially, *Metaph.*, Bk. xi.

[3] In Bk. viii. chh. i, vi, he maintains that motion is eternal — caused from eternity. Boedder, *Natural Theol.*, pp. 209–214, criti-cises his arguments. On Aristotle's philosophy and theism, see L. T. Cole, *op. cit.*, pp. 19–21; Zeller, *Aristotle and the Peripatetics;* Ueberweg, *op. cit.*, Vol. I. pp. 137–180; Prof. Patton, *op. cit.*, pp. 14, 15; Illingworth, *Personality*, pp. 64, 65.

[4] Ueberweg, *op. cit.*, Vol. I. p. 207; L. T. Cole, *op. cit.*, p. 22.

mind and providence, and based their conviction upon the order and harmony of the universe; but their position was pantheistic rather than theistic.[1] Neo-Platonic thought culminated in an ineffable abstraction — not in a personal God.[2]

Many traces can be discovered in ancient pagan literature of a dim consciousness that there is one supreme God.[3] This belief, however, was robbed of practical value by idolatry and grovelling superstition; and did not control the thinking of philosophers except as the unavoidable postulate of human reason. The fact that these philosophers employed the forms of theistic argument proves that theism is inseparable from reasoning about fundamental problems of being, and that it is the proper goal of such reasoning. On the other hand, their failure to arrive at an explicit theism illustrates our contention that the knowledge of God depends upon spiritual conditions, as well as upon reason. Logic cannot be violated by rational belief and knowledge; but it can be transcended by the human mind,[4] and mere logic is not an adequate basis of the knowledge of God.

[1] Ueberweg, *op. cit.*, Vol. I. pp. 194–200. L. T. Cole, *op. cit.*, p. 22. On both Epicureanism and Stoicism, see Zeller, *The Stoics, Epicureans and Sceptics.*

[2] Ueberweg, *op. cit.*, Vol. I. pp. 238–252; Bigg, *Christian Platonists of Alexandria.*

[3] The ancient fathers appeal to this, with numerous citations, in their apologies. Cf. Tertullian, *De Testim. Animae*, ii; St. Justin, *Apol.*, ii. 6; Theophilus, *Ad Autol.*, *init.* See Hagenbach, *Hist.* of *Christ. Doc.*, § 35, for other references.

[4] Cf. § 8, above.

§ 11. The conditions which were wanting in ancient philosophic thinking were supplied by the revelation of the Word-Incarnate, and by the Christian dispensation of grace. Christianity gave the cosmological, teleological, and idealogical thinking of the ancient world its true and theistic bearing, and made modern theism a possibility.[1] But the development of a scientific theism was delayed by various causes. Many of the best thinkers among the early Christians had experienced the futilities of pagan thought, and were inclined to abandon the use of logic altogether in vindicating their belief in God.[2] It was, of course, impossible for them to do this entirely, for human thinking, implicitly at least, is unavoidably theistic. The ancient Christian fathers devoted their attention to making known the Person and claims of Jesus Christ, and in doing this prepared the way for richer theistic developments.

Other causes besides the one above mentioned delayed the development of Christian theism. Practical considerations led early apologists to exhibit the absurdities and the moral futility of polytheism rather than to elaborate theistic arguments.[3] They rightly assumed that, so far as men who were susceptible to religious appeals were concerned, to win them from their allegiance to false gods meant to win them to

[1] Cf. ch. i. 6; ch. iii. § 3, above.

[2] Justin Martyr describes his experience with pagan philosophy, in *Dial. with Trypho*, ch. 2.

[3] L. T. Cole, *Basis of Early Theism*, pp. 46 *et seq.* A good example is to be seen in Clement Alex., *Cohort.*, ch. ii.

Christ, and to that knowledge of the true God wherein eternal life consists. Sincerely religious men did not need to be persuaded that personal Divinity existed and required their allegiance.[1] They needed only to learn that there is but one God, and that the gods which they were worshipping were but idols. The development of a scientific theism, necessary as it would become in time, was not a matter of immediate urgency. The only important constituency to which early apologists addressed themselves, other than the polytheistic, consisted of Jews, who did not need to be persuaded theistically. They only needed to be shown that Jesus Christ was the promised Messiah and the only-begotten Son of God — the Mediator between God and man.[2]

It would be erroneous, however, to infer that the fathers of the Church passed over theistic arguments altogether. It is hardly possible for Christian theologians to write freely without any reference to the natural evidences of God's being, attributes, and providential government. Traces of the more elementary theistic arguments are numerous in patristic literature — the appeal to consent, and the cosmological and teleological arguments.[3]

[1] The soul, Tertullian contends, in *De Testim. Animæ*, is naturally Christian. See Hagenbach, *Hist. of Christian Doc.*, Vol. I. p. 136.

[2] This kind of argument is found in St. Justin, *Dial. with Trypho*; Tertullian, *Apol. against the Jews*.

[3] Hagenbach, *Hist. of Christian Doc.*, Vol. I. pp. 133, 134; Vol. II. pp. 22–26, gives the chief references. Cf. L. T. Cole, *Basis of Early Christ. Theism;* Franzelin, *De Deo Uno*, Thes. vi–ix; Petavius, *De Deo*, lib. I. capp. i–iv.

The appeal to consent was connected with the contention that belief in God is natural and instinctive for man,[1] although often perverted and made practically ineffective by moral degeneration and superstition. But Clement of Alexandria, Origen, and others denied the possibility of demonstrating the existence of God by mere formal logic. The knowledge of God requires for its development and security the obedience of faith and divine grace. Clement laid down the truism that the first principles of reason cannot be demonstrated, since they constitute the bases of demonstration and belong to its premises rather than to its conclusion. The ultimate first principle is God, and His existence, therefore, cannot logically be the conclusion of a syllogism.[2] The ontological argument, for instance, can only terminate in an unknown abstract.[3] It is, we may add, the abstract, and to that extent unreal, conception of the Infinite which prevails in much modern thought that gives agnosticism some, at least, of its persuasive power.[4] Theistic arguments when employed by the fathers were employed *ad hominem* chiefly, and by way of confirmation and explanation of the Christian idea of God, rather than as formal proofs of His existence.

The conditions of western thought, however, were

[1] Hagenbach, *op. cit.*, Vol. I. pp. 135, 136.

[2] Clement Alex., *Strom.*, iv. 25; v. 12; viii. 3. Cf. Hagenbach, *op. cit.*, p. 139.

[3] Clement Alex., *Strom.*, v. 12.

[4] Cf. ch. ii. § 7, above.

more favourable to the development of theism than
those of the East, and St. Augustine made positive
contributions to theistic argument. Making use of
Platonic methods of thinking, he developed three forms
of idealogical argument. All forms of knowledge,
and even of probability, presuppose necessary truth.
Thus the probable is so regarded by virtue of its
resemblance to presupposed truth. The absoluteness of truth is necessarily postulated, and it must be
grounded in being. The absolute Being, Who is
Truth itself, is God.[1] He reasons in a similar way
about beauty. Beauty permeates the visible universe.
It is not always perceived as adequately as it should
be, but when discerned is seen to be what it is by virtue of participation in absolute and eternal beauty.
The source and standard of all beauty is the eternal
God.[2] Again, he started with the good as seen in
created things. A comparison between good and
evil shows that the essence of good lies in its being,
whereas evil is the privation of being. Every form
of good is what it is by participation in the *ens realis-
simum*, the Supreme Good, Who is absolute Being,
God.[3]

To sum up St. Augustine's idealogy, the changing
things of this world are what they are by participation
in that which changes not. They are contingent,

[1] St. Augustine, *De Lib., Arbit.*, ii. 2–15; *De Vera Relig.*, xxx, xxxi;
Soliloq., i. 3; *Confess.*, xii. 25. Cf. Flint, *Theism*, p. 272; Driscoll,
God, p. 78; Ueberweg, *op. cit.*, Vol. I. pp. 338–340.

[2] *Confess.*, VII. xvii. 23 (cf. X. xxviii. 39).

[3] *De Civ. Dei*, vii. 2 *et seq.*; *De Lib. Arbit.*, iii. 13, 36.

and their existence involves the non-contingent. They are imperfect, and the imperfect is seen to be what it is by contrast with the perfect, the existence of which is presupposed. The world exhibits itself as participative in the true, the beautiful and the good. These are not unreal, but centre in the supreme reality pre-supposed in all reason — that is, in God, who is Truth, Beauty, and Goodness in their ultimate perfection and reality.[1]

§ 12. Mediæval theism is best represented by St. Anselm and St. Thomas Aquinas. St. Anselm inherited St. Augustine's form of thought. In his *Monologium* he developed that writer's argument from the good; and in the *Proslogium* set forth the ontological argument in a form which is classic.[2]

Platonic forms of thought, hitherto prevalent, gave way somewhat in the thirteenth century to the Aristotelic; and St. Thomas Aquinas was most successful in employing the peripatetic philosophy in Christian interests. He dealt with theistic arguments very briefly, but his treatment of them determined the lines of theistic thought for ages, and has had much influence even to the present day.[3]

[1] On St. Augustine's general theistic position, see Ueberweg, *op. cit.*, Vol. I. pp. 333–346; Gratry, *Knowl. of God*, Pt. I. ch. iv (sees more in St. Augustine than is really there); Hagenbach, *Hist. of Christ. Doc.*, Vol. II. pp. 24–26.

[2] It is considered in ch. viii, below. On St. Anselm, see the biographies of him by Dean Church and Martin Rule.

[3] See his *Summa Theologica*, I. ii. 3 (given in Caldecott and Mackintosh, *Selections from the Lit. of Theism.* pp. 23–28. Cf. pp. 10–39). See also his *c. Gent.*, Bk. I. chh. x–xiii.

He set forth five arguments: (*a*) Aristotle's inference from motion and change to "a first source of motion which is moved by nothing else," which "all men understand to be God"; (*b*) The necessity of a first efficient cause to account for the observed order of causation — also found in Aristotle; (*c*) The argument from contingent to necessary being, upon which alone the existence of contingent things can be based; (*d*) The implication of perfect being which is found in the judgment that the things of this world constitute a rising series of imperfect beings — practically a development of St. Augustine's argument for the True, the Beautiful, and the Good; (*e*) All things work teleologically, but are not of themselves the source of the design with reference to which they are governed. There must be a supreme Governor of all, who is God.

St. Thomas argues partly on grounds of reason and experience, for the intelligence,[1] love [2] and will [3] of God, and thus lays foundations for modern discussions of divine personality.[4] He also considers the difficulty of evil on Augustinian lines. Evil is regarded as essentially privative. God is good since there is

---

[1] *Summa Theol.*, I. xiv., esp. art. 1.

[2] *Ibid.*, I. xx., esp. art. 1.

[3] *Ibid.*, xix., esp. art. 1.

[4] He defines *persona* as *rationalis naturae individua substantia*, following Boetius, *Ibid.*, I. xxix. 1. He defends the application of the name *persona* to God (in art. 3 of the same Q.), but in a more excellent manner than it is applied to creatures. The whole of question xxix is important.

no privation of essence in Him, and no accidents which can be the subjects of privation.[1]

Scholastic writers were unable to employ adequate inductions from natural phenomena, for physical science was undeveloped. Their reasoning, therefore, is somewhat particularist and abstract. But they were able, none the less, to formulate lines of argument upon which modern thought depends to a far greater extent than is usually acknowledged.[2]

§ 13. It is impossible within our limits to give an adequate survey of modern theism. Its richness is due to the fact that, inheriting the Christian idea of God, without which an adequate theism cannot be developed, and the theistic forms of thought of scholastic theology, modern theists have been enabled by a fuller knowledge of physical and human nature to employ wider inductions, and by the aid of modern critical philosophy to remove certain crudities of earlier theistic thought. The psychological and moral arguments have received more distinct formulation; agnostic arguments have challenged and caused a more thorough study of, and regard for, the laws of epistemology, and for the conditions of human thought;

---

[1] *Summa Theol.*, I. xlix. Cf. I. v–vi; and *c. Gent.*, Bk. I. ch. xxxix.

[2] The *Theologia Naturalis of* Raymond de Sabonde (early in the fifteenth century) is the only mediæval treatise which treats of the natural self-manifestation of God, in the manner of modern treatises of natural theology. See Caldecott and Mackinstoh, *Selections from the Lit. of Theism*, pp. 37–39. Windelband's *Hist. of Philos.* treats very fully of scholasticism. Cf. Baldwin, *Dic. of Philos.*, *s. v.* "Latin and Scholastic Terminology," by Royce.

and the evolutionary theory has immensely improved theistic argument, especially in its teleological aspects, by compelling theologians to emphasize the significance of the general order and history of nature rather than that of isolated natural phenomena. Modern theism exemplifies the law that every perversion of truth, or attack upon it, brings about in the end a more adequate and convincing exhibition of verity. "The truth is mighty and will prevail." If the present age is troubled with agnosticism and doubt, it has seen the development of an apologetic which can hardly fail to reduce their influence among thoughtful men.

Descartes (1596–1650 A.D.) was influenced by his mathematical genius to place an undue emphasis upon the necessity of a demonstrative basis for knowledge, and sought to build his philosophy upon the reality of thought. He laid down the premise *Cogito, ergo sum.* Analyzing thought, he based a theistic argument upon the idea of the Infinite. This idea, he said, cannot have been derived from experience, which is finite; nor can it have been invented by finite minds. It is innate, therefore, and must have been imparted to the mind by an infinite Creator.[1] His part in preparing the way for modern agnosticism has already been mentioned.[2]

Spinoza (1632–1677 A.D.) adopted Descartes' mathematical and demonstrative method, but in the interests

---

[1] His argument is considered in ch. viii. § 2, below.   On his general position, see Ueberweg, *Hist. of Philos.*, Vol. II. pp. 41–54.
[2] Ch. ii. § 2, above.

of a pantheistic view which he derived, with modifications, from mediæval sources and from Bruno. He
emphasized the principle of causation, as determining
all things without possibility of teleological variation.
He rejected teleology altogether, as excluded by the
law of necessity which is involved in causation. This
emphasis upon the principle of causation and the
invariability of its working has profoundly influenced
later thought in relation to divine government and
miracles. He declared God to be the First-Cause
and Substance of all things, infinite and eternal. His
infinitude, which was viewed quantitatively, was said
to exclude the existence of other substances. All
things are modes of divine substance and unalterably
determined by the law of causation. This doctrine
was supported by *a priori*, cosmological and mathematical considerations. He also anticipated the tendency which is seen in Schleiermacher, the Ritschlians,
and the pragmatists to divorce the interests of objective truth from those of religion and piety.[1]

Leibnitz (1646–1716 A.D.), while following the dogmatic rationalism of Descartes and Spinoza, substi-
tuted for Spinoza's one substance, and for Descartes'
dualism, a theory of multitudinous monads, severally
complete, and kept in harmony by divine and creative
arrangements. Their mutual relations are external and

---

[1] His system is given in its maturest form in *Ethica more Geo-
metrico*. See Flint, *Anti-Theistic Theories*, *pp.* 358–375, 546–551;
Ueberweg, *op. cit.*, Vol. II. pp. 55–78; Pfleiderer, *Philos. of Relig.*,
Vol. I. § I. ch. i.

mechanical.[1] His philosophy was popularized, with modifications, by *Wolff* (1679–1754 A.D.), whose influence was paramount in Germany until Kant's time.[2]

Eighteenth-century theistic thought was dominated in England as well as in Germany by mechanical views of the universe and its government, and by complacent belief in the capacity of reason to demonstrate God's existence with mathematical certainty. A bald intellectualism was in evidence. Revelation was considered exclusively in its supernatural forms, and was regarded by those who acknowledged its reality as purely external, and as consisting of a series of publications of divine truth, severally final. Deistic rationalists either regarded revelation as an authentication of moral truths otherwise discoverable by reason, or repudiated it as contrary to reason and to the established order of nature. The tendency to regard God as external to His world — as a *Deus ex machina* — was generally prevalent.[3] Theistic argument took the demonstrative form,[4] and this is especially seen in the *a priori* argument of *Samuel Clarke* (1675–1729 A.D.)[5] and the teleology of *Wm. Paley* (1743–1805 A.D.).

[1] On Leibnitz, see Ueberweg, *op. cit.*, Vol. II. pp. 92–114; Pfleiderer, *op. cit.*, Vol. I. § I. ch. ii.

[2] Ueberweg, *op. cit.*, Vol. II. p. 114, 116; Pfleiderer, *op. cit.*, Vol. I. § I. ch. iii.

[3] See Pfleiderer, *op. cit.*, Vol. I. § I. ch. iv; Geo. Fisher, *Hist. of Christ. Doctrine*, Period V. ch. i. A. S. Farrar, *Hist. of Free Thought*, chh. iv, v, gives a thoughtful survey of the 18th century.

[4] See Caldecott, *Philos. of Relig.*, pp. 114–119.

[5] Discussed by Flint, in *Encyc. Brit.*, *s. v.* "Samuel Clarke." It is to be found in the Boyle Lec. of 1704.

The latter writer, after the manner of Leibnitz, treated the contents of nature as if they were mutually independent and severally complete. The evidences of design were discovered in particular instances of adaptation, rather than in the general course of nature.[1]

In the meantime the empirical philosophy was promoted by *Locke* (1632–1704 A.D.),[2] and given more consistent formulation by *Hume* (1711–1776 A.D.). Hume also brought eighteenth-century scepticism to its final stage, carrying certain elements in the epistemology of Descartes, Locke, and Berkeley to their *reductio ad absurdum*.[3]

Immanuel Kant (1724–1804 A.D.) inherited the dogmatic rationalism of Leibnitz and Wolff, but was roused by the scepticism of Hume to throw off his "dogmatic slumber." He did not, however, wholly escape from dogmatism. His *Critique of Pure Reason*, wherein he undertook to prove the invalidity of the rational bases of theistic knowledge, and his *Critique of the Practical Reason*, in which he treated the ideas of God, of the world and of ego as necessary postulates of human thinking, have determined the

[1] *Natural Theology.* Paley's clear and persuasive style made his treatise the leading text-book on the subject during the first half of the nineteenth century. The *Bridgewater Treatises* elaborate Paley's argument. Paley was not so absurd as he is often said to have been, nor is the fundamental principle of his argument at fault. Cf. V. F. Storr, *Development and Divine Purpose*, ch. ii.

[2] On Locke's position, see Ueberweg, *op. cit.*, Vol. II. pp. 79–88; Pfleiderer, *op. cit.*, Vol. I. pp. 113–116. Cf. p. 18, above.

[3] Cf. ch. ii. § 2, above. On his position, see Ueberweg, *op. cit.*, Vol. II. pp. 130–135; Pfleiderer, *op. cit.*, Vol. I. pp. 127–133.

general course of theistic thought since his time.[1]
His adverse criticisms of the ordinary lines of demonstrative theistic arguments are vitiated to some extent
by his point of view; but they have proved to be of
great value, none the less, and have prepared the way
for the development of a richer and sounder theism.
Kant is indeed the real founder of present-day theistic
philosophy, in spite of his responsibility for the prevalence of theological agnosticism.

That portion of Kant's philosophy which treats
of the idea of God as a necessary postulate of practical
reason engaged the attention of his German successors, and *George William Hegel* (1770-1831 A.D.)
formulated a theory of transcendental dialectic which is
thought by many to give cognitive validity to the idea
of God by proving the identity of the ideal and the real.
His theistic philosophy is difficult to master, and his
followers have not agreed in their interpretations. But
his transcendental idealism has had an influence upon
theism hardly less important than that of Kant.[2]

[1] Cf. ch. ii. § 3, above. On his position, see Ueberweg, *op. cit.*,
Vol. II. pp. 137-194; J. Watson, *Extracts from the Writings of Kant;*
and *The Philos. of Kant Explained;* E. Caird, *Crit. Philos. of Imman.
Kant;* Pfleiderer, *op. cit.*, Vol. I. § I. ch. vi; Flint, *Agnosticism*, ch. iv.
Pt. IV (a searching criticism).

[2] On Hegel's position, see Ueberweg, *op. cit.*, Vol. II. pp. 231-243
(who gives a bibliography of his works, p. 234); J. H. Stirling, *The
Secret of Hegel* (a full exposition in 2 vols.); Pfleiderer, *op. cit.* Vol. II.
pp. 78-114; Caldecott, *Philos. of Relig.*, pp. 29-36. Among English
speaking writers who reflect the influence of Hegel may be mentioned
John and Edward Caird, J. H. Stirling, T. H. Green, T. B. Strong,
W. T. Harris, and Josiah Royce.

The evolutionary theory of *Charles Darwin* (1809–1882 A.D.), exhibited in his *Origin of the Species* (published in 1859), had a momentous effect on theism. It gave a heavy blow to Paley's method of looking for evidences of design in particular instances of adaptation; but led to the development of a more defensible teleological argument, based upon the general course and intelligible trend of natural evolution. It also indirectly brought about an abandonment of the deistic separation between God and His world. The immanence of God has come to be emphasized — sometimes pantheistically, and at the expense of divine transcendence and personality.[1]

The "New Knowledge," as it is called, as to the nature of matter, occasioned by investigations into the phenomena of radium, is too fresh for its effect upon theism to be determined with certainty.[2] It appears to us, however, to accentuate the drift away from materialism which has set in of late years, and to fortify the doctrine of spiritual causation of all things which theism embodies.

IV. *Its Methods*

§ 14. Our rapid survey of the history of theism leads us to look for a wide diversity of methods in modern theistic discussions. The vast enlargement

---

[1] Cf. pp. 155, 156, below.

[2] The phenomena in question are abundantly described in Duncan's *New Knowledge.* Cf. Prof. Pellat, *New State of Matter;* Whetham, *Recent Devel. of Phys. Science,* chh. vi, vii.

of knowledge of theistic data and the increased complexity of contemporary thought make it difficult to give a coherent summary of the methods and arguments which are to be reckoned with at the present time by theistic students. This treatise, however, will be incomplete without some sort of summary, however imperfect.[1]

Broadly speaking, theism has been either rational, or empirical, or both.[2] Rational theism emphasizes the validity of thought, the capacity of the reason to transcend the data of experience, and the rational validity of the higher knowledge thus obtained. Empirical theism, on the other hand, emphasizes experience as the real basis of knowledge, and professes to discover sufficient grounds of theistic belief without transcending its contents. Rational theists may either make the theistic hypothesis their original postulate, verifying it by inductive arguments, or attempt — unsuccessfully, we believe — to avoid presuppositions, and to arrive at theistic belief only as the conclusion of argument and the final chapter of their philosophy.

We shall find that many writers are either too individualistic or too comprehensive in their methods to be described either as rational or as empirical theists.

[1] In making such summary Caldecott's valuable *Philosophy of Religion* has been freely used, although some changes have been made in the arrangement of types. That book deserves careful study. Its survey is limited, with a few exceptions, to English and American writers since the reformation; but the variety of theistic types exhibited is practically exhaustive.

[2] Caldecott, *op. cit.*, pp. 4–7.

And we believe that those theists are right who refuse to regard either the rational or the empirical points of view, considered in isolation, as adequate. An adequate theism starts with experience of God, whatever view may be taken of the nature of such experience, and then makes the accepted fact of God's existence to be the postulate and subject-matter of rational methods of investigation and verification. At all events, the fact that the being of God is at least implicitly presupposed in all theistic argument, and in human reasoning generally, in our judgment is certain.

The classification of types which is here adopted is as follows. I. *Rational types:* (*a*) Demonstrative; (*b*) Transcendental; (*c*) Ethical; (*d*) Æsthetical; (*e*) Combined speculative and ethical. II. *Empirical types:* (*a*) Social; (*b*) Intuitional; (*c*) Mystical: III. *Classified by psychical faculties:* (*a*) Intellectual; (*b*) Emotional; (*c*) Volitional; (*d*) Comprehensive (Personalism). This last group constitutes an unavoidable cross division.[1]

---

[1] Caldecott classifies the intuitional with rational types, and our third group with empirical types.

A more comprehensive division of the attitudes adopted by philosophical thinkers towards the theistic problem — one which includes non-theistic writers — might be made as follows: (*a*) A natural and immediate consciousness of God; (*b*) His existence provable by *a priori* argument; (*c*) Provable, but by *a posteriori* argument; (*d*) Not capable of either proof or disproof (sceptical); (*e*) Exclusive dependence upon supernatural revelation; (*f*) Explicit anti-theism. This is an elaboration of Boedder's classification — *Natural Theol.*, pp. 9–12.

§ 15. (*a*) First among the rational types comes the *demonstrative*. Those who are thus classed conceive of the universe as exhibiting causation and purpose, and depend upon *a posteriori* arguments to establish the truth of theistic doctrine. The trustworthiness of human reason, and the reality of the external world, are accepted on *a priori* grounds; but the method of argument is *a posteriori*.[1] The *a priori* argument receives little attention by theists of this type:[2]

(*b*) *Transcendental* theism dates from Kant, but was developed by his successors, especially by Hegel. The necessary postulates of reason — Kant's transcendental ideas — are treated as "constructive of

[1] The Vatican Council declares, *Constit. Prima*, capp. i, ii (trans. in Wm. Humphrey's *His Divine Majesty*, pp. viii–xi), that the being of God can be established on grounds of natural experience and reason. This is the position of St. Thomas, *Summa Theol.*, I. i; *c. Gent.*, I. x–xiii. Among Roman Catholic writers are B. Boedder, (*Nat. Theol.*, 1891); R. F. Clarke (*The Existence of God*, 1887); and J. F. Driscoll (*Christian Philos.: God*, 1904). Among others are Locke (*Essay*, 1690), Bishop Pearson (*The Apos. Creed*, 1659); William Paley (*Natural Theology*, 1803); Thos. Chalmers (*Nat. Theol.*). Jas. McCosh (*Method of Divine Government*, 1850; *First and Fundamental Truths*, 1889); J. Tulloch (*Theism*, 1855), Eighth Duke of Argyll (*Philos. of Belief*, 1896); J. B. Mozley (*Essays*, 1878; *Univ. Serms.*, 1876; *Bamp. Lecs.*, 1865); R. Flint (*Theism*, 1876) and W. N. Clarke (*Can I Believe in God the Father?* 1899).

[2] Prominent exceptions are Leibnitz and Wolff in Germany, and Dr. Samuel Clarke (*A Demonstration of the Being and Attrib. of God*, 1704) and W. H. Gillespie (*The Necessary Existence of God*, 1833). Several writers, while denying the formal validity of the ontological argument, regard it as bringing to light the dependence of reason for its validity upon the truth of the idea of God. So T. B. Strong, James Lindsay, and R. Flint.

intelligent experience," and therefore as exhibiting realities. The data of experience become wholly without meaning on any other supposition. The most fundamental of the transcendental ideas is the idea of God. It "is necessary for the explanation of the ideas of self and the world — in themselves and in relation to each other." The idea of God as really existing is therefore inseparable from, and essential to, our trust in reason. The validity of reason stands or falls with the validity of this idea. This line of thought is *a priori*, and appeals too exclusively to mere intellect to be effective, unless co-ordinated with *a posteriori* argument. Transcendentalists are usually conscious of this; and treat the necessary postulate of God as unifying theistic proofs, so called, and as giving them their proper and coherent meaning and value.[1]

(*c*) *Ethical* theism of the rationalist type starts with "the sense of the reality of the deliverances of the moral

---

[1] Among the transcendentalists are John Caird (*Philos. of Relig.*, 1880); Ewd. Caird (*Evolution of Relig.*, 1892), T. H. Green (*Introd. to Hume*, 1874; *Proleg. to Ethics*, 1883), T. B. Strong (*Man. of Theol.*, 1892), J. H. Stirling (*Gifford Lecs.*, 1889–1890), A. W. Momerie (*The Being of God*, 1886), Jas. Lindsay (*Recent Advances in the Philos. of Relig.*, 1897), C. M. Tyler (*The Basis of Relig. Belief*, 1897), and Josiah Royce (*The Relig. Aspect of Philos.*, 1885; *The Conception of God*, 1895).

The transcendental method has influenced the theistic argument of many who cannot be regarded as being transcendentalists in the strict sense. For example, J. G. Schurman (*Belief in God*, 1890), A. J. Balfour (*The Foundations of Belief*, 1895), T. B. Saunders (*The Quest of Faith*, 1899), and W. E. H. Lecky (*The Map of Life*, 1899).

8

judgment; of the obligation to do right, to be virtuous, to love goodness and to pursue it." In brief,
the moral argument, so called, is given the primary
and interpretive place, and is sharply distinguished
from the arguments of causation and design. The
point emphasized is that the ideal which our sense of
obligation involves transcends all our moral achievements and therefore requires the assumption of a
transcendental source. Other arguments are employed, but in moral connections, and with attention to
their spiritual significance.[1]

(*d*) Under the *æsthetical* type come those who emphasize the theistic implication of the omnipresent
fact of beauty. St. Augustine had done this, but
was not followed in this regard by mediæval writers.
Beauty was given its place again in Scotland by Hutcheson and Reid. Kant paid some attention to it, and
Cousin emphasized it. The Romanticism of the early
part of the nineteenth century also had an influence
— not very effective in philosophy — in the same direction. The rarity of emphasis upon beauty in theism is
due to a frequent failure to realize its objective nature.
Empiricism has had a wide-spread effect of blunting
the sense of beauty. Theism, in consequence, has

[1] Kant's *Critique of Practical Reason*, and Butler's *Sermons on
Human Nature* look in this direction. The influence of German
idealism has combined with a revulsion from the arid intellectuality of eighteenth-century rational methods to give this type increasing prominence. Later examples are Abp. Temple (*Relations
between Religion and Science*, 1884), A. C. Fraser (*Philos. of Theism,*
1894–1896), and Andrew Seth (*Theism*, 1897).

been deprived of its own. By æsthetical theists beauty has been treated either demonstratively, as an effect to be accounted for, or idealistically, as unintelligible unless we postulate the Infinite as the source of its reality.[1]

(e) Those who are not satisfied with the demonstrative type of theism cannot invariably be classed strictly either in the transcendental or in the ethical group, but adopt a *combined speculative and ethical* theism. The validity of abstract reason is accepted; but practical and ethical considerations are employed also as constituting important elements in an adequate theistic argument.[2]

§ 16. We now come to *empirical* theism. Such theism rests upon the claim that the presence of the Infinite Being is objectively experienced, so that experience itself is a sufficient basis, apart from inferential proof, for the assertion that the Absolute and Infinite exists. Experience is manifold, and such a

---

[1] John Ruskin (*Modern Painters*, etc.) is the most prominent writer of this type. Seeley (*Natural Religion*) also dwells upon the significance of beauty. J. H. Kennedy (*Natural Theol. and Mod. Thought*, 1889) emphasizes the æsthetic argument at some length. J. B. Mozley, Dean Church, and Bishop Barry ought also to be mentioned.

[2] Examples are Richard Hooker (*Eccles. Polity*, Books I–IV, *passim*, 1594), Bishop Berkeley (*Works*, ed. by Fraser, 1871), who treats the world as consisting of sense symbols whereby the divine mind speaks to us, Bishop Butler (*Sermons*, 1726; *Analogy*, 1736), and, more recently, W. G. Ward (*Philos. of Theism*, 1884), John Fiske (*Cosmic Philos.*, 1874; *Man's Destiny*, 1881; *Idea of God*, 1885; *Through Nature to God*. 1899), and Prof. Le Conte (*Evolution*, Pt. III., 2d. ed., 1895). The last two enlist the theory of evolution.

claim need not, and does not, mean an assertion of open vision. It includes social theism, intuitional theism, and mysticism. The first dwells upon the experience of mankind at large, the last two upon individual experience.

(*a*) *Social* theism emphasizes the fact of general consent, as exhibiting experience of God on the part of mankind. This experience is varied. It issues in diverse notions of God, and is embodied in many religions. The universal prevalence of religion constitutes evidence of common consent and this consent is regarded as justifying individual belief in God.[1]

(*b*) The *intuitional* type is based upon belief that men are able when contemplating the phenomena of natural experience to look beyond and directly to perceive the Supreme Reality upon which all things depend. Kant described the idea of God as a necessary postulate of the reason, but the theists with whom we are here concerned regard it as an intuitive perception of reality, perceived through the transparent window of phenomena. Nature is for them not so much a mirror as a window. It affords confirmatory evidence; but intuition rather than inference is said to be the real basis of our knowledge of God. The

[1] Caldecott says that it is difficult to find English thinkers who are consistent social theists. But he discovers affinities to social theism in the positions of Matthew Arnold (*Literature and Dogma*, 1873; *God and the Bible*, 1875) and Benjamin Kidd (*Social Evolution*, 1894). It would be a mistake to suppose that all writers who employ the argument *e consensu gentium*, interpret consent as exhibiting experience of God. Cf. ch. iv. §§ 1, 2, below.

non-universality of this experience is explained by special subjective causes, such as sin and spiritual inertia.[1]

(c) *Mystical* theists resemble the intuitionalists in affirming the possibility of a direct perception of the Supreme Reality, but connect it with conditions and methods that intuitionalists do not consider to be either natural or normal. The mystic acknowledges his dependence upon supernatural assistance, but is apt to regard his experience of God as strictly normal.[2] It is the man who misses such experience who is abnormal in his estimation. Mystical theology speaks of a threefold way — purgative, illuminative and unitive — the last being realized in an ecstatic contemplation of God through the *media* of transparent symbols. Thorough-going mystics rarely concern themselves with theistic arguments, but are not precluded by their principles from accepting their value or even from making use of them to confirm faith. Many writers are mystical in that they acknowledge the possibility of the experiences claimed by mystics,

[1] Among intuitionalists are Lord Herbert of Cherbury (*Tractatus de Veritate*, 1624), Theodore Parker (*Theism*, 1842; *Disc. on Relig.*), J. D. Morell (*Philos. of Religion*, 1849), Samuel T. Harris (*Philosophical Basis of Theism*, 1887; *The Self-Revelation of God*, 1899), J. J. Murphey (*Scientific Bases of Faith*, 1873; *Natural Selection and Spiritual Freedom*, 1893) and W. Knight (*Aspects of Theism*, 1893).

[2] Not in the sense of ordinary, or common to the majority, but as being within the proper capacity of all who attain to the state which God has made attainable for mankind in this life by means of grace and ascetic self-culture. Cf. F. Granger, *The Soul of a Christian*, pp. 151 *et seq.*

without either regarding them as normal or claiming to have enjoyed them.[1]

§ 17. The above given classification of theistic methods is, we believe, *logically* complete and helpful. But it cannot in every case be applied successfully in classifying individual theists, for many of them do not exclusively employ any one of the methods which we have described. This should be remembered in considering many of the names mentioned in the foot-notes. It is what the writers named appear severally to emphasize that has determined their clas-

---

[1] Caldecott is not as successful as usual in treating of this type. Récéjac's *Bases of the Mystic Knowledge;* Inge's *Christian Mysticism;* Scott's *Aspects of Christian Mysticism;* F. Granger's *Soul of a Christian;* and T. T. Carter's *Life of Grace* are useful guides. Prof. James' *Varieties of Religious Experience* is very valuable, although somewhat alien in its point of view. Caldecott groups with this type those whom he calls "comprehensive intuitivists," who acknowledge some kind of direct experience of God and proceed to investigate the phenomenal world theistically: *e.g.* S. T. Coleridge (*The Friend*, 1818; *Aids to Reflection*, 1825; *Confessions of an Inquiring Spirit*, 1840), Julius Hare (*Univ. Sermons*), Frederick D. Maurice, Francis Newman (*The Soul*, 1849), H. B. Swete (*Faith*, 1895), W. B. Pope (*Higher Catechism of Theol.*, 1883); G. P. Fisher (*Grounds of Theistic and Christian Belief*, 1889, 1902), W. S. Lilly (*The Great Enigma*, 1892), Bishop Westcott (*Gospel of Life*, 1892; *Relig. Thought in the West*, 1891), Aubrey Moore (*Lux Mundi*, II., 1889; *Science and the Faith*, 1889; *Essays*, 1890), J. R. Illingworth (*Lux Mundi*, V. 1889; *Personality*, 1894; *Divine Immanence*, 1898), G. J. Romanes (*Thoughts on Relig.*, 1895), and H. P. Liddon (*Some Elements of Religion*, 1872). S. T. Harris (*Self Revelation of God*, 1886) may be added. Some writers refer the experience of God to a special faculty; some, like Schleiermacher, reduce it to emotion; and some consider it to be the result of harmoniously exercising all the psychical faculties together.

sification. And many theists are either too comprehensive in their methods [1] or too individualistic [2] to
be classed with any particular group.

It should be added also that certain writers are most
conveniently grouped in supplementary cross divisions, according to the psychical faculties which they
consider to be enlisted.[3]

(a) Many have either repudiated the part of emotion
and will in theism, or have practically ignored these
factors of spiritual knowledge, depending on a bald
intellectualism.[4]

(b) Others have considered the knowledge of God
to be exclusively *emotional* in form or basis.[5]

---

[1] For example, Bishop Barry (*Nat. Theol.*, 1876), J. J. Lias (*Is it Possible to know God?* 1883; *Nicene Creed*, 1897), R. Travers Smith (*Man's Knowledge of Man and of God*, 1884–1885), Jas. Martineau (*Study of Religion*, 1887), E. R. Conder (*Basis of Faith*, 1877), C. Voysey (*Theism*, 1895), J. R. Seeley (*Nat. Religion*, 1882) and W. L. Davidson (*Theism*, 1892–1893).

[2] Hobbes (*Leviathan*, 1651), who made God the supreme Governor, who is to be obeyed — a despot; and Deists, of whom Lord
Herbert of Cherbury is a type. Also those who reduce God to the
finite, *e.g.* F. C. S. Schiller (*Riddles of the Sphinx*, 2d ed. 1894).

[3] Caldecott classifies them with empirical theists, but this does not
seem to be strictly accurate. Personal experience of God is not the
point which they emphasize; and some of them would repudiate the
empirical point of view.

[4] Such was the deficiency of the demonstrative theists of the deistic
period; and Hegel and his followers betray the same tendency.

[5] Schleiermacher conceived of religion as essentially a feeling of
dependence. The Ritschlians make existential-judgments give way
to value-judgments in matters of religion. The tendency to pure
emotionalism is found among pietists of all types. The British
tendency, however, has been to disparage the part of feeling. Wm.

(c) A few have reduced theistic belief to an act of the *will*.[1]

(d) The best theistic writers of our day have insisted that all our faculties are exercised in the knowledge of God, and that truth in this direction requires for its attainment the action of man's entire psychical nature.[2]

Our survey will be incomplete, if we do not call attention to certain anti-theistic writers who discuss theistic arguments, and who, in some instances, serve the interests of what they repudiate;[3] and also to writers

---

J. Fox (*Works*, 1865, Vol. VIII) is an exception. He goes to the other extreme, on unitarian and pantheistic lines. The part of feeling is asserted in a more reasonable way by Flint (*Theism*), Illingworth (*Personality*), R. C. Moberly (*Reason and Religion*), and others.

[1] The most representative example, perhaps, is W. James (*The Will to Believe*, 1897). Cf. also H. B. Swete (*Faith*, Pt. II), who regards faith as "in the last analysis the act of the will and not of the intellect. Many who could not be classed with Prof. James insist upon the active nature of spiritual intelligence, and upon the part of will in theistic knowledge.

[2] J. H. Newman (*Grammar of Assent*, 1870) is the most notable example, especially as he disparages the part of formal logic in the interests of the "illative sense," and of a personal certitude which arises from the exercise of all our psychical faculties. Cf. also F. J. A. Hort (*The Way, the Truth, and the Life*, 1874–1893), E. A. Abbott (*The Kernel and the Husk*, 1888), A. J. Mason (*Faith of the Gospel*, 1887), and R. C. Moberly (*Reason and Religion*). Many theists, of various types, emphasize the part of all our faculties in belief.

[3] David Hume (*Dialogues concerning Natural Religion*, 1750; *Natural Hist. of Religion*, 1757), J S. Mill (*Three Essays on Religion*, 1873), G. J. Romanes (*Candid Exam. of Theism*, by Physicus, 1878), who abandoned his unbelief later, and Herbert Spencer (*First Principles*, 1860; Arts. in the *Nineteenth Century*, 1884). Spencer's works are very useful for theism.

who reject theistic argument, and the capacity of human reason to know God, in the interests of supernatural revelation.[1]

§ 18. The method of a theistic writer inevitably depends upon whether his aim is apologetical or systematic. An apologist seeks primarily to persuade, and will therefore adapt his method to his constituency and to his age. This is illustrated by the fact that, although the argument for the truth of Christianity which is based upon miracles is valid, and ought not to be neglected in a scientific treatise of theology, it is not usually emphasized in an age in which the miraculous element in Christianity is apt to be regarded as one of its difficulties. Similar considerations cause theistic treatises to be more or less restricted in scope.

It is the aim of a systematic theologian, on the other hand, when treating of theism, to embrace in one comprehensive scheme every important line of thought and argument which bears upon his subject. He seeks, of course, to make clear the persuasive value of the evidence of God's being and attributes; but he writes for believers in God, and scientific completeness and logical connection are his paramount considerations. The importance of each line of thought is estimated by its intrinsic validity and scientific relation, rather than by the estimate likely to be placed upon it by particular types of thinkers.

[1] Lord Bacon (*Advancement of Learning*, 1605), H. L. Mansel (*Limits of Relig. Thought*, 1858), and Scott-Holland (*On Behalf of Belief*, 2d ed., 1892, p. 89).

The aim of this treatise is scientific, for it is part of a work of Dogmatic Theology. We believe that each of the methods which we have been describing in the sections immediately preceding embodies valid thought and argument, which should be given due place and proportionate emphasis. Thus the part of each psychical faculty in the knowledge of God — whether intellectual, emotional, or volitional — requires acknowledgment at the outset. It also needs to be emphasized that the self-revelation of God, on the one hand, whether natural or supernatural, and the active operation of our minds under spiritual conditions of enlightenment, on the other hand, are essential prerequisites of theistic knowledge. Finally it ought to be confessed that no one can come to a just consideration of theistic arguments without theistic presuppositions. The state of the question has to be reckoned with, and that is determined by the fact of world-wide consent, and by the claim of countless millions to have come into experiential contact with God. That the being of God is the implicit postulate of every theistic argument is one of the most indubitable conclusions of modern psychological and critical investigation, and is undoubtedly an important factor in the general prevalence of religion and of theistic consent. It is not necessary to become a disciple of any school in order to acknowledge this.

These considerations determine our method. That God exists, and that He is the infinite, personal, all-powerful, wise and righteous Creator, Sustainer, and

Governor of all being, life, and history, is our avowed conviction at the outset. And this belief is laid down as our working hypothesis — one which occupies the field, and which can be verified by a multitude of pertinent facts and considerations, that are made available by experience and rational reflection. We are not inquirers, but investigators.

We are not pioneers in this investigation; nor do we expect to contribute anything substantially new to the subject. The labours of many of the greatest thinkers of our race, moreover, emancipate us from the necessity of marshalling in their multitudinous details the facts which have theistic bearing. These facts have been generalized in what are called theistic "proofs," and we shall devote our attention to these "proofs," considering them one by one.

The word "proof," as here employed, is not to be taken as committing us to any exaggerated view of the evidential force of the several theistic arguments. Our method is inductive. The proofs, which are mainly *a posteriori*, constitute generalizations of the several lines of investigation which appear to confirm the theistic hypothesis. Their evidential force is very unequal, and is not correctly estimated except when the proofs are considered in mutual connection as interrelated parts of a comprehensive induction. To put it in a conventional way, the force of theistic argument is cumulative. We do not consider any of the proofs to be sufficient in isolation. Considered together we reckon them — not as formally demonstrative in effect, but — as constituting an induction amply sufficient to justify theistic certainty, and to put men to a probation of whole-hearted surrender to the divine will and government.

CHAPTER IV

THE STATE OF THE QUESTION

I. *Consent and Experience*

§ 1. In several chapters which follow we shall consider the chief theistic arguments.[1] By way of preface this chapter will be devoted to the state of the question. This is obviously determined by the views hitherto prevailing, and by men's experience of God, if there has been such experience.

Traditional views are summed up in the phrase *consensus gentium*, or the fact that some sort of belief in the Divine has prevailed, so far as our sure knowledge extends, in every age, in every race, and in every clime.[2] The evidence of this fact consists mainly in

[1] For a bibliography of theism see note at the commencement of ch. iii, above, and notes in §§ 15–17, same chapter.

[2] For treatments of theistic consent, see Caldecott, *Philos. of Relig.*, Introd. § 2; Driscoll, *God*, chh. ii, iii; C. Harris, *Pro Fide*, ch. viii; Boedder, *Natural Theol.*, pp. 62–76; Illingworth, *Personality*, note 15, pp. 249–251; Blackie, *Atheism*, pp. 5–16; Staley, *Natural Relig.*, *pp.* 63–72; Stanton, *Place of Authority*, pp. 56–63; R. Flint, *Theism*, App. note viii; *Anti-Theistic Theories*, Lec. VII. Classical references are Cicero, *De Nat. Deorum*, i. 17; *Tusc. Quest.*, i. 13; *De Legibus*, i. 8; Seneca, *Epis.* 117; Lactantius, *Div. Instit.* Bk. I. chh. ii, v. Agnostic and adverse treatments are found in H. Spencer, *First Prins.*, Introd. §§ 1, 2, 4; J. S. Mill, *Theism*, pp. 155 *et seq.* Various works in comparative religion are referred to below.

Among the Christian fathers who consider the fact of consent,

the universal prevalence of religion. It is now acknowledged by the foremost specialists in the subject that no race, however debased, can be found in which religion is wholly wanting.[1]

§ 2. It is true that many religions require careful scrutiny before we can discover in them even the most elementary germs of belief in the Divine.[2] It needs also to be acknowledged that monotheism, which is the only true form of theism, appears usually to be confined — at least in articulate development — to the more highly cultivated races.[3] These facts have

which they often connect with a naturally implanted consciousness of God, are Justin M., *Apol.*, ii. 6; *Dial. with Trypho*, ch. 93; Clement Alex., *Strom.*, v. 12–14; *Cohort.*, vi. 59; Theophilus, *ad Autol.* init.; Minutius Felix, *Octavius*, ch. 32; Tertullian, *De Testim. Animæ*, ii; *Apol.*, xvii; Origen, *c. Celsus*, vii. 37; *De Princip.* iv. 37; St. Athanasius, *c. Gent.*, 35; S. Gregory Naz., *Orat.* xxxiv. 3–21; St. Augustine, *Confess.*, x. 27; *De Genes. ad Lit.*, IV. xxxii. 4–9; St. John Damasc., *Orth. Fid.*, I. iv.   Cf. Hagenbach, *Hist of Christ. Doc.*, § 35; Franzelin, *De Deo Uno*, Thes. vii.

[1] "Writers approaching the subject from such different points of view as Professor Tylor, Max Müller, Ratzel, de Quatrefages, Tiele, Waitz, Gerland, Peschel, all agree that there are no races, however rude, which are destitute of all idea of religion." Jevons, *Introd. to the Hist. of Religion*, p. 7.   Cf. Flint, *Anti-theistic Theories*, Lec. vii.   We have given a bibliography of comparative religion in *Introd. to Dog. Theol.*, p. 212, note 1.

[2] Liddon defines religion correctly as "the idea of an obligation by which man is bound to an invisible Lord." *Some Elements*, Lec. I.   Cf. our *Introd. to Dog. Theol.*, p. 214, note 1.   Max Müller, *Origin of Religion*, pp. 10 *et seq.*, discusses the etymology of "religion," and gives the chief modern definitions.   Cf. Baldwin, *Dic. of Philos.*, s. v. "Religion (Nature of)."

[3] Exceptions occur among the native Australians, African tribes, and American Indians. References to support this contention are

been urged as reducing, and even as nullifying, the theistic nature and value of the consent which we are considering.[1]

Obviously we are not justified by the facts, if we appeal to an explicit acknowledgment by all mankind of the one infinite God with whose existence and nature we are concerned. But this mistake cannot rightly be attributed to modern theistic writers.[2] Aristotle lays down the truism that "the real nature of a thing is whatsoever it becomes, when the process of its development is complete."[3] In order, therefore, to understand the true significance of the universal prevalence of religion, we need only to take note of the fact that theism, in the sense in which we use the term, is the ultimate form which religion assumes when developed according to its own nature. There are indeed religions which are the results of degeneration. But there is no real difficulty in identifying the

given by Driscoll, *God*, pp. 27, 28. In particular see Lang, *Making of Religion*, pp. 180 *et seq.*, and Macculloch, *Comparative Theol.*, ch. ii.

[1] Physicus (G. J. Romanes) dismisses the argument from consent with scant courtesy as "clearly fallacious, both as to facts and principles": *Candid Exam. of Theism*, p. 6.

[2] Thus Boedder, *Natural Theol.*, p. 62, is careful to limit the subject-matter of consent to "the existence of an intelligent nature superior to the material world and to man"; and argues that this universal belief must be based upon truth, and that the existence of a personal God is implied in such truth. Cf. pp. 195, 196 of the same work.

[3] Given by Staley, *Natural Relig.*, p. vi. Cf. Fairbairn, *Philos. of the Christ. Relig.*, pp. 214, 215; V. F. Storr, *Devel. and Divine Purpose*, pp. 223–226; Ladd, *Philos. of Relig.*, Vol. I. pp. 110 *et seq.*

system which most unmistakably exhibits the development of religion *after its kind* — Christianity. In any case, theism is latent in the inferior religions, whether we regard them as the seeds of future growth,[1] or as the result of a falling away from higher and purer forms. And this is borne out by the fact that a study of the languages employed by savages, and the knowledge gained by those who observe their practices and conversation at close range, show the existence of a latent consciousness of a Supreme Being, which superstition is not able wholly to eradicate.[2] To realize the nature and significance of this consensus, however, we should notice that it becomes more determinate and unqualified with the advance of knowledge and thought. The higher races possess the most definite theistic convictions.

§ 3. Atheistic philosophers undoubtedly exist, but they are exceptional, and their position can be accounted for by causes which prove the rule that the normal man shows an increasing tendency towards

---

[1] The contention that the religions of savage races exhibit religion in its primitive stage of development gains what plausibility it possesses from the theory of a purely natural evolution of religion, and from the assumption that primitive man was incapable of possessing an articulate consciousness of God. Recent investigation shows, however, that linguistic traces remain among the debased races, with other evidences, of the previous existence of higher and purer forms of religion. See Max Müller, *Science of Relig.*, pp. 71 *et seq.*; Lang, *The Making of Relig.*, ch. xv; Pfleiderer, *Philos. of Relig.*, Vol. III. pp. 15, 16. Ladd, *op. cit.*, pp. 134–136.

[2] Driscoll, *God*, pp. 39–42 (who gives numerous references); Lang, *Making of Relig.*, chh. ix–xv.

definite theistic belief as he advances in civilization.[1]
Three causes for the existence of atheism may be mentioned. (a) The first is moral and spiritual blindness,
due either to excessive absorption in scientific and non-
spiritual interests, or to lack of submission to the conditions and laws of spiritual knowledge. The natural
sciences are concerned exclusively with the conjunction
and sequence of phenomena, and the habits of scientific specialists sometimes bring about an atrophy of
the higher faculties.[2] (b) Again, a false and sceptical
conception of the nature and laws of belief and knowledge — one which is based exclusively upon abstract
speculation, and fails to accord with normal experience
— will shut out from consideration the manifold self-
revelation of God.[3] (c) Finally, personal circumstances
such as exceptional early education, unfortunate experiences with professing believers, and an exclusive
consideration of perverted religious systems, will
often create violent prejudice and blinding hate of the

[1] Blackie's *Natural Hist. of Atheism*, chh. iii, vi, surveys the
varieties of atheism, tracing them to (a) mental imbecility; (b) moral
incapacity; (c) indocility; (d) reaction from doctrinal caricatures.
Cf. Caldecott, *Philos. of Religion*, pp. 15, 16. S. Harris, *Self-Revel.
of God*, pp. 348–353; Flint, *Anti-Theistic Theories*, pp. 5–8 and
Lec. vii.

[2] Blackie, *op. cit.*, pp. 57–64. Darwin lamented that his absorption in physical investigations had destroyed his capacity to enjoy
poetry and beauty. *Life and Letters*, Vol. I. pp. 101, 102. Physical
scientists are more often theists than atheists, however; and materialism is much less in evidence to-day than formerly. See C. Harris,
Pro Fide, pp. 109–111. Cf. p. 27, note 3, above.

[3] On scepticism, see ch. ii., above.

9

truth.[1] Modern atheists are none the less at issue with the convictions of intelligent thinkers in general. They constitute exceptions which prove the rule.[2]

§ 4. The fact of theistic consent is one that ought to be reckoned with. To ignore it, or to adopt contrary convictions without accounting for its wide prevalence on grounds which justify such a course, is clearly unscientific. In saying this we do not urge any formal claim of authority, although universal consent in matters open to general experience cannot rightly be reckoned as having no authority whatever. What we emphasize is that consent implies reasons, whether valid or not, lying behind it, and a successful investigator will reckon with such reasons before arriving at final convictions.

The reasons which have been given to account for the origin of religion and belief in the Divine fall under two heads:[3] those which make for the truth of theistic doctrine, and those which have been urged as

[1] See Blackie, *op. cit.*, ch. vi. The late Robert Ingersoll's position was the result of reaction from the most narrow type of Calvinism, which he never ceased to treat as the real Christianity of history.

[2] C. Harris, *Pro Fide*, pp. 108, 109, states that out of 543 persons named in Comte's Positivist Calendar of those who have done the most good in the world, in his atheistic estimation, over 90 per cent were believers in supernatural religion. Cf. S. Harris, *Self-Revel. of God*, pp. 348-353.

[3] On this subject, see Franzelin, *De Deo Uno*, Thes. vi (gives the patristic views); Boedder, *Natural Theol.*, pp. 68-74; Driscoll, *God*, pp. 45-62; Calderwood, *Philos. of the Infin.*, pp. 47-48; Max Müller, *Origin of Relig.*; Jordan, *Compar. Relig.*, as cited below; S. Harris, *Self-Revel. of God*, pp. 353-364; Fairbairn, *Philos. of the Christ. Relig.*, Bk. I. ch. vi; Pfleiderer, *Philos. of Relig.*, Vol. III. ch. i.

nullifying the value of consent. We take up the latter ones first.

(a) It used to be urged that religion is of artificial origin, being devised by priests for their own advantage. Wider investigations have put such a view quite out of court. Particular forms of religion have had personal founders, but the work of such founders has always been confined to the reformation and development of existing religion.[1]

(b) It is more common now to treat religions as having natural causes, and as being the result of evolution. Jordan reduces evolutionary theories on the subject to the four heads of fetichism, spiritism, animism, and naturism.[2]

In all these theories the distinction between primitive forms of religion and the cause of the origin of

[1] Gautama, Zoroaster, Confucius, and Mahomet afford illustrations of our contention. The priestcraft theory was advanced by Pierre Bayle (1647-1706), and urged by deistic writers. See Ladd, *Philos. of Relig.*, Vol. I. pp. 141, 142; Boedder, *Natural Theol.*, pp. 69, 70; Fairbairn, *Philos. of the Christ. Relig.*, pp. 260-262.

Ignorance of natural causation has also been alleged, and fear excited by the more stupendous phenomena of nature. Fear could not have the Divine for its object unless belief in the Divine already existed. Theistic belief has been helped rather than hindered by the removal of ignorance of nature, and it is increasingly realized that a knowledge of natural antecedents does not solve the problem of causation, but brings it into bolder relief. Cf. Boedder, *Natural Theol.*, pp. 68-72.

[2] *Comparative Relig.*, pp. 223-231, 532-537. It would take us too far afield to discuss them in detail. No one of them can be clearly proved to be the primitive form of religion, which is prehistoric and has left no interpretable traces within the sphere of anthropological investigation.

religion has been disregarded. It is a truism that to re-trace processes of development is not to account for origins. The forms of religion have been various, and to a considerable extent have been determined by environment and circumstances.[1] But the cause of the birth of religion lies deeper than the phenomena of which anthropologists take note. To describe the evolution of religions, therefore, is not to account either for the origin of religion in general or for theistic belief.[2]

§ 5. We turn to theories which are favorable to theistic doctrine. The chief of these may be called revelational, psychological, and evidential.

(c) According to the revelational theory the origin of religion is due to a primitive and supernatural revelation from God.[3] That such a revelation occurred is the common belief of those who accept, as we do, the essential truth of Genesis.[4] But this reve-

---

[1] Fairbairn, *op. cit.*, pp. 216–226.

[2] Fairbairn, *op. cit.*, pp. 192, 193, 196, 197, 209, 210, 228, 229. The general theory that religion is to be accounted for by natural evolution is maintained by Tylor (*Primitive Culture*, ch. ii), Spencer (*Prins. of Sociology*), W. E. H. Lecky, C. P. Tiele, Huxley and others. Its inadequacy is pointed out by Pfleiderer (*Philos. of Relig.*, Vol. III, pp. 7–16); De La Saussaye (*Science of Relig.*, ch. ii); Driscoll (*God*, pp. 49–55); Jordan (*Compar. Relig.*, pp. 223–231); and Ladd (*Philos. of Relig.*, ch. vi). Modern views are epitomized in Baldwin, *Dic. of Philos.*, *s. vv.* "Religion (Evolution of)" and "Religion (Psychology of)."

[3] Very generally maintained prior to the development of the science of comparative religion.

[4] Care should be taken to distinguish between belief in primitive revelation, and the theory that religion depended upon such revelation for its origin.

lation does not come technically within the scope of theistic argument, and hardly accounts for the universal persistence of religion, even among races which have long ceased to retain in memory the contents of the revelation to which we refer.[1] Clearly supernatural revelation alone does not account for the consent with which we are concerned.[2]

(d) What may be called the psychological theory is that man is so constituted by psychical nature that he inevitably acquires a consciousness of personal relations with the Divine, and practises some kind of religion under all conditions of his development. In brief, man is a religious animal, and the idea of God is certain to arise in his mind whenever his experience affords occasion for reflection. Without religion he cannot realize himself.[3] That this is true cannot be

[1] Many religions, indeed, claim to be based upon revelation; but the mutual inconsistencies of these alleged revelations forbid the supposition that they represent reliable traditions of primitive revelation. S. Harris, *Self-Revel. of God*, p. 456; Flint, *Theism*, pp. 338, 339.

[2] The theory is now being generally abandoned. See Jordan, *Compar. Relig.*, pp. 214–223, 525–532, who cites Max Müller, *Science of Relig.*, p. 41; A. B. Davidson, in Hastings' *Dic. of the Bible, s. v.* "God"; Fairbairn, *Studies in the Philos. of Relig. and Hist.*, pp. 13, 14; R. Flint, *Theism*, pp. 22, 23; Schurman, *Belief in God*, p. 81. To these may be added De La Saussaye, *Science of Relig.*, pp. 18–23.

[3] S. Harris, *Self-Revel. of God*, pp. 345–365; Christlieb, *Modern Doubt*, pp. 140–143; J. L. Spalding, *Relig., Agnosticism and Education*, pp. 7–15; Driscoll, *God*, pp. 60–62; Calderwood, *Philos. of the Infin.*, pp. 46–56; A. H. Strong, *Syst. Theol.*, Vol. I. pp. 58, 59; Wm. Humphrey, *His Divine Majesty*, pp. 27, 28; Ladd, *Philos. of Relig.*, ch. x; Liddon, *Some Elements*, Lec. I. pp. 5–7; Aug. Sabatier, *Philos. of Relig.*, pp. 3–4.

gainsaid. "The heart is restless until it finds rest
in Thee, O God." [1]

(e) The evidential theory is that the evidence of
God's existence, and of our relation to Him, is so universal and obvious that only the fool can say in his
heart "There is no God." [2] As St. Paul says, "That
which may be known of God is manifest in them, for
God manifested it unto them. For the invisible things
of Him since the creation of the world are clearly seen,
being perceived through the things that are made,
even His everlasting power and Divinity." [3] That
such is the case is a leading contention of this volume.

The conclusion to which we are driven is somewhat
as follows. The general prevalence of religion in
every age and race, and the theistic consent which is
at least implicit in religion, cannot be accounted for
by mere natural evolution, or by any non-theistic
theory of their origin. The truth is that the religious
nature of man, and the self-manifestation of God in
every department of human experience, constitute
together the only credible explanation of the origin
of religion and of the phenomena of theistic belief. [4]
The evidences available seem to show that mankind
was originally monotheistic, however undeveloped

[1] St. Augustine, *Confess.*, Bk. I. ch. i. Cf. Tertullian, *The Soul's
Testimony;* and John Fiske's argument from the evolution of man as
a religious animal, in *Through Nature to God*, ch. x.

[2] Psa. xiv. 1; liii. 1. Cf. Rom. i. 18, 22.

[3] Rom. i. 19, 20. Cf. Psa. xix. 1–4, 7.

[4] See S. Harris, *Self-Revel. of God*, chh. iii–v, xxvi; Ladd. *Philos.
of Relig.*, chh. x, xiv, xv.

and childlike primitive monotheism may have been; and the Christian belief in a primitive supernatural revelation has not been shown by recent investigation to be false.[1] But the tendency to fall away from monotheism has been wide-spread; and the preservation and development of the true religion has been due primarily to supernatural causes — to a series of divine dispensations culminating in the Incarnation and the establishment of the Christian Church.

§ 6. It is now in order to consider the theistic bearing of the *consensus gentium*. Its evidential value is undoubtedly limited, but we believe that this has been unduly disparaged. As has been hinted already,[2] the formal authority of this *consensus* cannot be regarded as determining the question of the truth of theism, nor may we deny the necessity of investigating its causes. The weight of general consent is considerable, especially in matters which are open to the consideration and investigation of all; but men are not infallible, and the saying *vox populi vox Dei* cannot be accepted without qualification. Yet the presumptive value of universal consent is too great simply to be dismissed without consideration.[3] What mankind has generally believed, at least impliedly, and

[1] Fairbairn, *Philos. of the Christ. Relig.*, p. 204, points out how impossible it is for history to reach the first man, or to describe his state. Cf. ch. i. § 2, above.

[2] See above, § 4.

[3] Cicero, *De Natura Deorum*, I. xvii, regarded its authority as infallible. Cf. Stanton, *Place of Authority*, pp. 56–63, for a sounder view.

what has been held with a tenacity and definiteness which have increased in proportion to men's advance in enlightenment, ought to be regarded as holding the field until it has been shown to be based upon mistaken grounds and to be false.

We shall return to this last contention,[1] but desire to emphasize two very significant characteristics of theistic consent to which we have alluded. In the first place, the subject-matter of this consent is not necessarily technical, nor such as eliminates from consideration the common judgment of non-experts. On the contrary the data which have to be reckoned with are level to the apprehensions of all men, and the theistic inference, as history shows, is not recondite. Moreover, this inference is a practical one which affects every human being at many points. In brief the truth of theism is pre-eminently a question which has to be determined, if at all, by general judgment, rather than by the investigations of specialists.

The other characteristic which we wish to emphasize is the persistence and growing strength and definiteness of theistic consent. It has persisted in spite of moral causes opposed to it, in spite of diverse human conditions, and in the face of skilful attacks upon its rationality. It has more than persisted; it has shown its greatest vitality among the intelligent. So true is this that we may discover in a general way the boundaries of civilization by ascertaining the extension of definite belief in monotheism among men.

[1] See §§ 10, 11, below.

A concluding consideration is this: as has been shown in our last section, when we investigate the causes of theistic consent, we discover that no theory of its origin is adequate or defensible which does not allow for the religious nature of man, for the inevitableness of his belief in the Divine, and for the conviction of men in general that theistic belief is justified by evidences which obtrude themselves in every department of experience. In brief, the presumption is very strong indeed that, if we are guided by the normal reason of mankind — that is, if we are humanly rational, — we must inevitably become theists. An anti-theistic position must be based upon some deviation from human reason,[1] or upon some failure to do justice to the facts of every-day experience.[2]

§ 7. Connected with the *consensus gentium* is the claim of multitudes of men to have had personal experience of God.[3] This experience is variously described. Some think it to be due to the exercise of a special

[1] We say reason rather than logic, for reason, as we have shown in ch. iii. § 8, is larger in its scope and capacity than such lines of argumentation as are described by the laws of formal logic.

[2] Thus pantheism, the only serious rival of theism, refuses to do justice to the facts of moral experience.

[3] Cf. ch. iii. § 16 (*b*), above; Caldecott, *Philos. of Relig.*, pp. 5, 6 and chh. i, vii, ix, x; S. Harris, *Self-Revel. of God*, Pt. I, esp. ch. ii; W. Knight, *Aspects of Theism*, chh. viii–x; Lilly, *The Great Enigma;* G. P. Fisher, *Grounds of Belief*, p. 24; Inge, *Christian Mysticism;* Newman, *Grammar of Assent*, ch. v. § 1. These writers expound the experience of God, but for testimonies to its inspiring reality we ought to look chiefly to devotional literature. Cf. Psa. xxvii. 4; xxxiv. 8; lxvi. 16–20; xc. 1; cxxxix. 7–10; St. John xiv. 9; xvii. 3; Acts iv. 19, 20; 1 St. John i. 1, 3; iv. 16.

faculty of intuition;[1] others to be the result of progress
in the spiritual life and distinctly supernatural.[2] Some
again reckon it as emotional, and as expressing itself
in a sense of dependence.[3] Others describe it as involved in the processes of moral judgment.[4] A baldly
intellectual view of it is taken by some.[5] Finally it
is described as enlisting all our personal faculties —
the most reasonable view, especially if the factors of
divine grace and God's self-manifestation to the soul
are acknowledged.[6]

§ 8. Two very obvious objections are made to our
dependence upon an appeal to personal experience in
theistic argument: (a) that it is purely personal, and
cannot be depended upon by those who have it not;
(b) that it belongs to the supernatural order, which
does not come within the sphere of theistic discussion.
Such objections are valid in so far as they forbid our
reckoning personal experiences of God among formal
arguments for His existence. Yet, when we consider

[1] See Caldecott, op. cit., ch. x. Coleridge, Hare, Maurice, and
the Cambridge Platonists are examples.

[2] The mystics, strictly so called. Cf. ch. iii. § 16 (c), above.

[3] Schleiermaker and others who identify religion with feeling.
The inadequacy of this view is shown by Liddon, Some Elements,
Lec. I. i. 1.

[4] Newman, who does not, however, exclude other factors.

[5] A view congenial to the philosophy of Hegel. Theodore Parker,
and perhaps W. Knight and Bp. Berkeley, thus interpret our experience of God.

[6] H. P. Liddon (Some Elements), Bp. Westcott (Gospel of Life),
Aubrey Moore (in Lux Mundi, VIII), Jas. Martineau and S. Harris
(Self-Revelation of God).

these alleged experiences in connection with the *consensus gentium*, and the arguments by which it is supported, we are not justified in regarding them as having no confirmatory value. This ought to be acknowledged, especially when we reckon with the number of testimonies which are given — a number beyond computing.

The fact that many are lacking in such experiences does not nullify the testimony of those who claim to have enjoyed them. The higher experiences of men depend upon conditions which are not universally present, and manifold causes can be found to account for the absence of experience of God in those who are perhaps highly intelligent, but whose spiritual culture has been either deficient or misdirected. As W. Knight points out, "the higher powers are those which are most easily deranged, or thrown out of order." "While the reports of every faculty must submit to the severest tests for verification, the evidence of no faculty is to be set aside merely because it is possessed by few."[1] The testimony of experts is at least as weighty in spiritual investigation as it is in other fields, but the experts must be spiritual.

§ 9. A possible confusion of thought should be mentioned as necessary to be avoided in this connection. The experience of God with which we are concerned is not equivalent to open vision. That no

[1] *Aspects of Theism*, pp. 110–114. Cf. *Introd. to Dog. Theol.*, ch. iv. § 6, where it is shown that the spiritual faculty is potentially present in all, although not universally cultivated.

mere man has seen God is beyond reasonable dispute.[1]
Experience is more manifold than vision. Men seek
after God, and haply find Him,[2] who confess that they
have never seen Him. The sight of God is to be
realized under higher conditions than any which
this life affords.[3] The Christian believer, however,
experiences a divine communion and fellowship in
prayer which constitutes the most real element in his
life; and he also experiences promptings, inspirations,
and providences which he is unable to describe in
terms which do not imply personal contact between
God and the soul.[4] Whether the causes of such experiences can be taken note of in a purely scientific
investigation or not, the fact that multitudes of intelligent people insist upon their reality is too easily verified to be regarded as wholly negligible by reasonable
students of the theistic problem. It constitutes a
datum to be reckoned with.

II. *The Burden of Proof*

§ 10. Theistic investigation should take note of the
facts of the *consensus gentium* and of the claim of

[1] St. John i. 18; Heb. xi. 1; 2 Cor. iv. 18; v. 7; Rom. viii, 24, 25.
Cf. *Introd. to Dog. Theol.*, p. 88 and ch. v. § 16 (*d*). Also below,
ch. x. § 4.

[2] Cf. Acts xvii. 27.

[3] 1 Cor. xiii. 9–12; 1 St. John iii. 2. Cf. Theophilus, *Ad Autol.*,
i. 2–8 — a classic passage.

[4] Such descriptions are very numerous in Holy Scripture. We
have referred to a few examples, p. 121, note 3, above. These
descriptions exhibit real experiences, whatever view may be taken of
inspiration.

enlightened millions to have come experientially into contact with the infinite God. The reason is that these facts determine conclusively the state of the theistic question. The theistic hypothesis is in possession. This is to put it very mildly; for it has been in possession from the remotest antiquity, throughout the world, and in every field of enlightened experience, and the strength of its possession is altogether unique. Countless human beings, indeed, acknowledge that it is so fundamental, so abundantly verifiable, and so far-reaching, that no one can live rightly on any other basis. If need be, it is confessed, men ought to die for it rather than acknowledge its falsity. Men will die, no doubt, for false beliefs; but this belief is so wide-spread, and so deeply connected with human enlightenment, that it may reasonably be regarded as grounded in man's deepest instincts, and as being an inevitable concomitant and distinguishing characteristic of normal human thinking.

§ 11. Granting that these facts do not constitute formal proofs of the theistic hypothesis, we are constrained by the fundamental laws of logic to insist that they determine on which side lies the burden of proof. It is irrational to reject a hypothesis like this without adequate proof of its falsity.[1] We say more.

[1] John Stewart Mill, who was certainly not prejudiced in favour of our position, none the less acknowledges the principle in question when defining the point of departure of scientific induction. He says, "When mankind first formed the idea of studying phenomena according to a stricter and surer method than that which in the first instance they had spontaneously adopted, they did not, conformably

In view of the undeniable fact that men's moral principles are determined by their belief touching the truth of theistic doctrine, so that an irrational attitude on the question is likely to preclude the adoption of correct moral principles and to make wickedness appear justifiable, it must be confessed that a rejection of theism without sufficient proof of its falsity is immoral.[1] The only refuge from this conclusion lies in scepticism, the rejection of human reason.

to the well meant but impracticable precept of Descartes, set out on the supposition that nothing had been already ascertained." *Logic*, Bk. III. ch. iv. § 2.   However ready some thinkers are to assume that previous ignorance is the true basis of theistic investigation, they do not apply such a principle to other fields of induction.   See Illingworth, *Personality*, pp. 76, 77.   Liddon, *Some Elements*, pp. 48–51; Mason, *Faith of the Gospel*, ch. i. § 3; Blackie, *Atheism*, ch. i, esp. pp. 21–25.

[1] That is, materially and logically speaking.   It would be obviously unjust to impute immoral motives to all atheists, or to assume that they are necessarily conscious of the logic of their position.   Men often continue to be controlled by lofty ideals after they have abandoned the premises by which alone these ideals can be vindicated. Inherited ideals and the influences of Christian civilization are often more powerful than logic.   Yet the logic of convictions is certain ultimately to be realized in practice, if these convictions are maintained with sufficient energy and persistence.   An atheistic community would not fail to become an immoral one.   It should be noted that theistic doctrine is not only the real foundation of morality; but, if true, determines its central elements.   We are made for God, and He is our chief end.   A non-religious morality is an emasculated shadow of itself.   On the moral and probationary implications of theistic evidence, cf. Butler, *Analogy* (Gladstone's Edit.), Pt. II. ch. vi. §§ 10 *et seq.*   On the whole subject, see Flint, *Theism*, pp. 7–12 and note II, pp. 329–335; J. Caird, *Philos. of Relig.*, ch. ix; Romanes, *Thoughts on Relig.*, pp. 144, 151, 152.

Atheists, if they are rational, are forced to shoulder the burden of proving that there is no God.[1] It is generally admitted that if God's existence can be proved in any sense of that term, its proof is largely *a posteriori* — based upon an induction of the facts of human experience. It follows that to disprove God's existence one must show that no facts exist which can be employed reasonably in such an induction. In brief, a universal negative must be established. And since the possible sources of theistic evidence are world-wide in their range, this negative cannot be established on any other basis than that of universal knowledge — that is, exhaustive knowledge of every realm of fact which the universe contains, — fortified by a capacity for interpretation and generalization which has never been realized by any child of man.[2]

[1] This burden has never been shouldered. Atheists devote themselves to criticising theistic arguments. A thorough-going attempt to demonstrate the non-existence of God has never been made. Flint, *Anti-Theistic Theories*, pp. 8, 9. On the subject of atheism, see Flint, *op. cit.*, chh. i, vi, vii; Blackie, *Natural Hist. of Atheism;* Christlieb, *Modern Doubt*, Lec. iii. Pt. I. *Catholic Encyc.* and *Jewish Encyc.*, *s. v.* "Atheism." The most respectable attempt to overthrow the theistic position is, perhaps, *A Candid Exam. of Theism* by Physicus (G. J. Romanes). The author emerged from his nightmare of unbelief before his death, as can be seen in his *Thoughts on Religion*, edited by Chas. Gore. Hume's *Essays*, Kant's *Critique of Pure Reason*, and Mill's Essay on *Theism* are also to be consulted for the more important objections to the validity of theistic arguments.

[2] Flint, *Anti-Theistic Theories*, pp. 8–14, 446–450; Chalmers, *Natural Theol.*, Vol. I. Bk. I. ch. ii; Christlieb, *Modern Doubt*, pp. 143, 144.

The conclusion of the matter is that a normal human being does not come to theistic investigation as an inquirer to whom the conclusion is as yet problematical. He comes rather as possessed of normal human reason; as unavoidably postulating, therefore, the conclusion which he seeks to verify;[1] and as accepting the law of common sense that beliefs in general possession are to be regarded as presumptively true and reasonable until found to be inconsistent with human knowledge. We defer to the judgment of enlightened mankind; we refuse to take for granted that our experiences of God are subjective illusions; and we trust the normal reason of men — the reason which is found to work in everyday life — as the only reason by which any hypothesis whatever can be put to proof.

[1] Mulford, *Republic of God*, pp. 1–5. Whatever deficiencies may be found in Kant's critical philosophy, his doctrine that the idea of God is a necessary postulate of practical reason has rightly determined the course of modern theistic thought to an important extent. *Critique of Practical Reason*, Transcendental Dialectic, Bk. II. ch. ii. §§ 3–5, 8. Cf. ch. iii. §§ 13, 15 (*b*), above. To assume *as a hypothesis* what we seek to prove is not bad logic, but is a method constantly employed in physical science. But such procedure makes theistic argument a process of verification rather than of demonstration.

CHAPTER V

THE COSMOLOGICAL ARGUMENT

I. *Positive Statement*

§ 1. The cosmological argument presupposes the truth of the necessary and *a priori* postulate that there must be an adequate ground of being, and that no ground is adequate which is not absolute and unconditioned. It applies this postulate to the world of our experience. The world must have such an absolute and unconditioned ground; and, being finite and conditioned, cannot be its own ground, which must be other than itself.[1] All other *a posteriori* arguments

---

[1] On the cosmological argument, see St. Thomas, *Summa Theol.*, I. ii, 3; *c. Gent.*, I. xiii; Hastings, *Encyc. of Relig.*, *s. v.* "Ætiology"; *Cath. Encyc.*, *s. v.* "Cause"; Illingworth, *Personality*, pp. 89–93, 251–255; Flint, *Theism*, ch. iv; Martineau, *Religion*, Bk. II. ch. i; Dorner, *Christian Doctrine*, Vol. I. pp. 248–259; Mozley, *Essays*, Vol. II. pp. 414–444; Calderwood, *Philos. of the Infin.*, ch. vii; W. S. Jevons, *Prins. of Science*, ch. xxxi; Driscoll, *God*, chh. vi–viii; Porter, *Human Intellect*, Pt. IV. ch. v; Boedder, *Natural Theol.*, pp. 32–46. Criticisms are to be found in Kant, *Critique of Pure Reason*, Transcendental Dialectic, Bk. II. ch. iv; Hume, *Human Understanding*, § vii; J. S. Mill, *Theism*, pp. 142–154; *Logic*, Bk. III. ch. v; Physicus, *Candid Exam. of Theism*, pp. 6–9; Knight, *Aspects of Theism*, pp. 53–58; Davidson, *Theism and Human Nature*, Lec. xi. Pt. II.

The Patristic forms of the argument are given with references by Petavius, *De Deo*, I. i–ii; and Thomassinus, *Dogmata Theol.*, Lib. I. cap. xxi. Cf. Athenagoras, *Plea for Christians*, xv, xvi; Tertullian,

can be seen to be involved in the cosmological. They are in fact specific applications of its logic to the several spheres of experience, or so many departments of theistic interpretation involved in that postulate. Thus the teleological and moral arguments are not independent of the cosmological; but illustrate it, and exhibit its force.[1]

The forms of the cosmological argument are various.

(a) Motion is a universal phenomenon of the cosmos. It implies a Mover, and the implication is not adequately realized except by hypothecating an unmoved Mover of all.[2]

(b) The world is transitory and mutable in all its aspects. It must have for its ground something which is eternal and immutable.[3]

De Spectac, ii; *Adv. Marc.*, i. 17; v. 16; *Scapula*, ii; St. Augustine, *Confess.*, X. vi; *De Civ. Dei*, II. iv; VIII. vi; *De Lib. Arbit.*, II. xvii; *De Gen. ad Lit.* VIII. xx–xxvi.

A very complete bibliography of Causation is given in Baldwin, *Dic. of Philos.*, pp. 602–607.

[1] Caldecott, *Philos. of Relig.*, pp. 26, 27; Boedder, *Natural Theol.*, pp. 31, 32.

[2] Aristotle is the father of this argument, *Metaphysics*, Bk. XI. ch. vii; *Physics*, VIII. vi. It was popular with scholastic writers. St. Thomas, *Sum. Theol.*, I. i. 3; *Contra Gent.*, I. xiii. It is urged by Driscoll, *God*, ch. viii, who gives and answers the objections. See Owen, *Dogmatic Theol.*, p. 69.

Aristotle regarded motion as co-eternal with its cause. Cf. Boedder's discussion of his argument: *Natural Theol.*, pp. 209–214; Davidson, *Theism*, pp. 45, 46.

[3] St. Augustine, *De Civ. Dei*, VIII. vi; XI. iv; St. John Damasc., *De Orth. Fid.*, i. 3; Driscoll, *God*, pp. 140–146.

(c) All that we see is contingent and dependent for reality upon something else. The ultimate reality upon which everything depends must be independent of this law — self-existent and necessary.[1]

(d) The things which we contemplate are relative, conditioned, and finite — that is, they are determined and limited as to their essential nature by their relations to other things. There must be an ultimate ground of determination — an Infinite and Absolute which is self-determined and unconditioned, and unlimited by anything else than itself.[2]

(e) The phenomena of the universe are necessarily understood to be grounded for reality in *noumena*, and the reality of *noumena* is perceived to be grounded in an ultimate reality in which they rest for their own reality.[3]

(f) Everything which we observe is perceived to be imperfect, and to be measured by unrealized potentialities; and the imperfect and unrealized cannot be apprehended as such except on the supposition that a real perfect exists in which no potentialities are unrealized.[4]

[1] John Caird, *Philos. of Relig.*, ch. v; Driscoll, *God*, ch. vi; Illingworth, *Personality*, p. 84; S. Harris, *Self-Revel. of God*, ch. xi.

[2] John Caird, *op. cit.*, pp. 126 *et seq.*; St. Anselm, *Monol.*, iii; Illingworth, *Personality*, pp. 89–93.

[3] John Caird, *op. cit.*, pp. 126 *et seq.* This line of argument, in the hands of Spinoza, lends itself to a pantheistic conclusion — that is, by neglecting the truth that, although all substance depends for reality on God, creaturely substance is none the less distinct in being, and possesses a derivative reality of its own.

[4] The historical source of this argument is to be found in Aristotle's

(g) The universe is perceived to be a system of effects, and therefore must have a cause. This is the ætiological argument; and, as it is the most common and illuminative form of the cosmological argument, it requires especial attention.

§ 2. The *ætiological argument* [1] starts with the generalization that the universe, as we know it, whether viewed in its particulars or in its totality, does not contain within its own essence the ground of its existence and phenomena. The inference is that it is an effect, and depends for its reality and existence upon a cause other than itself. Involved in this inference is the *a priori* postulate that all reality is grounded in necessary and self-existent being; [2] so that, if any thing is seen not to be self-existent, it must be regarded as dependent in causation upon what is self-existent and necessary.

---

distinction between δύναμις and ἐνέργεια, and his treatment of the latter as prior to the former. *Metaphysics*, VII. vi; XI. vii. Cf. Boethius, *De Consol. Philos.*, iii. 10; St. Anselm, *Monol.*, chh. i., ii., iv.; St. Thomas, *Summa Theol.*, I. i. 3; Descartes, *Medit.* iii; Illingworth, *Personality*, p. 252. What is termed the "way of eminence" in conceiving of divine attributes is dependent on the validity of this argument. Cf. ch. i. § 9, above; and ch. x. § 3 *fin.*, below.

[1] The ætiological form of the cosmological argument can be found in the writers mentioned above, in the first note of this section — especially St. Thomas, Flint, and Martineau. Herbert Spencer acknowledges the necessity of inferring the existence of a First-Cause, although he adds that its nature is unthinkable. *First Prins.*, ch. ii. § 12.

[2] Materialists and pantheists assume that an eternal ground of reality exists, and their assumption, so far as it goes, supports the ætiological argument. Their failure lies in their theories as to the nature and identity of the "world-ground."

This dependence is sometimes described in terms of a regress of causes; but, in strict language, the intermediate links are merely moments in the process of efficient action of a cause which is not itself an effect, but self-existent and self-determinative. In other words the mind is not compelled to trace the process of causation backward *ad infinitum* in order to reach the real cause.[1] Each particular effect constitutes in itself a sufficient *a posteriori* basis of the inference that nothing can really explain its occurrence or reality except an uncaused or self-existent cause. The argument, in brief, is independent of the problems connected with sequence in causation and temporal considerations. The principle that causation forbids the separation in time of cause and effect is not prejudiced. God is called "First-Cause," it is true, but the ætiological argument does not require us to use the word "first" in a temporal sense. The necessary thought involved is simply this, that the cause of the universe precedes it *in the order of causation* and is not thus preceded by a cause of itself. The causation of the world is an existing fact, and the cause and effect coexist, that is, so far as the causal relation is concerned.[2]

---

[1] Cf. § 6, below.

[2] The notion that they coexist in all relations — that is, that the universe never began to be, although eternally dependent upon God for its existence (maintained by Martineau, *Religion*, Vol. I. pp. 381–392) — is inconsistent with the idea of causation as applied to finite being. Cf. p. 142, note 1, below.

It should be added that to call God First-Cause is not to postulate

Again, the ætiological argument does not necessitate that we should conceive of the cause as external to the effect. The cause of the world must be *other* than the world: but it can be and, as is suggested by considerations which are not now before us, must be immanent in the world as well as transcendent.[1]

Such, in brief, is the ætiological argument; the conclusion of which is that a Cause of the world exists which is seen on analysis of the idea of causation to be no other than the supreme infinite and personal God in whom we believe. This will appear more clearly when we treat of the teaching of the cosmological argument.[2]

the necessity of His having created the world, but to insist that whatever in fact exists, other than God, owes its existence to Him. Causation in final analysis is an act of will — not of necessity.   Cf. §§ 4, 11, below.

[1] It is a remarkable blunder of some of the ablest modern writers which leads them to criticise the traditional form of the ætiological argument — and the teleological argument as well — as implying that the Cause of the world is external and remote.   Christian theists have never argued for the existence of an *extra*-mundane God, but for a *supra*-mundane God.

The truth of divine immanence has always been a veritable truism of Christian theologians, both East and West.   But catholic writers realize that divine immanence and transcendence are counter truths, neither of which can rightly be understood except in connection with the other.   The error of our day is an exclusive emphasis upon divine immanence, which is as one-sided as the deistic position.   Cf. p. 165, note 2, below.

[2] In §§ 9–12 below.

II. *Objections*

§ 3. It is desirable, however, before considering this teaching, to deal with objections.

(*a*) The most fundamental objection concerns the *a priori* postulate that a necessary ground of things must exist. Kant concedes that, "on the supposition that something exists, I cannot avoid the inference that something exists necessarily." But urges that this necessity cannot be shown to be objective. He says that "the unconditioned necessity of a judgment [that something exists necessarily] does not form the absolute necessity of a thing." That is, the inference from necessity of *judging* that necessary being exists to the *fact* of its existence cannot be established as true by the reason.[1]

The objection is valid in so far as it indicates the impossibility of demonstrating that the reason can be trusted in its fundamental postulates. Reason must start with something which it takes for granted, and its first premises lie beyond demonstration. The assumption that necessary being must exist is such a premise, and cannot directly be demonstrated, since it is a necessary premise of all demonstration. But

[1] *Critique of Pure Reason*, Transcendental Dialectic, Bk. II. ch. iv. As Kant points out, the cosmological argument postulates the ontological argument from necessity of thought to objective reality. Another criticism of this method of argument is contained in Knight, *Aspects of Theism*, ch. iv. Kant's criticism is translated in Caldecott and Mackintosh, *Selections from the Literature of Theism*, pp. 183 *et seq.* Physicus raises the same objection, *Candid Examination*, pp. 4–6.

the difficulty is not insuperable. We cannot reason either for or against the truth of any judgment except on the supposition that reason is to be trusted in its unavoidable premises. Whatever, therefore, is necessarily postulated in all reasoning is necessary for reason, and what is necessary for reason cannot be treated as otherwise than true by reason. In brief, a necessary postulate of demonstration has the same validity for rational minds as does any possible demonstration. The two stand or fall together. We must accept our necessary postulates as axiomatic, or else we must reject the validity of all reasoning, including the reasoning of Kant himself. All that any argument can achieve is to satisfy the requirements of reason — of actual human reason. It ought to be clear that to start with a necessary postulate of reason should not prejudice this result, but is necessary for its accomplishment. And when the requirements of reason are satisfied, a refusal of assent is irrational — not less so because we cannot demonstrate the fundamental trustworthiness of reason.[1]

[1] See Flint, *Agnosticism*, pp. 225, 226; C. Harris, *Pro Fide*, pp. 7, 8. We return to this in discussing the ontological argument, ch. viii. § 4. Cf. Boedder, *Natural Theol.*, pp. 32–33; Mozley, *Essays Hist. and Theol.* Vol. II. pp. 416–422; Pfleiderer, *Philos. of Relig.*, pp. 158–164. He says, p.159, "It is certainly open to us to ask, if an idea *can* serve only as a regulative principle of a true knowledge of the actual, if it must not at the same time be a constitutive principle of explanation, or a real foundation of the actual." Again, p. 161, "The issue of the *Dialectic of Pure Reason*, according to which ideas may be not only possible, but even necessary to thought, without our being able to predicate objective truth of them, is evidently

§ 4. (*b*) Hume objected that no idea is valid unless derived from sensible experience, and that the idea of causation cannot thus be derived. We never observe causation, as usually defined, but what we thus describe is in reality mere phenomenal sequence.[1] Mill reiterated this objection, and declared that the so-called law of causation is nothing else than the uniformity of nature or the invariability of physical sequences.[2]

A double reply can be made. In the first place valid ideas are not derived exclusively from sensible experience, but also from internal experience — that is, from consciousness of our psychical activities of mind, emotion, and will. And the idea of causation is derived in the first instance from internal experience.[3] The

the fundamental principle of the purest *Scepticism,*" etc. Cf. also Porter, *Human Intellect*, pp. 521–523.

[1] He accounted for the illusion of causation by custom and repeated connection in thought. *Inquiry Concerning the Human Understanding*, § vii; *Treatise of Human Nature*, Bk. I. § 14. Given by Porter, *Human Intellect*, p. 574. Dr. Thos. Brown also identifies causation with the constant connection of two objects in time. *Inquiry into the Relation of Cause and Effect*, esp. Pt. I. § 1.

[2] *Logic*, Bk. III. ch. v; *Theism*, pp. 142–154. In the latter he says, "The Cause of every change is a prior change . . . for if there were no new antecedent, there would be no new consequent. . . . It is thus a necessary part of the fact of causation . . . that the causes as well as the effects had a beginning in time": pp. 143, 144. See also Physicus, *Candid Examination*, pp. 6–9.

[3] Romanes, *Thoughts on Relig.*, pp. 124–126; Driscoll, *God*, pp. 122, 123; Martineau, *Religion*, Vol. I. pp. 188–189; C. Harris, *Pro Fide*, p. 7 (*b*); Calderwood, *Moral Philos.*, p. 184, 185 (who gives other references for and against our contention); McCosh, *Intuitions*, pp. 258–262.

phenomena which we describe by the term causation consist of voluntary acts of power by which subsequent events are determined; and it is the volitional and determinative aspect of the phenomena in question which in fact leads us to identify and describe them as causal. Whatever, in brief, is seen to determine which of alternative possibilities is to be realized is perceived to be a cause, and our perception of such causation is intuitive and more complete than any of our external perceptions.[1]

This brings us to our second reply; which is that, having thus derived the idea of causation from intuition, we are able to distinguish clearly in external experience between mere phenomenal sequence and physical causation. A phenomenon which is observed to determine the occurrence of other phenomena is perceived to be what is called a physical cause. But in so far as an essential element in determination — volition — is wanting, we call it a secondary cause. By this we mean that its determinative quality is involuntary and derivative. We are obliged to look further for the real cause, which intuitive knowledge teaches us must be will. To determine between

[1] The intuitive nature of our perception of causality was denied by Mill, who was answered at some length by Wm. Geo. Ward, *Philos. of Theism*, Ess. viii. Ward's argument is given in Wilfrid Ward's *Wm. Geo. Ward and the Catholic Revival*, pp. 327–343. Cf. also Porter, *Human Intellect*, pp. 572–573.

The intuition of causality within ourselves enables us to identify effects, wherever they come within our observation. And the basis of our identification is not mere analogy, but knowledge of the nature of causation.

alternative possibilities is necessarily a volitional act.[1]
We thus distinguish between sequence and causation
even when contemplating invariable sequences. Not
every invariable sequence constitutes in itself a causal
connection, although we assume, of course, that the
sequence has a cause somewhere.[2] Thus the fact that
days are invariably followed by nights is not understood to mean that days are causes of nights; whereas
we readily perceive that the expansion of mercury
which invariably follows an increase of heat is caused
by that increase — that is, of course, in the secondary
or derivative sense above explained.[3] The assumption
that we distinguish rightly between causal relations
and mere sequences constitutes a necessary basis of
scientific induction, so that a denial of the validity of
the idea of causation is thoroughly unscientific.[4]

[1] On the volitional nature of causation, see Martineau, *Religion*,
Vol. I. pp. 188–202; Vol. II. pp. 227–248; Driscoll, *God*, pp. 123, 124;
Fraser, *Philos. of Theism*, pp. 190–193; Fisher, *Grounds of Belief*,
pp. 28, 29; Illingworth, *Personality*, pp. 86, 87; *Divine Immanence*,
pp. 126–129; Romanes, *Thoughts on Relig.*, pp. 124–126; Flint,
Theism, pp. 129, 130; Calderwood, *Moral Philos.*, pp. 184, 185.

[2] Just so far as we perceive that physical sequences are invariable,
we gain peculiar reasons for believing that they are determined
rather than determining. That is, they are not causes but effects.

[3] On the fact that we distinguish causation from sequence in
nature, see Wilfrid Ward, *Wm. Geo. Ward and the Catholic Revival*,
pp. 343, 344; Steenstra, *Being of God*, pp. 36–38.

[4] On the whole objection see Martineau, *Religion*, Vol. I. pp.
137–146; Wm. Geo. Ward, *Philos. of Theism*, Essay viii; Driscoll,
God, pp. 122–126; Flint, *Theism*, pp. 97–101; W. S. Jevons, *Prins.
of Science*, pp. 221–226; Porter, *Human Intellect*, pp. 574–578;
Boedder, *Natural Theol.*, pp. 160, 161.

Prof. Huxley, in *Chas. Darwin's Life and Letters*, by F. Darwin,

§ 5. (c) A third objection comes from Kant, and is in the form of a dilemma: If the law of causation is universal, God is subject to that law, and has a cause. On the other hand, if it is not universal, the world in its totality may constitute an exception.[1]

The answer is not far to seek. Kant confuses the law that all things must have an ultimate and necessary ground of their existence and reality with the law of causation, which applies only to things which do not possess this ground in themselves.[2] It is because all our experience forbids the supposition that the universe possesses its ultimate ground of existence in itself, that we are compelled to find that ground elsewhere — that is, to look for its cause. But the ultimate ground of existence, just because it is ultimate, must contain its own ground of existence in itself. Therefore we perceive that it is uncaused.[3]

Vol. II. p. 200, says, "The one act of faith in the convert to science is the universality of order, and of the absolute validity, in all times and under all circumstances, of the law of causation. . . . But such faith is not blind, but reasonable, because it is invariably confirmed by experience, and constitutes the sole trustworthy foundation for all action." Cf. Schurman, Belief in God, pp. 50–60, 65, 66.

[1] Critique of Pure Reason, Transcendental Dial., Bk. II. ch. iv. For a translation of his epitome of the objection, see Caldecott and Mackintosh, Selections, p. 206.

[2] The two laws may be expressed as follows: (a) Nothing exists without an ultimate ground of its existence, whether this ground be within its own essence or extraneous; (b) Everything that does not possess the ground of its existence in itself is an effect, that is, it requires a cause. These laws warrant the inference that the world, since it does not possess the ground of existence in itself, requires a cause.

[3] McCosh, Intuitions, pp. 271–272; C. Harris, Pro Fide, pp. 5, 6.

§ 6. (*d*) This line of thought also meets the well-worn but really superficial objection that the law of causation, if valid, requires us to hypothecate an infinite regress in causation.[1] It does nothing of the kind.[2] It requires simply that we shall postulate a real cause — that is, one which is not itself an effect.[3]

§ 7. (*e*) Another objection is that the universe as a whole cannot be proved to be an effect. The origination of its substance is really inconceivable, and its permanence is a necessary postulate of scientific induction.[4]

It is true that no formal proof that the universe as

---

[1] Schurman, *Belief in God*, p. 151; Knight, *Aspects of Theism*, pp. 53–55; Calderwood, *Moral Philos.*, pp. 224, 225; Mulford, *Republic of God*, pp. 7, 8; Mill, *Theism*, pp. 143, 144. Mill says, "The cause of every change is a prior change; and such it cannot but be; for if there were no new antecedent, there would not be a new consequent. If the state of facts which brings the phenomenon into existence had existed always or for an indefinite duration, the effect also would have existed always," etc.

[2] The notion that it does is based on the identification of causation with physical sequence, in which, as Mill shows (see previous note), the very existence of the antecedent involves the consequent. But if causation is volitional, the cause produces its effects only when it wills. It is not a new cause that is necessary for a new effect, but a determining agent. See Martineau, *Religion*, Vol. II. pp. 246–248; Fraser, *Philos. of Theism*, pp. 190–193.

[3] Mozley, *Essays Hist. and Theol.*, Vol. II. pp. 424–432; Boedder, *Natural Theol.*, p. 55; Flint, *Theism*, pp. 119–124; Illingworth, *Personality*, pp. 87–89; Fisher, *Grounds of Belief*, pp. 27, 28; Stirling, *Philos. and Theol.*, p. 126. Cf. p. 133, above.

[4] J. S. Mill, *Theism*, pp. 142, 143; Physicus, *Candid Examination*, pp. 6, 7. Kant's form of this objection is explained by Pfleiderer, *Philos. of Relig.*, Vol. III. pp. 256, 257. Mill concedes that creation by a sovereign will cannot be disproved: *op. cit.*, p. 137.

a whole is an effect can be afforded.   But all the actual
knowledge which we have of the universe shows that
it constitutes a system of mutable and finite things,
that is, of effects; and no possible combination of finite
effects can constitute a self-existent universe.[1] Its
origination is unimaginable — not inconceivable, — [2]
for it transcends sensible experience; but so is its self-
existence.   Scientific induction does not postulate an
endless past for the world, but a continuance, for the

[1] On the indications that the universe had a beginning, see Flint,
Theism, pp. 101–118; Chalmers, *Natural Theol.*, I. v; Profeit, *Creation of Matter*, esp. last ch. Boedder, *Natural Theol.*, pp. 145–148
(a metaphysical arg.), and pp. 159–160.

It has been maintained that the universe is eternal, but none the
less causally dependent on God. So Martineau, *Religion*, Vol. I.
pp. 381 *et seq.*; Fraser, *Philos. of Theism*, pp. 125–131; A. K. Rogers
Religious Concep. of the World, pp. 164–167. It is true that causation does not necessarily involve temporal sequence (Cf. V. F. Storr,
Devel. and Divine Purpose, pp. 95–98); that physical causes, so
called, may coincide in duration with their effects; and that the universe may be regarded as everlasting — that is, as coming into exist-
tence with time, so that no time ever existed when temporal things
were not. But to be an effect means to have a beginning, and to be
a true and ultimate cause — that is, an uncaused cause — means to
be without beginning and eternal. The eternity of God does not
mean that He existed alone through *ages prior* to creation. It means
that His life and being transcend temporal measures. The transcendent element in eternity, necessary as it is to the idea of infinite
Being, is beyond any imagination of ours. We can say, however,
that temporal sequence does not describe the causal relation between
God and creatures.

[2] Only such things as can be pictured in the concrete are imaginable, whereas any proposition that conveys *meaning* to the mind
comes within the conceivable. Cf. *Introd. to Dog. Theol.*, ch. v.
§ 6, and also ch. ii. § 2 of this volume.

present at least, of the existing system of natural causation, so called, the uniformities of which it describes.[1]
Natural sciences deal with processes now going on, or
now verifiable. They are not concerned with ultimate origins.[2] To believe that the universe is self-
existent involves either dualism, or materialism, or
pantheism. Each of these alternatives has graver
difficulties than theistic doctrine.[3]

§ 8. (*f*) Finally, there is the objection against
inferring the existence of an infinite God from the
consideration of finite phenomena. This objection
sometimes takes an agnostic form, and is then based

[1] We often speak of the "permanent element" in nature which
underlies its constant changes. The word "permanent" is used
relatively. It is impossible to discover evidence that any element
in nature is absolutely permanent — without origin and indestruct-
ible. All that has been shown is that, whatever matter may be in
its essence, we have never observed either its origination or its destruction. Whether it can be originated or destroyed is a problem
that natural science has not been able to solve. Cf. Gwatkin, *Knowl.
of God*, Vol. I. pp. 11, 12; T. R. Birks, Modern *Physical Fatalism*,
chh. v, vi (on the reality and indestructibility of matter).

On the uniformity of nature, what it means, the limits of its
validity, and its significance for theology, see Baldwin, *Dic. of Philos.*,
s. v. "Uniformity"; Mozley, *Miracles*, chh. ii, iii; Abp. Temple,
Relations between Religion and Science, pp. 7–33, 92–96, 225–228.
Cf. our *Introd. to Dog. Theol.*, ch. ii. §§ 4, 5.

[2] Prof. Huxley says, *Nineteenth Century*, Feb., 1886, pp. 201, 202,
"It appears to me that the scientific investigator is wholly incom-
petent to say anything at all about the first origin of the material
universe. The whole power of his organon vanishes when he has to
step beyond the chain of natural causes and effects. No form of
nebular hypothesis that I know of is necessarily connected with any
view of the origination of nebular substance."

[3] We consider these alternatives in ch. ix, below.

upon a denial of human capacity to transcend the finite in our inferences and conceptions.[1] It also takes the logical form, that to infer an infinite cause to account for finite phenomena is to put more into the conclusion than the premises warrant. An infinite cause, it is urged, is unnecessary for finite effects, however vast.[2]

We have met the agnostic form of this objection by anticipation in our second chapter,[3] and it is unnecessary to repeat what has there been said. We need only to call attention to the fact that the infinite nature of the cause which we infer does not involve the supposition that the act of inference itself is infinite. All human acts of inference are in themselves necessarily finite. But our inability to form an adequate notion of an infinite cause does not debar us from perceiving that such a cause exists, and is required in order to account for the world of effects. If the term infinite were really meaningless, as agnos-

[1] The alleged contradictions of thought involved in hypothecating an infinite cause are presented by Hamilton and Mansel, and are summarized by Spencer, who quotes freely from these writers. See *First Prins.*, ch. ii. §§ 12, 13; ch. iv. § 24.

[2] This objection has often been urged in the interests of dependence upon supernatural revelation, and in opposition to what is mistakenly thought to be subversive rationalism. In modern philosophy it is usually advanced ostensibly against the teleological argument, as if that argument were self-complete and concerned with proving the infinity of the ultimate Cause. See ch. vi. § 13, below. The objection is found in Knight's *Aspects of Theism*, pp. 62, 63; and was urged by Hume, Kant, and Hamilton.

[3] See ch. ii. § 7, above.

tics assert, and if we were unable to form any true notion whatever of an infinite cause, the objection would be valid. To repeat our reasons for believing that a finite notion of an infinite being is possible, and attainable by us, would be superfluous.[1]

The logical form of the objection derives its plausibility from the mistaken assumption that the nature of the effects — their vastness — constitutes the basis of the inference that their ultimate Cause is infinite. It is true, of course, that the nature of the phenomena considered by theists teaches that their cause is mighty beyond our imagining; and this helps our minds to rise to the apprehension of infinite almightiness. But omnipotence, or infinite power, is a different notion from power to perform finite works, however great they may be. There is a distinct step when we pass from indefinitely great finite power to infinite power; and an argument for the existence of the former cannot of itself prove the existence of the latter. This ought freely to be acknowledged. The whole difficulty is removed, however, by a correct understanding of the ætiological argument. What is immediately inferred from the existence of effects is simply this, that these effects, whether small or great, must have a real, that is ultimate, cause. It is the further consideration

[1] See ch. ii. § 6, above. Pfleiderer says, *Philos. of Relig.*, Vol. III. p. 254, that "any act of thought that is conscious of the finiteness of the individual objects it deals with, has therewith at once transcended the limits of the finite, and has along with the notion of finiteness embraced also its correlative, infinity." Cf. John Caird, *Philos. of Relig.*, p. 130; Porter, *Human Intellect*, p. 659.

that a cause is not real or ultimate, if it is itself an effect, which justifies the inference that it must be uncaused and self-existent,[1] and an uncaused self-existent being is infinite — that is, unlimited by anything else than its own eternal essence.[2]

The conclusion of the matter is that no objection can overthrow the validity of the cosmological argument, so long as we accept the necessary postulates of human reason and employ normal methods of inference. And the impossibility of formulating the argument as a demonstrative syllogism does not nullify the force of this conclusion.[3]

[1] Calderwood, *Philos. of the Infin.*, p. 384; Illingworth, *Personality*, p. 86.

[2] Illingworth, *op. cit.*, p. 92; Ladd., *Philos. of Relig.*, Vol. II. p. 113; S. Harris, *Self-Revel. of God*, p. 154. St. Thomas, *Summa Theol.*, I. vii. 1, concludes that God is infinite because He has not received His being from another, but is Himself His own subsisting esse. On the whole objection, see Boedder, *Natural Theol.*, pp. 151, 152; Calderwood, *op. cit.*, pp. 383, 384 (Cf. p. 226); S. Harris, *Self-Revelation of God*, pp. 241–243.

[3] It is to be emphasized, as fundamental to our entire theistic argument, that we do not pretend to fulfil all the requirements of formal logic or of *a priori* criticism, but to make use of the rational postulates and methods of inference which in fact govern men's judgment in every-day life. No higher reason can be demanded for belief than that which is found to be normal and unavoidable in human thinking generally. We do not need to impugn the normal methods of reason in order to estimate the validity of theistic argument. Cf. Newman, *Grammar of Assent*, ch. viii. § 1, concluding remarks.

III. *Teachings*

§ 9. It remains for us to summarize the implications and teachings as to the nature of God involved in the cosmological argument. Some of them have been referred to in the course of our discussion, but they need to be exhibited in connected order.[1] They may be summed up very briefly by saying that, if the cosmological argument is valid, the Cause of all things must be ultimate, adequate, voluntary, and one.

(*a*) When we say that the Cause of the universe must be *ultimate*, we mean simply that He must be a real cause — one that is not merely a link in a series of effects. The notion of an infinite regress of causes is inconsistent with a rational ætiology, and temporal sequence is not a correct description of the relation between the ultimate cause and the phenomena of the universe. This cause, in order to be ultimate, must be itself uncaused, that is, self-existent and self-determined.[2] This is only another way of saying that it must be infinite, in that it is limited by nothing but itself, and is eternal.[3]

§ 10. (*b*) The cause of the universe must also be

[1] The implications of the cosmological argument are discussed by Martineau, *Religion*, Bk. II. ch. i. § 8; Mozley, *Essays Hist. and Theol.*, pp. 433–444; Flint, *Theism*, pp. 124–130; C. Harris, *Pro Fide*, ch. ii. Attention should be called to J. S. Mill's discussions of the teaching of nature concerning its Author : *Theism*, pp. 176–195. He concedes that nature appears to indicate a Being of great power and knowledge, but one whose power, knowledge and benevolence are limited.

[2] See above, § 6.   [3] See above, § 8.

adequate, which means sufficient to account for the universe and its phenomena, in whatever aspect of reality we may contemplate them. Thus the power and energy which the universe exhibits must proceed from power and energy in the ultimate cause, for it is obvious that such phenomena cannot proceed from anything which is without power and energy. This power must be sufficient to account for all power, whether actually existing or possible, because if any power should manifest itself that does not now exist, the argument with which we are concerned shows that it would necessarily proceed from the ultimate ground of power — the cause of the universe. God is, therefore, the ground and source of all power, so that His power cannot be limited by anything except by power itself. Such power answers to the idea of infinite power or omnipotence.[1] This does not mean that God has power to do any imaginable thing, but that He possesses and is sovereign over all power. Anything that power can do, the power of God can do and can control.[2]

If God is an adequate cause of the universe He must

---

[1] The argument for infinite power is not based upon the vastness of its effects (Cf. pp. 145, 146, above), but upon its being the sum and source of all power, whether actual or hypothetical.

[2] See Flint, *Theism,* pp. 127–129; Davidson, *Theism,* pp. 456–463; Ladd, *Philos. of Relig.,* pp. 123–126. Cf. the theological definitions of omnipotence in St. Thos., *Summa Theol.,* I. xxv; Pearson, *Apos. Creed,* pp. 75–83; Wilhelm and Scannell, *Manual,* Vol. I. pp. 208–210; Martineau, *Religion,* Vol. I. pp. 375–377. Divine omnipotence is considered in its place, ch. xii. § 1, below.

possess in Himself the grounds of possibility of all its contents and phenomena, including life, personality, and being itself. He must be a living cause, for life cannot proceed from a cause that is without life. Spontaneous generation, if it were found to occur, would not nullify this principle. It would merely show that, under certain conditions, life is produced by God without the mediation of previously existing forms of physical life. In its ultimate analysis, the law that life must proceed from life would not be violated.[1]

The universe contains persons, and an impersonal being obviously cannot be the cause of personality,[2] or of the characteristic capacities and functions of persons. These functions include intelligence, feeling, and will. The ground of intelligence, feeling, and will must therefore be contained in God. In brief, God is personal, and this conclusion is not less necessary to satisfy the requirements of ætiology because we cannot adequately comprehend the mode of infinite intelligence, feeling, and will. As will appear in

[1] Cf. pp. 267, 268, below, where references are given.

[2] This argument is not based upon the supposition that a cause must resemble its effect, but upon the necessity of an adequate cause. After all justice is done to the symbolical and inadequate significance of the term person as applied to God, the fact remains that, if He were impersonal, He could not create persons. Cf. Walker, *Christian Theism*, pp. 31–33; McCosh, *Intuitions*, pp. 274, 275; C. Harris, *Pro Fide*, pp. 18, 19; Martineau, *Religion*, Vol. I. pp. 383–389; S. Harris, *Self-Revel. of God*, pp. 341–345; Boedder, *Natural Theol.*, pp. 35–46, 161–165. The personality of God is considered below, in ch. x, §§ 6–8.

another connection, these functions are not necessarily impossible for an infinite being, and our inability to picture or define their divine exercise does not establish any necessary contradiction between personality and infinitude. It is the finite mode of personal functioning that is impossible for an infinite nature.[1]

The universe exists, and its existence, as well as its phenomena, requires an ultimate cause. This is so whatever view we may adopt as to the nature of the universe and of what is called matter or substance.[2] The coming into being of things, as distinguished from their manipulation and development, requires a cause. God is therefore a creative Cause. The metaphysical puzzles connected with the phrase *ex nihilo* [3] may be too deep for our solution, but until we solve them we have no basis for repudiating the truth that finite being has not the ground of its existence in itself, but must have a Creator.[4] If, therefore, the cosmological

[1] See below, ch. x. §§ 7, 8. Cf. Knight, *Aspects of Theism*, ch. xi; C. Harris, *Pro Fide*, pp. 21, 22.

[2] The discovery that matter is radio-active, and that atoms are not its ultimate constituents, has reopened the whole question of the nature of matter, and some are inclined to describe it in the terms of electrical energy.

[3] Creation *ex nihilo* does not mean that nothing is a something from which substance proceeds, but that God created substance without the use of pre-existing materials. If God created all things, primitive substance must have been thus created. Inasmuch as we are ignorant as to what in ultimate analysis substance is, it is foolish to say that such creation is impossible.

[4] Cf. § 7, above, on the objection that the substance of the universe cannot be proved to be an effect, and the references there given.

Taking the writer of Genesis "to imply that where nothing of a

argument is valid, a God exists who is the almighty, living, and personal Creator of all the universe.

§ 11. (c) The cause of the universe must be *voluntary*, not only because the universe contains persons and their ultimate cause must be personal, but also, as has been shown above, because we cannot conceive of any causation except as a determination of which among alternative possibilities shall be realized.[1] The only causation which we can observe from within — our own causal activity — is seen to take the form of volitional determination; and the only means we have for distinguishing external causation from mere phenomenal sequence is our perception that this same element of determination between alternatives is operating. Determination of this kind is necessarily volitional; and therefore a real cause is not conceivable in its final analysis except as a will. The cause of the universe is therefore a voluntary Cause, and is not to be confused with the physical links of causation wherein we detect the working of His will.[2]

material nature previously existed, this substance appeared," Prof. Huxley says, "That is perfectly conceivable, and therefore no one can deny that it may have happened." *Nineteenth Century*, Feb., 1886, pp. 201, 202. J. S. Mill says, *Theism*, p. 137, "There is nothing to disprove the creation and government of nature by a sovereign will."

[1] Cf. § 4, above, and the references there given, on the volitional nature of causation.

[2] V. F. Storr, *Development and Divine Purpose*, pp. 282–285, suggests that the appearance of incompatibility between the uniformity of nature and will-causation is due to an assumption, based upon human analogies, that will is essentially capricious and mutable.

§ 12. (*d*) Finally, the Cause of all things must be *one*. This is suggested by the fact that the universe constitutes an order, in which all events are inter-related in causation. The unity of nature is a neces-sary postulate of science, and this postulate implies the unity of nature's Cause.[1] To hypothecate a plural-ity of causes is to prefer a complex solution of the cosmological problem to one which is relatively simple — obviously an unscientific procedure.[2] Moreover, the conclusion already justified, that the Cause of the universe is infinite, points in the same direction. An infinite being cannot be limited by anything else than itself. The consequence is that, if such a being exists at all, every other being must be dependent upon it for reality. An independent reality, such as another infinite would be, would constitute an external lim-itation.[3]

We might proceed to show that the nature of the

In the divine will, which is eternal, there "can be no variation, neither shadow that is cast by turning." The will of God is perfect and persistent, and is the cause of all law and order in the universe.

[1] Walker, *Christian Theism*, pp. 25, 26; Martineau, *Religion*, pp. 379–381; Flint, *Theism*, pp. 124–127; St. Thomas, *Summa Theol.*, I. xi. 3.

[2] The principle of parsimony of causes was described by William of Occam in the fourteenth century. *Entia non sunt multiplicanda præter necessitatem.* Cf. St. Thomas, *Summa Theol.*, I. xi. 3. As Sir Wm. Hamilton puts it, "Neither more, nor more onerous causes are to be assumed, than are necessary to account for the phenom-ena." See C. Harris, *Pro Fide*, p. 5, note 1; Martineau, *Religion* pp. 377–379; Baldwin, *Dic. of Philos.*, *s. v.* "Parsimony (Law of) "

[3] Franzelin, *De Deo Uno*, pp. 294–296. Divine unity is con-sidered in its place, ch. x. § 9, below.

effects which we observe in the world requires us to infer that God is an infinitely intelligent Designer, the Source and perfect Standard of righteousness, and the moral Sovereign of mankind. The cosmological argument is indeed so comprehensive in its data and bearing that all theistic arguments may be regarded as contained in it. But convenience and ordinary practice alike require that we should consider separately its teleological and moral aspects, under the heads of the teleological and moral arguments.

CHAPTER VI

THE TELEOLOGICAL ARGUMENT

I. *Statement*

§ 1. The teleological argument postulates the principle of causation, and is immediately based upon the evidences of intelligent purpose which are generally to be observed in nature. The inference which is made from these evidences is that the Cause of the universe is an infinitely intelligent and wise Person, who orders all effects harmoniously and in accordance with a plan which we can partially investigate and interpret.[1]

---

[1] This argument was formulated by Socrates (Xenophon, *Memorabilia*, i. 4); and Plato (*Philebus*). Aristotle as well (*Physics*, ii. 8; *Metaph.*, i. 4); and Cicero (*De Nat. Deorum*, ch. ii). None of these writers reached a determinate theistic doctrine.

It is given in Psa. xix. 1–4; xciv. 9, 10; and is implied or at least involved in Job xxxvii–xli; Psa. viii; civ; Isa. xl. 21–26; Wisdom xiii–xv; St. Matt. vi. 25–32; Acts xiv. 15–17; xvii. 23–28.

Patristic references might be multiplied. The following are select examples: Athenagoras, *Plea for Christians*, xvi; Minuc. Felix, *Octav.*, xviii; Tertullian, *Adv. Marc.*, I. xi–xiv; Theophilus, *Ad Autol.*, i. 5, 6; Lactantius, *Divine Inst.*, iii. 20; *Anger of God*, x; Clement Alex., *Cohort.*, x; St. Athanasius, *c. Gent.*, xxvii. 3, xxix, xxxv–xxxvii; *De Incarn.*, ii. 2; St. Gregory Naz., *Orat.*, ii, xxviii. 6; St. Augustine, *De Ordine*, i. 2; *De Vera Relig.*, xxix; *De Civ. Dei*, xi. 4. Cf. Illingworth, *Divine Immanence*, ch. i. §§ ii, iii. S. Thomas Aquinas condenses the argument in *Summa Theol.*, I. ii. 3, *resp. dic.* 5; and the

The form which this argument takes at a given moment is necessarily determined by existing scientific conceptions of nature; and since these conceptions have changed, the teleological argument has undergone modification and reconstruction — especially since the general adoption of the evolutionary hypothesis. The primary data of the argument remain the same — innumerable indications of adaptation, or adjustment of means to ends. But, whereas the emphasis was formerly upon particular instances of adaptation, especially in the organic world, attention is now paid to the general order of nature and the purposeful method of its development. The theory of a special creation of each several species has been abandoned, and the newly developed science of biology assumes that existing forms of life have been evolved out of simpler forms. Thus the living unity

scholastic method *in re* is modernized by Boedder, *Natural Theol.*, pp. 46–62.

Among modern treatments see Caldecott, *Philos. of Relig.*, pp. 22–27; Baldwin, *Dic. of Philos.*, *s. vv.* "Teleology," "Mind and Body"; Fisher, *Grounds of Belief*, ch. ii; Paul Janet, *Final Causes;* Jas. Orr, *Christian View of God*, pp. 97–103; V. F. Storr, *Devel. and Divine Purpose;* W. Profeit, *Creation of Matter;* Gwatkin, *Knowl. of God*, Vol. I. Lec. iii; O. Lodge, *Life and Matter;* Illingworth, *Divine Immanence*, ch. ii; Martineau, *Religion*, Bk. II. ch. i. §§ 5–7; Fairbairn, *Philos. of the Christ. Relig.*, pp. 27–37; J. Caird, *Philos. of Relig.*, ch. v; Tennant, in *Camb. Theol. Essays*, pp. 89–99; S. Harris, *Self-Revel. of God*, ch. xii; Flint, *Theism*, Lecs. v, vi; App. notes, xiii–xxiv. Paley's *Natural Theol.* is, of course, of the highest historical importance. The *Bridgwater Treatises* elaborate his method of argument. For full bibliography of teleology, see Baldwin, *Dic. of Philos.*, Vol. III. pp. 645–6.

of nature is emphasized, and the indications of design in particular things are interpreted in relation to a plan which is seen to govern the whole biological order of development. Again, whereas in the eighteenth century the world was conceived of as a machine, and God was looked upon as an external mechanic, the organic aspects of the universe are now emphasized, and the truth of divine immanence is in especial favour.[1]

In brief, men now think of the universe as a growing organism, so to speak; and as a drama, the meaning of which becomes more and more intelligible as its underlying purpose is progressively realized. The belief that the world is a cosmos, in which uniformity prevails, is not abandoned; but the biblical conception — that it is an *æon*, an unfolding drama — is more adequately understood.[2]

§ 2. The teleological argument may be viewed as advancing through three stages — signified by the phrases: (1) adaptative relations; (2) cosmic unity; (3) progressive continuity; — and as proving that all things are ordered by intelligence.

(*a*) The argument starts with particulars — countless examples of adaptation — which have been thought to manifest design.[3] Nor do they cease to

[1] Cf. p. 93, above.   See also V. F. Storr, *Devel. and Divine Purpose*, chh. ii, iii; Flint, *Theism*, pp. 195-199; Martineau, *Religion*, pp. xiv-xvi.   Darwin's own attitude is shown in his *Life and Letters* (by F. Darwin), Vol. I. ch. viii.

[2] Cf. *Introd. to Dog. Theol.*, p. 45 and note 1 *in loc.*

[3] Such was the form of Paley's argument.   See his *Natural*

suggest design to unprejudiced modern thinkers. Such thinkers, however, are not always willing, in view of the Darwinian hypothesis, to acknowledge that particular adaptations in nature *require* teleological interpretation.[1]

§ 3. (*b*) The argument proceeds to a second stage. Induction is made use of to show that nature is at unity with itself; and that all things work together in accordance with laws, so as to constitute a cosmos, wherein part is adjusted to part and life to environment in a complex but harmonious and interrelated system of things, which cannot be regarded as arising from accident or mere chance.[2] The coincidence of con-

---

Theology. It has been supported by the phenomena of instinct, especially of bees, whose wonderful structures give evidence of forethought and design which cannot be attributed to bees, but must be ascribed to the Maker of bees.

[1] Cf. § 10, below.

[2] The absurdity of the theory that all things are ordered by chance becomes obvious when seriously applied to the more intelligible particulars of experience. It then becomes a foil to the teleological view, making its rejection to appear obviously unintelligent. Cf. Clarke, *Can I Believe in God the Father?* pp. 30–33; Fisher, *Grounds of Belief*, pp. 43–45. Cf. Hastings, *Encyc. of Relig.*, *s. v.* "Accidentalism." Moreover, if intelligence is apparent *anywhere* in nature, it is, in view of the unity of nature, probably dominant *everywhere*. To interpret a unity by its least intelligible aspects is plainly unreasonable. Cf. Martineau, *Religion*, Vol. I. pp. 254–258.

Another important thought is that whereas matter is of use for spirit — for mind — spirit is of no use for matter. Therefore matter and its laws are to be interpreted by mind and not *vice versa*. Cf. Illingworth, *Divine Immanence*, ch. i.

Finally, it is a truism that mere force is blind, yet it works for the production of an intelligible universe. The inference is obvious —

ditions, the balance of forces, and the orderly relations of natural laws appear more and more marvellous in their intelligible unity with the progress of the inductive sciences.[1]

§ 4. (c) The third stage of the argument reckons with the historical continuity of nature. The universe is seen to unfold itself through the ages as if it meant something. It is evidently developing in accordance with an intelligent plan, and is fulfilling a progressive purpose to which all things minister. The goal of the ages is seen to be spiritual, and is identified more and more clearly with the destiny of man.[2]

These facts are patent to all, although we owe their fuller exhibition to modern science. The conclusion to which they point is level to the humblest understanding, when invincible prejudice or sceptical philosophy does not blind the judgment. An intelligible universe, one that appears more and more intelligible

that intelligent will is in control of physical force. Cf. Fisher, *Grounds of Belief*, pp. 47, 48; V. F. Storr, *Devel. and Divine Purpose*, pp. 194–197. The mechanical view of nature is utterly inadequate, and (as Huxley acknowledges, in *Darwin's Life and Letters*, pp. 201, 202) it need not be held in a form which excludes an original ordering of the universe by intelligence. See Jas. Ward, *Naturalism and Agnosticism*; V. F. Storr, *op. cit.*, pp. 168–186.

[1] On the whole argument from order, see V. F. Storr, *op. cit.*, ch. v; S. Harris, *op. cit.*, pp. 367–372; Knight, *Aspects of Theism*, pp. 59–62; Flint, *Theism*, Lec. v; Martineau, *op. cit.*, Vol. I. pp. 254–302.

[2] See V. F. Storr, *Devel. and Divine Purpose;* S. Harris, *Self-Revel. of God*, pp. 272–281, 287–292.

with the increase of investigation, is obviously one that is ordered by intelligence. It is the revelation of a mind, and ought to convince every thoughtful observer that the Cause of the universe is as intelligent and wise as He is all powerful.[1]

II. Objections

§ 5. We come to objections.[2]

(a) It is urged by Kant that the teleological argument, so far as it is valid, can only prove the existence of an overruling Architect and Fashioner of nature. That this Architect is the Creator of the world is not shown.[3]

[1] On the thought that an intelligible world is necessarily the product of intelligence, see Fairbairn, *Philos. of the Christ. Relig.*, pp. 27–38; W. Profeit, *Creation of Matter*, chh. i, ix; S. Harris, *Self-Revel. of God*, pp. 256–266; A. K. Rogers, *Religious Concep. of the World*, pp. 121–151 (from Berkeley's standpoint).

[2] Anti-theistic and sceptical criticisms of the teleological argument appear in Spinoza's *Ethics;* Hume's *Dialogues Concerning Natural Religion;* Kant's *Critique of Pure Reason;* J. S. Mill's *Theism;* Physicus' *Candid Exam. of Theism.* Adverse criticisms of the argument from a theistic standpoint can be found in Knight's *Aspects of Theism*, ch. v; Mulford's *Republic of God*, pp. 8–19; John Caird's *Introd. to the Philos. of Religion*, ch. v.

Theistic discussions at large of objections are contained in Fisher's *Grounds of Belief*, pp. 47 *et seq.*; Flint's *Theism*, Lec. vi; S. Harris' *Self-Revel. of God*, pp. 294–340; Martineau's *Religion*, Vol. I. pp. 302–374; Boedder's *Natural Theol.*, pp. 154, 155, 165–195; Driscoll's *God*, pp. 161–178; and in many other theistic works.

[3] Kant's *Critique of Pure Reason*, Transcendental Dial., Bk. II. ch. iv; translated in Caldecott and Mackintosh's *Selections.* Cf. Knight, *Aspects of Theism*, pp. 63, 64. This objection had been urged by Hume, *Dialogues*, and is echoed by J. S. Mill, *Theism.*

Such an objection came naturally enough from Kant, because he had just been professing to show that the cosmological argument "contains a perfect nest of dialectical assumptions which transcendental criticism does not find it difficult to expose and to dissipate." The teleological argument is a branch of the cosmological, and it is to the more fundamental elements of that argument that we look for justification of the belief that the Designer of the universe is its Creator.[1] It should be added that the results of modern investigation establish the contention that matter bears the marks of manufacture quite as unmistakably in its elementary and primitive forms as in its combinations. All available evidence, in brief, supports the conclusion that the Designer of the laws of matter is the Cause of matter itself.[2]

§ 6. (b) A second objection is that the universe is finite, and the intelligence and wisdom displayed in it are finite. We may not, therefore, infer that the Designer of the universe possesses infinite knowledge and wisdom. We shall consider this objection when we discuss the teaching of the teleological argument.[3]

§ 7. (c) It is also urged that an argument based

[1] Flint, *Theism*, pp. 170, 171; Pfleiderer, *Philos. of Relig.*, Vol. III. p. 259; Jas. Orr, *Christian View*, pp. 102, 103; Fisher, *Grounds of Belief*, p. 49; Martineau, *Religion*, Vol. I. pp. 307, 308.

[2] W. Profeit, *Creation of Matter*, esp. ch. xi; Martineau, *op. cit.*, pp. 305-313; Fisher, *op. cit.*, p. 49; Storr, *Devel. and Divine Purpose*, pp. 197, 198; Flint, *op. cit.*, pp. 170-174. Cf. pp. 150-151, above.

[3] See § 13, below, where references are given. Cf. also ch. v. § 8, above, where a similar objection is considered in relation to the cosmological argument.

upon contrivances — upon adjustments of means to ends — depends for its theistic value upon a universal presence of these contrivances in nature. In order to prove that the universe in its totality is designed we ought to show that everything in the universe exhibits adaptation of means to ends. Failure to demonstrate purpose in any instance constitutes a vitiating limitation of the universal induction required in order to demonstrate that the whole universe is designed. It is notorious that the purpose of many things is unknown. In fact it is easy to discover things which appear to be useless and purposeless.[1]

This objection assumes that the argument which starts with the fact of adaptations in nature is confined in its data to such adaptations, and depends for its force upon universal induction. The fact is that the teleological argument is much richer than this, and depends for its convincing force upon its more advanced stages.

The unity of nature, and the interrelation of its parts and processes, now taken for granted by intelligent men generally, obviates the necessity of discovering separate uses for everything. Each element and object in nature is to be interpreted in relation to the whole, and with reference to the general end for which the universe has been created. And it is not to be

[1] Chas. Darwin urged this objection, *Variation of Animals and Plants*, vol. II. p. 431; His *Life and Letters* (by F. Darwin), Vol. I. pp. 314, 315; Vol. II. p. 382. In a letter to Asa Gray he alleges rudimentary organs in man as examples. Cf. Physicus, *Candid Examination*, pp. 37, 38; Knight, *Aspects of Theism*, pp. 67–75.

expected that, with our imperfect knowledge of the divine mind, we should be able to discover the place and function of each part in the whole. The existence of innumerable adaptations does, however, suggest design, and the wider study of nature as a whole converts the suggestion into certainty that its phenomena and their complex unity cannot be accounted for without hypothecating some kind of intelligence.[1]

§ 8. (d) Somewhat related to the objection which we have been considering is one that at first appears more formidable. It is urged that the universe bears upon itself many marks of imperfection — mal-adjustments, failures, and much waste. Many of its contrivances are defective, and some of them have been immensely improved upon by human invention. Why could not an infinite God, it is asked, have created a perfect world? It seems incredible that He should have created difficulties in order to display skill in overcoming them.[2]

Our reply, in the first place, is that the excellence of anything should be estimated with reference to the purpose for which it is made. A world which was perfect in itself, considered as its own end, might be quite unsuited for the end which the existing world was intended to fulfil.[3] The world, we have abundant

---

[1] On the whole objection, see Martineau, *Religion*, Vol. I. pp. 330-337; Boedder, *Natural Theol.*, pp. 182-192; V. F. Storr, *Devel. and Divine Purpose*, pp. 138-144.

[2] J. S. Mill, *Religion*, pp. 28-30, 35, 36; *Chas. Darwin's Life and Letters* (by F. Darwin), pp. 310, 311; Mulford, *Republic of God*, pp. 8-19; Knight, *Aspects of Theism*, pp. 66, 67.

[3] The supposition that the existing world is the best possible was

reasons for believing, was made for man and in particular for the development of human character. The very imperfections, so called, of nature appear to constitute useful factors in the achievement of such a purpose; which, apparently, could only be fulfilled by the presence of such difficulties and probationary conditions as a world like this affords.[1]

maintained by Leibnitz, Malebranche and Rosmini. That it cannot be the best in the abstract is inferred from its finitude by St. Thomas, *Summa Theol.*, I. xxv. 6; and the whole subject is discussed by Boedder, *Natural Theol.*, pp. 121–126. The position of Leibnitz is epitomized in well-known lines of the poet Pope:

> "All discord, harmony not understood;
> All partial evil, universal good;
> And spite of pride, in erring reason's spite,
> One truth is clear, whatever is, is right."

The wasteful cruelty of nature is set forth by Tennyson:

> "Are God and Nature then at strife,
> That Nature lends such evil dreams?
> So careful of the type she seems,
> So careless of the single life;
>
> 'So careful of the type'? but no,
> From scarpèd cliff and quarried stone
> She cries, 'A thousand types are gone,
> I care for nothing, all shall go.'"

The obvious reply is that this process, of struggle and survival of the few, in fact works for the perfecting of things; and this is a higher end than the happiness for the moment of individual beings.

[1] See Butler's *Analogy*, Pt. I. ch. v, espec. the latter portion, for a classical treatment of this. There is abundant reason for doubting the possibility of constituting a world which shall at once be suited for free and progressive creatures and be perfect in itself. Infinite power is after all limited by the nature of power, which is meaningless

Again, it appears to be a part of the divine purpose to enlist man's participation in the ordering of nature, and in its improvement for his own ends. The fact that man can improve upon nature may reasonably be regarded as pointing to such a conclusion.[1]

Finally, we need to remember that the world is in the making, and necessarily exhibits the imperfections which appear in things not yet completed. And we have no standing ground for objecting that the divine end might have been fulfilled by immediate fiat.[2] Processes such as we see going on about us may be an essential part of the divine plan.[3]

§ 9. (e) A somewhat different objection is that to base a theistic argument upon instances of adaptation observed in nature involves the assumption that conditions which imply design in human art have the same implication when observed in divine creations. The argument, it is alleged, is based upon a fallacious analogy. If God is intelligent, His intelligence, *ex hypothesi*, is infinite, and cannot operate

when applied to the impossible. Cf. ch. xii. § 1, below; Boedder, *Natural Theol.*, pp. 171–174.

[1] The primitive charge to man is, "Subdue it [the earth]; and have dominion over the fish of the sea, and over the fowl of the air, and over every living thing that moveth upon the earth." Gen. i. 28.

[2] J. S. Mill's objection, *Theism*, pp. 176, 177: answered by Boedder, *Natural Theol.*, pp. 170–173; Martineau, *Religion*, Vol. I. p. 325; Flint, *Theism*, pp. 177–180.

[3] On the whole objection, see Martineau, *Religion*, pp. 337–374; Boedder, *op. cit.*, pp. 170–182, 192–195; V. F. Storr, *Devel. and Divine Purpose*, pp. 144–146; S. Harris, *Self-Revel. of God*, pp. 295–316; Flint, *Theism*, Lec. viii; and pp. 413–422.

after the manner of human intelligence. To attribute contrivances to Him is to reduce His mind to finite limitations. An infinite mind cannot be regarded as planning in the human manner, or as resorting to means and contrivances to accomplish its ends.[1]

So far as this objection is valid it applies to what is after all but the first stage of the teleological argument, considered as if it were logically complete. It may be acknowledged that natural adaptations of means to ends, considered apart from the general constitution of nature, do not necessarily require for their causation the kind of intelligence which the theistic hypothesis requires us to attribute to the Creator of the world. But they do suggest, upon the basis of analogy, the operation of an intelligent Cause of some kind; and they do so not less inevitably because Darwinists have alleged the possibility of an alternative explanation — the survival of the fittest. It is because what is thus suggested is corroborated by our investigation into the general constitution and development of nature, that the validity of the original and spontaneous inference from adaptations is seen to be established.

It is a mistake to suppose that, in order to attribute theistic meaning to adaptations in nature, we must assume that divine intelligence resembles our own in its methods of operation.[2] Our inferences as to divine

[1] J. S. Mill, *Theism*, pp. 168, 169 (cf. pp. 176, 177); Physicus, *Candid Exam.*, pp. 43, 44; Knight, *Aspects of Theism*, pp. 64, 65.
[2] Or that God is an external mechanic. Whether God operates

intelligence are governed not by any laws of resemblance between Him and His handiwork, but by the necessities of adequate causation. Adaptations suggest intelligence of some kind in the Author of nature, and a deeper study of nature at large corroborates the suggestion. The relation between the divine mind and these adaptations, or the methods of divine causation, is a distinct question. If the world is made for man, its physical sequences and adaptations are part of its suitability for human understanding and utilization. Were there no adaptations in nature, man could not adapt nature to his purposes. In brief, the world exhibits adaptations not because the mind of its Creator resembles human minds, but because intended for the intelligent use of such minds. And the fact that men can detect many adaptations in the universe, and utilize them, constitutes real evidence of the wisdom of its Creator, without compelling us to describe divine intelligence in the terms of its products — the contrivances, so called, of nature. They are called contrivances analogically, and not because the mind of their Cause is a contriving mind in the anthropomorphic sense of the phrase.[1]

from without (a purely deistic conception) or from within (true but often caricatured pantheistically) is not determined by the nature of the inference from adaptations, but by other considerations. Cf. Flint, *Theism*, pp. 181, 182; V. F. Storr, *Devel. and Divine Purpose*, pp. 204, 205; Boedder, *Natural Theol.*, pp. 167–170; Jno. Caird, *Introd. to the Philos. of Relig.*, pp. 146, 147; Martineau, *Religion*, Vol. I. pp. 328, 329. Cf. p. 134, note 1, above.

[1] V. F. Storr, *op. cit.*, pp. 26–28, 131–134, 200–203, 205–209; Flint, *Theism*, pp. 177–180; Martineau, *Religion*, Vol. I. pp. 313–328;

§ 10. The teleological argument has been immensely enriched by the forms of thought which the evolutionary hypothesis has accentuated.[1] But the theory

Boedder, *op. cit.*, pp. 170–173. Cf. p. 189, below, on the bearing of this upon the problem of evil in a world created by God.

[1] The evolutionary hypothesis in general teaches that all existing forms of substance and life have developed gradually out of primitive elements and conditions by means of the forces and laws which still operate. As applied to the organic world, it teaches the descent of higher forms of life from lower ones — there being no break of physical continuity in the process.

The Darwinian theory, published in 1859, Chas. Darwin's *Origin of the Species*, constitutes one of several explanations of the method of evolution. Scientific thinkers accept it as the best working hypothesis available — not as demonstrated. Cf. Wallace, in *Contemporary Review*, Aug., 1908. The theory is described by the terms "variation," "heredity" and "natural selection" or "survival of the fittest": —

(*a*) There is a tendency of all organisms to vary indefinitely — in Darwin's estimation, fortuitously. No individual is altogether like its parents, or like any other individual.

(*b*) Ancestral characteristics, none the less, are perpetuated to a large extent in offspring. Variability and heredity alike prevail.

(*c*) Organisms are propagated more abundantly than the food supply warrants; and a "struggle for existence" is inevitable, which results in eliminating every type of organism which is unable successfully to adjust itself to its environment, and to maintain itself against its rivals. This process is called "natural selection" — the name being suggested by the analogy of "artificial selection."

See *Encyc. Brit.*, *s. vv.* "Evolution," "Biology" and "Embryology"; Baldwin, *Dic. of Philos.*, *s. vv.* "Evolution," "Variation," "Selection," and "Existence (struggle for)"; Chas. Darwin, *Origin of Species; Descent of Man;* Herb. Spencer, *First Principles; Principles of Biology;* Thos. Huxley, *Man's Place in Nature;* Mivart, *Genesis of Species;* Jno. Fiske, *Cosmical Philosophy;* Romanes, *Darwin and After Darwin;* A. R. Wallace, *Exposition of the Theory of Natural Selection;* R. H. Lock, *Recent Progress in the Study of Variation,* etc.

of natural selection suggested an objection to teleology which was at first thought by many to be fatal.

(*f*) This objection is that the phenomena of adaptation upon which the teleological argument is based are accounted for by natural selection — that is, by undesigned variations and a survival of what is fittest to maintain itself under the conditions of its environment. The hypothesis of design, therefore, is not required by the facts; and any argument which depends for its validity upon such a hypothesis is futile.[1] The further point has been made that, from the nature of things, nothing can maintain itself unless it is capable of adjusting itself to its environment. Consequently the bare fact of the existence of things, quite apart from any particular theory of their origin or development, necessitates the phenomena of their adaptation to environment and mutual adjustment.[2]

Dr. Weismann of Germany denies that "acquired characters" can be transmitted to offspring, and his contention finds support. This view confines the process of evolution to the germ cell. See Baldwin, *Dic. of Philos.*, s. vv. "Acquired Characters," and "Weismannism." The recent investigations of Bateson and De Vries sustain the view that evolution proceeds by large and sudden steps. See R. H. Lock, *op. cit.*, ch. v.

[1] Darwin himself was inclined to believe in design, but could not overcome this difficulty. See his *Life and Letters* (by F. Darwin), Vol. I. ch. viii. His language on the subject is given by Boedder, *Natural Theol.*, pp. 182–195. This difficulty had been formulated as a passing suggestion, not developed, by Hume, in his *Dialogues Concerning Natural Relig.*: See Pfleiderer, *Philos. of Relig.*, Vol. I. p. 128.

[2] See Prof. James, *Pragmatism*, pp. 109–115. Cf. Gwatkin, *Knowledge of God*, pp. 60–63.

Many theistic writers have conceded, unwarrantably, we think, that the Darwinian theory has nullified Paley's argument for design from particular instances of adaptation in nature. What Darwinism has really done is to show that the teleological argument requires fuller development, if its validity is to be made clear to this age. And the new theory has supplied the conceptions which facilitate such a development. The theistic significance of adaptations has not been undermined, but links in the teleological argument have been supplied which the older knowledge of nature did not even suggest, much less show to be needed for the vindication of Paley's *naïve* inference.[1]

It has become apparent that the character, progressive effect and cosmological unity of natural adaptations must be reckoned with in order to establish their teleological meaning. The theory of special creations obscured this necessity and induced a habit of treating everything as separately designed. This habit has given way, in the light of larger knowledge, to an emphasis upon the biological and organic conception of the world as one growing thing. Nothing exists exclusively for itself, and the teleological meaning of

Such an argument is unsafe for those who repudiate design on the plea that adaptations are the result of variation and survival of the fittest. For, if nothing can even exist except under conditions of adaptation, adaptation is primitive and cannot have been caused by variation.

[1] The effect of Darwin's theory on Paley's argument is described by V. F. Storr, *Devel. and Divine Purpose*, chh. ii, iii; and Flint, *Theism*, Lec. vi.

adaptations cannot be realized adequately except in relation to nature as a whole. Biological science has brought out the living unity of things, and a purely mechanical interpretation of adaptations is no longer convincing. So much in general.

As to the specific objection that adaptations are due to natural selection and survival of the fittest, we reply, condensing J. B. Mozley's words, that that which survives does not owe to natural selection its existence, but only its sole existence as distinguished from the fate of a rival that perishes. Natural selection comes in after and upon the active developments of nature to prune and thin them; but it does not create a species; it does not possess one productive or generative function.[1] In brief, it merely describes the process of world development in a certain limited aspect. It accounts neither for the fundamental fact that a variable nature exists and develops, nor for the upward and obviously intelligent and interpretable quality of the development. We say "obviously intelligent," because the process of natural evolution has never been, and cannot be, described in harmony with the results of

[1] J. B. Mozley, *Essays*, Vol. II. pp. 395–407. Cf. Gwatkin, *Knowledge of God*, Vol. I. pp. 16–18; Fairbairn, *Philos. of the Christ. Relig.*, Bk. I. ch. i. §§ III, IV; Orr, *Christian View*, pp. 100, 101. Flint, *Theism*, pp. 194 *et seq.*, points out the fallacy of supposing that an analysis of the *process* of development explains its causation. Cf. Baldwin, *Dic. of Philos.*, *s. v.* "Origin *versus* nature," where it is shown that the origin of a thing does not indicate its nature. Cf. Knight, *Aspects of Theism*, pp. 127, 128. The explanation of a process is to be found in its end, not in its beginning: Storr, *op. cit.*, pp. 221–233.

scientific investigation, except in terms that imply an immanent intelligence which directs every event to the fulfilment of one all-embracing purpose.[1]

Mere survival of the fittest to survive might as well issue in degeneration as in progress.[2] It does not account for the orderly nature of the cosmos and the complex unity of its laws. The variations in nature, it is clear, are not fortuitous, but are directed and controlled in a manner which is seen to make the world more and more full of meaning.[3] Their results are intelligible when, and only when, interpreted in terms that imply intelligence behind them.[4]

[1] It is so described by all evolutionists. Storr, *op. cit.*, pp. 83, 84.

[2] Cf. Prof. Huxley's acknowledgment of this, *Darwiniana*, Vol. II. pp. 90, 91, quoted by Storr, *op. cit.*, pp. 60, 61. As Storr says, *in loc.* "For the explanation, then, of progress we are thrown back upon the fact of variability," and upon the problem as to whether "variations in the direction of progress . . . give us any ground for believing that there has been somewhere at work a principle of design or purpose." Cf. Flint, *Theism*, pp. 202, 203.

[3] The extent of variation of a given organism is determined by the law of that organism; and the variations which produced it were in turn limited in the same manner by earlier organisms. In brief, variation has always been under law, and the general result has been progress. See V. F. Storr, *op. cit.*, ch. iv.

[4] For general discussions bearing on the Darwinian objection, see V. F. Storr, *Devel. and Divine Purpose;* Flint, *Theism*, pp. 194–209; Fisher, *Grounds of Belief*, pp. 45–55; Temple, *Bamp. Lecs.*, Lec. iii; A. Moore, *Science and the Faith*, pp. 186–200; Iverach, *Theism*, Lecs. i–iv; Ladd, *Philos. of Relig.*, ch. xxxviii; Gwatkin, *Knowledge of God*, Vol. I. Lec. iii; Jevons, *Evolution*, chh. xii, xiii; Boedder, *Natural Theol.*, pp. 182–195; Orr, *Christian View*, pp. 97–103; Fairbairn, *Philos. of the Christ. Relig.*, Bk. I. ch. i. §§ III, IV; Profeit, *Creation of Matter*, chh. x, xi; Ward, *Naturalism and Agnosticism*, Vol. I. pp. 203 *et seq.*; Illingworth, *Personality*, pp. 94–99.

§ 11. (g) The general theory of evolution of the universe out of primitive matter and force has suggested the materialistic objection of Physicus, that matter, with its inherent qualities, and force afford sufficient explanation by their undirected development not only for every form of being and life, but for the so-called laws of nature, in accordance with which the process of evolution has advanced. These laws, it is said, are the results of the evolution of primitive matter and force, in which we may discern the promise and potency of every stage of natural history. Evolution proceeds, therefore, in accordance with non-intelligent and irreversible principles; so that, if we were sufficiently intelligent, we could predict with absolute certainty the course of all future events. Nature is wholly to be interpreted in mechanical terms, it is urged, if a scientific understanding of its contents and processes is to be acquired.[1]

It is undoubtedly true that natural scientists feel compelled, in order to simplify their inquiries, to eliminate from consideration every factor or supposition which cannot be interpreted mechanically. But this limitation is self-imposed in order to facilitate a restricted line of investigation. The consequence is that the conclusions of natural scientists are limited in the sphere of their validity to the mechanical aspects of nature. But the assumption which scientists sometimes make, that nature has no other aspects than the purely mechanical, is quite unwarranted, and is incon-

[1] Physicus, *Candid Exam.*, ch. iv, pp. 51-63.

sistent with many facts of experience.[1] That intelligence and will exist is proved by the existence of the sciences, and by the laborious attention which men give to their development; and every effort to describe mind and will in exclusively mechanical terms is doomed to hopeless failure.[2] That psychical activities are conditioned by mechanical concomitants is a fact of constant experience. But that the psychical transcends the mechanical and cannot be explained thereby, is as certain as any content of experience.[3]

[1] The inadequacy of a purely mechanical description and interpretation of nature is proved elaborately by J. Ward, *Naturalism and Agnosticism;* and by O. Lodge, *Life and Matter;* Cf. V. F. Storr, *Devel. and Divine Purpose,* pp. 168–186; Whetham, *Recent Devel. of Phys. Science,* pp. 16–20; Ladd, *Philos. of Relig.,* pp. 243–251.

[2] Cf. Flint, *Anti-Theistic Theories,* pp. 147–150; V. F. Storr, *op. cit.,* p. 180; Fairbairn, *Philos. of the Christ. Relig.,* p. 49.

[3] Jas. Orr, *Christian View,* pp. 146–150, gives three reasons which establish this beyond controversy: (*a*) The energy which is used in the cerebral changes that attend psychical activity is all expended in these changes. None of it disappears by passing over into an "unseen universe" of mind. The law of "conservation of energy," therefore, does not permit the inference that mental phenomena are physical products (Herbert, *Modern Realism Examined,* pp. 43, 57; Kennedy, *Natural Theol. and Modern Thought,* pp. 48, 49, 79, 80; S. Harris, *Phil. Basis of Theism,* pp. 439–442); (*b*) No laws of succession can be discovered between the two sets of phenomena. They appear as heterogeneous concomitants simply (Cf. Orr, *op. cit.,* notes *G* and *H* of Lec. iv); (*c*) Self-consciousness, if it were a product of physical causation, would exhibit merely a stream of successive and separate physical phenomena, whereas it reveals a persistent subject or ego. "Were we simply part of the stream, we would never know it" (Green, *Prologom. to Ethics,* Bk. I; Lotze, *Microcosmus,* pp. 157, 163; Seth, *Hegelianism and Personality,* pp. 3–5). The radical unlikeness of mental phenomena (which are connected logically) and

But there is another reply. Assuming for argument's sake that mind is a mechanical product, this can be accounted for only on the supposition that mind — no one can disprove that it exists — is germinally contained in its mechanical antecedents. That is, the primitive materials of evolution were potentially intelligent. If so, whence did this potential intelligence arise? If the position is taken that it is an attribute of matter, and that matter is eternal, then nature is intelligent and personal[1] — a conclusion which points to pantheism. The alternative is the theistic doctrine that the potential principle of intelligence in nature is the immanent and transcendent God and Creator of all things — a doctrine which is free from the immoral implications of pantheism and from its inadequacies.[2]

cerebral changes (which are connected by the laws of physical energy and motion) is generally conceded.

[1] Two fallacies lie near the surface: (a) that the process of natural development, once ascertained, accounts for the origin of its primitive materials and forces; (b) that the results of evolution can be higher in nature than their physical antecedents, without any higher cause operating to produce such results. Blind forces obviously cannot produce intelligence except under intelligent manipulation. J. S. Mill's supposition that although mind cannot *consciously* be produced except by mind, it can perhaps be produced *unconsciously*, *Theism*, p. 152, if it means anything, begs the question. It must mean that, although purely physical causes cannot operate consciously, they can produce conscious operation. If unconscious causes produce conscious activity they then begin to act consciously. Cf. Boedder, *Natural Theol.*, pp. 161–164.

[2] In addition to J. Ward, *op. cit.*, and O. Lodge, *op. cit.*, see, on this whole objection, Fairbairn, *Philos. of the Christ. Relig.*, pp. 48–55; Profeit, *Creation of Matter*, ch. xi; Flint, *Theism*, pp. 183 *et*

III. *The Wisdom of God*

§ 12. It ought to be clear that, so far from over-throwing the teleological argument, the objections which have been brought against it in modern days enable theistic believers to exhibit its validity more convincingly than ever. The hypothesis that this world is created and controlled in its development by an intelligent and wise God is verified with a completeness which is in proportion to the intelligence and success with which the constitution and course of nature have been investigated.

The question remains, What is the extent and degree of divine intelligence and wisdom which the teleological argument establishes? It is generally conceded that, if the argument is valid, it proves that the Creator is at least sufficiently intelligent to have produced the world and all its contents and arrangements. This means much. It means that divine intelligence transcends human intelligence as much at least as the conception and plan of the universe transcends our capacity adequately to understand and define. The deepest and most unfathomable meanings of nature, the vastest extent of its arrangements, their multitudinous complexities and harmonies, and the intellectual attainments of all the wisest of men who have lived in the past or who will live hereafter, all these, in their ultimate expla-

seq.; and *Anti-Theistic Theories*, pp. 129–175, 488–504; Fraser, *Philos. of Theism*, pp. 43–61; Christlieb, *Modern Doubt*, pp. 145–161.

nation, are products of divine wisdom and elements in a divine plan and purpose.[1]

§ 13. It has been said, however, and by those who concede all this, that nature is after all finite; so that to infer that the mind which is revealed in and by means of it is infinite in knowledge and wisdom, is to make our conclusion larger than its premises warrant. An infinite mind, it is acknowledged, will account for the wisdom displayed in the ordering of nature; but, it is urged, so will a mind of finite capacity. The law of parsimony forbids us to hypothecate infinite wisdom when finite wisdom satisfies the requirements of induction.[2]

If the teleological argument stood by itself, instead of being a branch of the cosmological argument, such an objection would be unanswerable; but when that argument is presupposed, as it is in any sound theistic argumentation, the difficulty is easily met, and in two ways. The infinitude of God, as we have seen,[3] is one of the necessary conclusions of the cosmological argument. The self-existent Cause of all things must be infinite. But if God is infinite, He cannot be limited externally in any of His attributes. If He were

[1] See Flint, *Theism*, pp. 175-177; Martineau, *Religion*, Vol. I. pp. 383-389.

[2] This objection was given in § 6, above, and its consideration postponed to this stage in our argument. It has been urged in somewhat similar terms against the cosmological argument. Cf. ch. v. § 8, above. As here considered, the objection is raised by Kant. Cf. Knight, *Aspects of Theism*, pp. 62, 63.

[3] Cf. ch. v. § 9, above.

thus limited in knowledge and wisdom, He would *ipso facto* be finite. Infinitude admits of *no* external limitation.[1]

Again, it ought to be acknowledged that, if the mind which is exhibited in nature is the mind of One who is the real and ultimate Cause of all possible reality — the cosmological argument, if valid, proves this, — then that mind is possessed of all possible knowledge and wisdom. That is, all the knowledge and wisdom that could be displayed in any operations whatsoever would have to be attributed to that mind. *Ex hypothesi*, if any knowledge or wisdom should come into actuality which does not now exist, it could have no other ultimate source than the Cause of all things — God. This means that the knowledge and wisdom of God are not, and cannot be, externally limited. They are limited only by the possibilities of knowledge and widsom as such, and that which has no external limitations is infinite.[2]

[1] The objection is considered by Flint, *Theism*, pp. 174–177; V. F. Storr, *Devel. and Divine Purpose*, pp. 198–200; Fisher, *Grounds of Belief*, p. 50; and by many others.

[2] Cf. ch. v. § 10, above, where by a similar argument it is shown that the power from which all possible power proceeds must be infinite. See Psa. xciv. 9, 10. Cf. St. Thomas, *Summa Theol.*, I. xiv. 9. Royce says, *Conception of God*, p. 8, "An Omniscient Being" [omniscience is infinite knowledge] "would be one who simply found presented to Him, not by virtue of fragmentary and gradually completed processes of inquiry, but by virtue of an all-embracing, direct, and transparent insight into His own truth, — who found thus presented to Him, I say, the complete, and fulfilled answer to every genuinely rational question." See, on divine knowledge and wisdom, ch. xii. §§ 3, 5, below.

13

CHAPTER VII

THE MORAL ARGUMENTS

I. *Conscience and History*

§ 1. Like the teleological argument, the moral arguments presuppose, and exhibit aspects of, the cosmological. They also presuppose divine intelligence, and therefore depend for validity upon the teleological argument. The moral argument, strictly so called, may be regarded as having three stages.[1]

(*a*) It begins with a consideration of the phenomena of conscience, which may be defined as the faculty of the mind wherewith we judge practically of the moral quality of actions, as to whether they are

---

[1] The ancients did not give the moral argument a separate consideration. Raymond of Sebonde, in his *Natural Theol.*, reasons that, as man is a responsible being who cannot distribute justice to himself, he must be under a superior being who can. Kant gave the moral argument the primary place, *Critique of Judgment*, § 86; and his emphasis upon the moral imperative has given this argument greater prominence in modern theism. For general discussions of it, see Flint, *Theism*, Lecs. vii, viii; and App., notes xxv–xxxv; Caldecott, *Philos. of Relig.*, pp. 46–52; Liddon, *Some Elements*, pp. 67–71; J. Orr, *Christian View*, pp. 108–111; Fairbairn, *Philos. of the Christ. Relig.*, pp. 83–93; Dorner, *Christian Doctrine*, §§ 23, 25, 26; Martineau, *Religion*, Bk. II. chh. ii, iii. 2; Fisher, *Grounds of Belief*, pp. 55–59; Calderwood, *Philos. of the Infin.*, ch. viii; Illingworth, *Personality*, pp. 103–112, 260–264; Conder, *Basis of Faith*, pp. 383–431.

righteous or sinful.[1] Two facts are indisputable: (1) that our reason is compelled to assume the eternal validity of the distinction between right and wrong; (2) that the sense of personal accountability for doing what is right and shunning what is wrong cannot be escaped by any sane human mind. The voice of conscience may indeed be partially stifled by persistent wrong-doing, but the sense of right and wrong, and the sense of accountability, cannot wholly be destroyed so long as reason retains its seat.[2]

The inferences which these facts justify are simple and practically unavoidable, even by those who endeavour to overthrow their theoretical validity. The distinction between right and wrong is true if human reason is at all to be trusted; and the fundamental teleology of the universe requires that we should do

---

[1] In calling conscience a faculty, we do not mean that it is a separate organ. It is simply a particular species of capacity and functioning of a mind which is one and indivisible in its activities. Cf. ch. ii. § 10, above; and *Introd. to Dog. Theol.*, ch. iv. § 4.

On the conscience, see St. Thomas, *Summa Theol.*, I. lxxix. 13; Jeremy Taylor, *Ductor Dubitantium*, Bk. I. ch. i; Bishop Butler, *Serms. on Human Nature*, ii; Elmendorf, *Moral Theol.*, IV. i, p. 499; Gury, *Compend. Theol. Moralis*, Pt. I. § 36; Janet, *Elements of Morals*, § 10. Cf. Rom. ii. 15.

[2] The chief ethical theories which are inconsistent with this position are the hedonistic or utilitarian and the Spencerian or evolutionist. Cf. § 4 (*b*), (*d*), of this chapter. Kant regarded the dictates of conscience as categorical imperatives which cannot be evaded or merged into anything else. See Martineau, *Religion*, Bk. II. ch. ii. §§ 1, 2; Gwatkin, *Knowledge of God*, Vol. I. pp. 43, 44; Illingworth, *Reason and Revel.*, pp. 237-240; Baldwin, *Dic. of Philos.*, *s. v.* "Obligation."

right and avoid wrong-doing. The sense of personal accountability is illusory and meaningless, unless a personal being exists whose authority over human conduct is beyond appeal, and whose will is the final standard of righteousness. It is possible to be lacking in a clear realization of our relation to the supreme will, but the logic of a sane human mind can never justify a denial thereof. We cannot be morally accountable to an impersonal object, to a stone, to a mere force, or to an abstract law. No other hypothesis can satisfy the requirements of moral sense except the doctrine that the Cause of the universe is a personal and righteous God to whom we must render full account for our lives and characters, in the light of the manifestations to us of His will.

We are compelled to describe the relation of conscience to human conduct in terms of authority.[1] But authority over our conduct has no meaning except as possessed by a person other than ourselves. When we attribute authority to the conscience, therefore, we do so metaphorically. The authority of conscience is really the authority of God; and the voice of conscience is simply our rational judgment as to what is the will of God in relation to our conduct under the particular circumstances of the moment.[2] That judg-

[1] Bishop Butler says of conscience, "Had it the power as it has manifest authority, it would absolutely govern the world": *Serms. on Human Nature*, ii.

[2] Cf. Calderwood, *Handbook of Moral Philos.*, pp. 66–68; Porter, *Moral Science*, §§ 112–114; Bp. Sanderson, *Conscience and Law* (transl. by Wordsworth), pp. 29–32.

ment may err in particulars, but we recognize its
derivative authority none the less, because of the
self-evident axiom that we ought to do what seems
to be right and shun the doing of what seems to be
wrong.[1]

§ 2. (b) This is the moral argument in its strictest
sense; but it is enriched and confirmed by signs that
the moral sovereignty of God is a real working force
in the course of human events.

This appears in the first place in personal experience. The justice of God works undeniably in award-
ing happiness or misery to individuals in accordance
with their deservings, as registered by the judgments
of conscience. Wickedness may triumph in superficial respects — especially hidden wickedness, — and
triumphant malice has its pleasures. But the happiness of the wicked is never unalloyed. Even the
most atrophied conscience imparts to its sinful pos-
sessor a sense of incompleteness and non-finality of
present gratification which constitutes an intimation
of impending woe and a persistent nightmare.[2] On
the other hand, the righteous enjoy consolations of
which the wicked have no experience. Their sorrows,

---

[1] That "probability is a very guide of life" in this connection is
shown in ch. iii. § 9, above. On the argument from conscience, see
Flint, *Theism*, pp. 214–226; Martineau, *Religion*, Bk. II. ch. ii. § 3;
Kant, *Critique of Judgment*, § 86; Driscoll, *God*, pp. 87–91; Wilf.
Ward, *W. G. Ward and the Catholic Revival*, pp. 341–345.

[2] On the mixture of pleasure and misery, and the predominance
of the latter, in malice, see Chalmers, *Natural Theol.*, Bk. III. ch. iii;
Flint, *Theism*, pp. 403–406. Cf. Job. xxi.

often severe, are seen to be temporary, and to work for their ultimate good.[1]   Hope displaces fear; love, even when seemingly despised, brings growing joy; and a self-approving conscience robs every evil of its terrors and of its finality.   In short, God has so constituted things that virtue, even in this probationary life, is self-rewarding and vice self-punishing.[2]

§ 3.   (c) The moral sovereignty of God and its righteous working are evident in human history at large.   There is, to use Matthew Arnold's often quoted language, a "Power not ourselves that makes for righteousness."[3]   To see that this is so one must, of course, take a broad view of the general course of things. Moreover, the advance of the interests of righteousness does not depend for proof upon any alleged superiority of moderns over the ancients in living up to their ideals of righteousness.   It lies rather in the improvement of moral ideals and in the increasing power and success of moral principles in determining public sentiment and social customs and conditions.   No intelligent student of the history of civilization can fail to see that moderns are at a decided moral advantage over the ancients in all that concerns the knowledge and practice of righteousness; and that it is now far more difficult for one to commit the grosser sins

[1] Heb. xii. 5–11; Rom. viii. 28.

[2] On this argument, see Flint, *Theism*, pp. 227–229.

[3] *Literature and Dogma*.   On this form of the moral argument, see Flint, *Theism*, pp. 229–232; Martineau, *Religion*, Bk. I. ch. v; Martensen, *Christian Dogmatics*, § 40; Pfleiderer, *Philos. of Relig.*, Vol. III. pp. 267–271.

with even seeming impunity than it was in earlier stages of human history.

The success of moral forces can be seen in the changed relations between different social classes, the improved condition of women, the abolition of slavery, the softening of methods of penal justice and of rules of warfare, the elaboration of international law in the interests of peace, and the development of public philanthropies. No doubt the great stream has its eddies and backward currents, but the direction in which the main current flows is quite unmistakable.

Now the power which has thus made for righteousness is obviously superhuman; for the natural propensities of men, when left without restraint, make for moral degeneration. Righteousness in the abstract has never been able to realize itself in the concrete without the assistance of personal influence and overruling circumstances.[1] The only hypothesis which can satisfy the conditions of the problem is that divine providence has manipulated conditions and events in such wise that the paths of righteousness have become more clear and easy to tread, while the paths of wickedness have become less and less easy to pursue with impunity. It is God that ruleth, in spite of, and even by means of, human weakness; and the manner of His government proves that He is righteous in all His ways.

§ 4. Several objections have been made against the moral argument.

[1] See Jordan, *Compar. Relig.*, pp. 351–353. Cf. Rom. vii. 14–23.

(a) It is said that the human will is a law unto itself, and that what is called conscience is nothing but an aspect of the will's functioning. This, however, is too plainly contrary to experience and sound psychology to need elaborate refutation. Consciousness bears witness that the judicial and volitional functions of the soul are distinct, and that the will is under moral laws which the conscience practically interprets for its direction. This is proved especially by the fact that the conscience and the will are often in antagonism, the former demanding implicit conformity to its judgments, the latter refusing such conformity. The theistic implications of conscience remain unaffected, therefore, by such an objection.[1]

(b) Another objection is based upon utilitarian grounds. Utilitarianism makes happiness the supreme aim of human conduct, implying that the sense of duty and of moral accountability are illusory. If such a theory is true, the moral argument has no valid basis in experience.[2]

But consciousness bears unmistakable testimony to the truth that men possess a sense of duty which cannot be identified with a mere perception of the

[1] See Flint, *Theism*, pp. 218, 219.

[2] On the principles of modern utilitarianism, see H. Sidgwick, *Outlines of the Hist. of Ethics*, pp. 236–253, who refers to Abraham Tucker, *Light of Nature Pursued* (1768-1774); Gay's dissertation prefixed to Law's trans. of King's *Origin of Evil* (1731); Paley's *Moral and Polit. Philos.* (1785); Bentham's *Works;* J. S. Mills' *Utilitarianism.* See also Baldwin, *Dic. of Philos., s. v.* "Utilitarianism"; Calderwood, *Handbook of Moral Philos.*, Pt. I. Div. I. ch. ii.

advantages of pleasure or happiness. The idea of duty is unique, and the sense of obligation does not invariably sanction the pursuit of happiness. The judgments of conscience and utilitarian considerations are often opposed to each other. In such cases, we perceive that the conscience, rather than our desire for happiness, should determine our conduct.[1]

(c) A third objection is based upon the fact that the conscience cannot always be trusted to give sound moral judgments, so that our sense of obligation to conform our lives to its dictates is plainly in need of qualification. The evidence of the conscience's fallibility is to be seen in the fact that the consciences of different men often disagree in their judgments. Savages, for instance, feel authorized and even required by their consciences to perform actions which the consciences of civilized men judge to be wrong.

No one will be influenced by such an objection who understands the real purport and basis of the moral argument. It is not based upon any supposed infallibility of the conscience, but upon the universal recognition that righteousness ought to be practised and that we are accountable for the discharge of this obligation. That the conscience may err in determining particulars of duty does not weaken the force of the intuition that we ought to do what is right, so

[1] Utilitarianism is criticised by Calderwood, *op. cit.*, pp. 130–152; Cf. Lecky, *European Morals*, ch. i; Blackie, *Four Phases of Morals;* Fairbairn, *Philos. of the Christ. Relig.*, pp. 63–68, 78–81; Martineau, *Types of Ethical Theory*, Vol. II. pp. 304–359.

far as we can ascertain it, and that we are accountable for so doing.[1] It is this sense of duty and accountability which implies the existence of a supreme moral Governor. It should be added, however, that, although the individual conscience is fallible and requires education, men are not left to grope blindly after the laws of righteousness. The proof of this is that men's moral ideals tend constantly to general agreement among progressive peoples. Consciences tend to become more and more trustworthy in their judgments with the advance of enlightenment and the development of the rational experience of mankind.[2]

(d) Another objection treats conscience as the product of evolution. It is urged that its beginnings may be discerned in man's brute ancestors, so that, having a non-rational origin, it may not be regarded rightly as possessing authority over human conduct, even in the derivative and metaphorical sense.[3]

Something might be urged as to the lack of evidence that conscience has had such an origin, but it is quite unnecessary. Evolutionists do not mistrust human reason in general, although they consider it to be a

[1] The authority of conscience is not based upon inerrancy of its judgments, but upon the fact that these judgments embody what we are able to learn of duty in each case.

[2] On the objection based upon errors of conscience, see Flint, *Theism*, p. 226; E. R. Conder, *Basis of Faith*, pp. 398, 399.

[3] The evolutionary theory of morality appears in Herbert Spencer's *Data of Ethics*. It is expounded by Martineau, *Types of Ethical Theory*, Vol. II. pp. 367–376; and treated at length, both historically and defensively, by C. M. Williams, *Review of Evolutional Ethics*.

product of evolution. The fact is that the origin of conscience has no bearing on its present nature and authority. It is what it is whatever may have been its antecedents; and to repudiate its authority on evolutionary grounds is inconsistent, unless we are also to repudiate human reason, of which it is an essential constituent and function.[1]

§ 5. (e) The most formidable, in fact the only serious, objection to the moral argument is based upon the existence of evil in a world created and governed by One who is *ex hypothesi* at once righteous and almighty. To put the objection in one of its most ordinary and representative forms, How can we maintain that the Almighty is righteous in all His ways in the face of the evidence that He has created possibilities of sin which He knew would become actualities? If He were perfectly righteous would He not necessarily have excluded such possibilities and actualities from His handiwork? Is not the fact that He has failed to exclude them fatal to the contention that He is both almighty and righteous; and must we not deny either the perfection of His righteousness or the doctrine of His omnipotence?[2]

These questions reduce themselves to one: — Is the existence of evil possible in a world created and ordered by an almighty and all-righteous God? Our

---

[1] The evolutionary objection is answered by Martineau, *op. cit.*, Vol. II. pp. 376–424; V. F. Storr, *Devel. and Divine Purpose*, pp. 236–238; Fairbairn, *Philos. of the Christ. Relig.*, pp. 68–74.

[2] J. S. Mill, *Theism*, pp. 186–195. The objection is found in innumerable popular works by infidels.

answer will depend upon the manner in which we attempt a solution of the problem.[1] If we attempt to solve it in the abstract, we may easily be led to adopt a conclusion which is inconsistent with theistic belief. But such a method cannot be rationally justified, for our knowledge of certain primary elements of the problem is too inadequate to enable us to grapple with it successfully when formulated in an abstract manner.[2]

[1] A historical survey of the attitudes which have been adopted towards the problem of evil is given by Fairbairn, *Philos. of the Christ. Relig.*, Bk. I. ch. iii. Cf. T. B. Strong, *Manual of Theol.*, pp. 222–230; Pfleiderer, *Philos. of Relig.*, Vol. IV. pp. 1–22.

The chief positions desirable to notice are as follows: (*a*) Dualism, especially in its Gnostic and Manichæan forms, which declares evil to reside intrinsically in matter and flesh; (*b*) Pantheism, which either explains evil away or ascribes it to God; (*c*) Optimism, which treats this as the best of all possible worlds; (*d*) Materialism, especially in modern physical fatalism, which makes evil a necessary phase of evolution and thus precludes a moral interpretation of it; (*e*) Pessimism, the gospel of despair; (*f*) The Christian view, which, amid variations in its speculative definition, does justice more adequately than any other view to the terrible reality of evil, but provides a practical solution of the problem which evil raises by its doctrines of redemption and grace. The theological treatment of this subject belongs to our treatise on Creation, in a subsequent volume.

[2] Cf. Illingworth, *Reason and Revel.*, pp. 232–237. The speculations of St. Augustine have to a large extent determined the views of western theologians since his time. *De Vera Relig.*, ix; *De Civ. Dei*, xii. 4–7; *De Ord.*, ii. 20. Evil, according to him, is not a positive entity but the negation of good. Its cause is deficient rather than efficient. Every being, as being, is good; and evil is a deficient relation in things which in themselves are good. Gen. i. 1, 31. This view is found in earlier writers, although not in a developed form: *e.g.* Clement Alex., *Strom.*, iv. 13; vi. 17; St. Athanasius, *c. Gent.*,

We cannot comprehend the meanings of the temporal issues of divine causation as they appear when these issues are viewed from the divine and eternal standpoint; nor do we understand sufficiently the part which the permission of evil [1] plays in the divine plan and purpose. We know this much, that, to an eternal mind and will, the effects which we are obliged to describe in terms of temporal sequence, or of means and ends, are one and all realized in an eternal now; so that nothing *stands between* the divine purpose and its fulfilment. The end is present in the beginning, and *the nature of the end* determines in eternity the significance and moral quality of divine causation in all that happens. In this connection the distinction between means and ends is valid only in relation to temporal sequence and from a temporal point of view. To allege, therefore, that God makes the end justify the means which He employs is meaningless. Such a description is inapplicable to eternal operations.[2]

iv.–vii. St. Thomas expounds it: *Summa Theol.*, I. xlviii. 1–4, and elsewhere. Such a position has the value of partial truth, but is inadequate to account for positive malice. It does not, however, as modern writers contend — *e.g.* J. Caird, in *Fundamental Ideas of Christianity*, Lec. ix — evaporate the reality of evil. Christian doctrine traces the origin of moral evil to creaturely wills, and makes the whole problem a moral one. Cf. on St. Augustine's theory, W. Bright, *Lessons from the Lives of Three Great Fathers*, pp. 271–275.

[1] Divine permission here means non-prevention — not divine connivance or sanction.

[2] T. B. Strong, *Manual of Theol.*, pp. 233–238. Those who object to the teleological argument that the Infinite and Eternal cannot be thought of as contriving means to ends (cf. ch. vi. § 9, above) are

We are also ignorant of the bearing of evil upon the question of divine omnipotence. We certainly have no knowledge which warrants the assertion that, if God is righteous, the existence of evil proves His power to be finite. Infinite power means fulness of power up to the limits of the idea of power. Some achievements are impossible from the nature of things. That is, they do not come within the category of power at all. To be unable, for instance, to make a fact not a fact is no evidence of finiteness of power; and it may be, so far as we know, that to develop a kingdom of saints without the incidental possibility that evil should appear as a by-product, so to speak, is equally outside the range of power as power.[1]

Such considerations are speculative, and are often more baffling to the imagination than satisfying to the

surely inconsistent in urging the objection to the moral argument which we are now considering.

If to create moral beings with knowledge that they will sin is necessarily evil, those human beings who produce children, knowing as they must that these children will not be sinless, are guilty.

[1] Illingworth, *Reason and Revel.*, p. 224; Fairbairn, *Philos. of the Christ. Relig.*, pp. 152–163; Le Conte, in *The Conception of God*, p. 72; Liddon, *Some Elements*, pp. 154, 155; T. B. Strong, *Manual of Theol.*, pp. 230–232; Fraser, *Philos. of Theism*, pp. 266–272. Fraser says, "To argue that the ideal of the universe cannot be perfect, and that the Universal Power cannot be ever active and infinitely good, if moral evil, with naturally consequent suffering, is found anywhere in it, implies, does it not, that 'God' cannot be God, if we find a planet containing personal agents on moral trial? A circle destitute of the essential properties of a circle could as well be supposed to exist, as a finite person on moral trial, who is wanting in what is essential to a person on moral trial."

reason. The problem of evil, so far as we can grapple successfully with it, is a practical one, and should be dealt with on practical lines.[1]

A sound instinct assures us that the evidence of divine goodness which conscience affords justifies the habit of judging the moral quality of the divine plan by the nature of the end which it appears to subserve, that is by the tendency of things considered in their totality. The considerations which we have given to show that a "Power not ourselves" "makes for right-eousness," both in individuals and in the general course of history, ought to be regarded as establishing prac-tically the righteous nature of the general tendency of things and of the divine purpose.[2]

Coming to details, we can see that what are called physical evils often subserve beneficent purposes. Pain serves to warn us off from fatal dangers, and is a needed stimulus to action. Its disciplinary effects are often conspicuous, such as the refining, toughening,

[1] Fairbairn says, *Philos. of the Christ. Relig.*, p. 132, "the belief in God is an excellent thing when we face evil as something to be vanquished; but when we face evil as something to be explained, the belief is itself surrounded with difficulties." The philosophy which works should be considered to be true, even though attended by prob-lems which defy speculative solution.

[2] To explain evil as being merely an inevitable imperfection of what is still in the making — metaphysical evil — would be to ex-plain it away. But it is permissible to believe that the possibility of evil is caused and justified by the incompleteness of the realization in time of the divine purpose. We say "in time," for in eternity the end is realized in the beginning. On the trend of all history towards the realization of perfect right, see Martineau, *Religion*, Vol. II. pp. 118–130. Cf. Flint, *Theism*, pp. 258, 259.

and ripening of spiritual character and the enlargement of human sympathies.[1] Certainly neither pain
nor death are what a malevolent God would have
made them to be.[2]

Moral evil is seen invariably to proceed from creaturely wills, and in practical judgment we inevitably
lay the blame on creatures.[3] Only when we venture
into the speculative sphere, and grapple with problems
which are too deep for us, are we tempted to make God
responsible for them. If we confine ourselves to practical considerations, we can see that the possibility of
sin is involved in human probation, which in turn
appears to be an essential factor in the development
of saints.[4] We can also see that moral evil is fighting a
losing battle, and this obviously by reason of an overruling providence, which compels the very sins of
men to subserve the interests of righteousness. Super-

---

[1] See Fairbairn, *op. cit.*, Vol. I. pp. 132–146; F. A. Dixey, in
Oxford House Papers, 2d Series, pp. 99–119; Le Conte, in *The Con-
ception of God*, pp. 72–74; Flint, *Theism*, pp. 245–252; Martineau,
Religion, Vol. II. pp. 56–99, esp. pp. 92–99.

[2] See Clarke, *Outline of Christ. Theol.*, pp. 120–123, 127, 128, for
a consideration of the kind of world this would be if God were bad.

[3] The only point of view from which we can justify this is theistic.
If there is no God and Judge over all, there is no moral responsibility. Moreover, in blaming our neighbours for sin, we blame
them alone. If we think of God, we think of Him as Judge, not as
guilty.

[4] We must not add suffering to sin, whether momentary or lasting,
as enlarging the problem. Sin is the only problem. Suffering is
either an effect or a remedy of sin, or at least an incident of a world
in which sin is possible. Cf. Illingworth, *Reason and Revel.*, pp. 221,
222.

natural revelation teaches us that sin has occasioned the most glorious manifestation of divine love and sanctifying grace that history has known or imagination has ever pictured.[1]

The sum of the matter is that if evil appears to be an inevitable by-product of the evolution of a kingdom of righteousness, it is not permitted to go utterly to waste; but is utilized in spite of itself for enriching the proper products of spiritual evolution.[2]

II. *Truth, Beauty and Religion*

§ 6. The phenomena of truth, beauty and religious aspiration are suitably considered in connection with the moral argument, for they exhibit moral and theistic implications which fortify that argument and enrich its teaching.

Truth pertains to the significance of things, and lies in the agreement of this significance with reality.[3]

---

[1] The permission of sin and the doctrine of redemption and superabounding grace, if that doctrine is true, are necessarily to be considered together. See Fairbairn, *Philos. of the Christ. Relig.*, pp. 167, 168; Illingworth, *Reason and Revel.*, p. 228; Liddon, *Some Elements*, p. 155. Cf. St. Augustine, *De Civ. Dei*, xiv. 26, 27; xxii. 1.

[2] On the problem of evil, see Flint, *Theism*, Lec. viii; Illingworth, *Reason and Revel.*, ch. xii; Martineau, *Religion*, Bk. II. ch. iii. § 2; Clarke, *Outline of Christ. Theol.*, pp. 153–158; Fairbairn, *Philos. of the Christ. Relig.*, Bk. I. chh. iii, iv; Pfleiderer, *Philos. of Relig.*, Vol. IV. pp. 1–45; Fraser, *Philos. of Theism*, Pt. III; T. B.Strong, *Manual of Theol.*, pp. 222–238; Liddon, *Some Elements*, Lec. iv; Butler, *Analogy*, Pt. I. ch. vii; Calderwood, *Moral Philos.*, pp. 256–259.

[3] Truth consists, St. Thomas says, *in adaequatione intellectus et rei*.

14

When apprehended and formulated truth takes the form of a judgment or proposition; and a proposition is true or untrue according as it agrees or disagrees with the reality or realities with which it is concerned. A true proposition describes what is, or has been, or will be, whether its subject-matter is entity, relation, or event.[1] Truth is objective, in so far as it is concerned with reality, and does not exist except as signifying it and agreeing therewith.[2] It is also relative, both because it signifies the relation of agreement, and because all signification whatsoever is relative to mind. Truth has no meaning, except as either proceeding from or apprehended by mind. It cannot be interpreted except in the forms and terms of intelligence. Apart from personality, therefore, truth has no existence.[3]

Truth is everywhere exhibited in nature, and objectively so. Nature never lies. The laws by which scientists describe natural phenomena are so many witnesses, through their persistent validity and re-

[1] On truth see Baldwin, *Dic. of Philos.*, *s. v.* "Truth and Falsity and Error"; Fleming, *Vocab. of Philos.*, *s. vv.* "Truth" and "Truths, First or Necessary, and Contingent"; Thos. Reid, *Intellectual Powers*, Ess. vi; St. Thomas, *Summa Theol.*, I. xvi.

[2] This position is opposed, in the sphere of religion to the Ritschlian theory of mere value-judgments; and in every sphere to the pragmatic view that truth consists in the practical utility of propositions — expounded by Prof. James, *Pragmatism.*

[3] Scepticism obviously, and, in effect, subjective idealism as well, exaggerate the relativity of truth and make it to be merely what man troweth. If thought constitutes reality, there is no reality except thought.

peated verification, of the unvarying agreement of these phenomena with the realities to which they introduce us. Widening experience teaches us that natural laws, rightly interpreted, are never violated; and this means that nature embodies truth. This truth is certainly objective, and no investigators of nature are able to proceed successfully, except on the supposition that nature signifies what it does independently of our mental apprehension of its meaning. Whence, then, does the truth of nature arise? As we have seen, truth has no existence except in relation to personal intelligence, producing and apprehending it. The truth of nature, therefore, since it is not the creation of our minds, implies the existence of another mind than ours from which it proceeds.[1]

A similiar conclusion is involved when we consider human reason. Except from the point of view of scepticism — which nullifies every theory whatsoever, including the sceptical — our reason in its fundamental laws is trustworthy. That is, rational processes are true, and are fundamentally in harmony with objective reality. This truthfulness of reason demands a cause, and the cause must be personal. Moreover, the truthfulness which characterizes nature and reason alike must also characterize their personal cause. God is this Cause, and His truthfulness is exhibited in all His handiwork.

It is possible to make the further inference that

[1] On the reign of truth in nature, see Chadbourne, *Natural Theol.*, Lecs. viii–x. Cf. Fraser, *Philos. of Theism*, pp. 114–117, 152, 153.

God is eternal and absolute. The very nature of truth requires this. Its participative subject-matter may indeed be relative and contingent, but to describe any thing or proposition as true is to measure it by a standard that is neither relative nor contingent, but eternal and absolute. But truth has its source in God, and the source of truth cannot be less abiding or less absolute than truth itself.[1]

§ 7. Beauty is that by reason of which we admire things; and both our capacity to admire and the realities which we admire imply that beauty is real and objective. We do not indeed identify beauty with the things which we admire, but we are unable to avoid the supposition that beauty is objectively real, and that natural phenomena are beautiful because they participate in real beauty.[2] Men have been found who are more or less insensible to beauty, but they are surely abnormal. The admiration of beauty is sufficiently universal to be regarded as normal, and as establishing its reality. Some have attempted to

---

[1] On the argument based upon the reign of truth see St. Augustine, *De Vera Relig.*, xxx, xxxi; *De Lib. Arb.*, II. viii, xii, xiv; *Solil.*, I. iii; *Confess.*, xii. 25; Driscoll, *God*, pp. 70–79; Fraser, *Philos. of Theism*, pp. 114–117; and Pt. II. Lec. viii.

[2] On beauty, see Baldwin, *Dic. of Philos.*, s. vv. "Beauty" and "Æsthetic"; *Encyc. Brit.*, s. v. "Beauty": Fleming, *Vocab.*, "Æsthetics." Among classical treatments are Francis Hutcheson, *Inquiry into the Original of our Ideas of Beauty and Virtue*, 1725; Thos. Reid, *Intell. Powers*, Ess. viii; Kant, *Critique of the Judgment;* Burke, *The Sublime and the Beautiful;* Cousin, *The True, the Beautiful and the Good;* Ruskin, *Modern Painters*, Vol. ii. A fuller bibliography is given by Baldwin, *Dic. of Philos.*, Vol. III. pp. 710–744.

identify beauty with utility;[1] but our admiration of the beauty of things is often most intense when we are least able to discover their utility. The distinction between beauty and utility is made too universally and is too obvious successfully to be denied. Some again have tried to reduce the phenomenon of beauty to pure subjectivity.[2] It is true that beauty has an ideal element, and has significance only in relation to persons who are capable of admiring it; but, unless we repudiate the testimony of consciousness, we are compelled to interpret the admiration of beauty as arising from the perception of something which is admirable in itself, that is, objectively beautiful. This is true of the products of art, of music, and even of thought, language, and personal character, as well as of natural phenomena.

Now, as has been said, we do not identify beauty with the sensible objects which we admire. They are apprehended as really beautiful, but because participating in an ideal quality by which they are trans-

---

[1] *E.g.*, Berkeley, *Alciphron;* and Hume. Cf. Caldecott, *Philos. of Religion*, pp. 53, 54.

[2] Cf. Caldecott, *op. cit.*, p. 54. The association theory traced the sense of beauty to association with past pleasure. For example, the beauty of a peach is based upon pleasure derived from eating peaches. Begg, *The Development of Taste*, refutes the theory.

A concise history of theories is contained in Knight, *Philos. of the Beautiful*, i. Kant, in *Critique of the Judgment*, holds that (*a*) The beautiful, as distinguished from the good and the agreeable, is the object of disinterested satisfaction; (*b*) It is a quality of things and universally pleasing; (*c*) It is purposive, but not to be judged by any particular ends; (*d*) It is intrinsically pleasing and ought to please all.

cended. Beauty, in short, is in its ultimate analysis an ideal standard by which we æsthetically value things. Like truth it appears to transcend all finite things and to be absolute. No other source of beauty can be conceived except the Cause of all things, God. If the handiwork of God is beautiful, He Himself must be beautiful and admirable; and, since He is altogether infinite, He must be infinitely beautiful and glorious.[1] "The heavens declare the glory of God";[2] but there are higher types of beauty than can be observed in the heavens. The beauty of personal character is the highest beauty which comes within our admiring experience. The character of God must be regarded as the source of such beauty, and He must be thought of as altogether lovely in Himself.[3]

§ 8. The argument that the practically universal aspiration of men to communion with the Divine cannot rightly be regarded as illusory, but implies the reality of the Divine, is an ancient one.[4] Its force,

---

[1] "The world itself by its well ordered changes, and by the fair appearance of all visible things, bears a testimony of its own, both that it has been created, and also that it could not have been created save by God, whose greatness and beauty are unutterable": St. Augustine, De Civ. Dei, xi. 4.

[2] Psa. xix. 1. Cf. Psa. lxxvi. 4; Eccles. iii. 11; Wisd. xiii.

[3] On this argument, see Tyrwhitt, Natural Theol. of Natural Beauty; Caldecott, Philos. of Religion, pp. 52–58, 187–196; Knight, Aspects of Theism, ch. xiii; Conder, Basis of Faith, pp. 272–275. We consider the beauty of God in ch. xii. § 12, below.

[4] Cf. St. Augustine, Confess., vii. 10; De Doc. Christ., i. 8. 9; De Civ. Dei, ii. 10.

which is confirmatory only, and has not been very highly estimated by theistic writers in general, has been made more apparent by the theory of evolution.

Herbert Spencer says,[1] "Considering all faculties, . . . to result from accumulated modifications caused by the intercourse of the organism with its environment, we are obliged to admit that there exist in the environment certain phenomena or conditions which have determined the growth of the feeling in question [religious aspiration]; and so are obliged to admit that it is as normal as any other faculty. Add to which that as, on the hypothesis of a development . . . the end towards which the progressive changes directly or indirectly tend, must be adaptation to the requirements of existence; . . . this feeling is in some way conducive to human welfare."

John Fiske develops this line of thought into a theistic argument.[2] "All life upon the globe . . . represents the continuous adjustment of inner to outer relations." Thus when the eye had been developed, "there came into existence . . . for those with eyes to see it, a mighty visible world that for sightless creatures had been virtually non-existent." With the appearance of man, the development took on a psychical nature, through adjustments "by the aid of ideal representations of environing circumstances. . . . The whole worth of education is directed toward cultivating the capacity of framing associations of ideas that

---

[1] *First Prins.*, ch. i. § 4.
[2] In *Through Nature to God*, pp. 180 *et seq.*

conform to objective facts. It is thus that life is
guided." "Every stage of enlargement has had reference to actual existences outside . . . so as to harmonize with some actually existing external fact.
Such has been Nature's method, such is the deepest
law of Life that science has been able to detect."
"Now there was a critical moment in the history of
our planet . . . when the process of evolution was
being shifted to a higher plane, when civilization was
to be superadded to organic evolution, when the last
and highest of creatures was coming upon the scene,
when the dramatic purpose of creation was approaching fulfilment. At that critical moment we see the
nascent human soul vaguely reaching forth toward
something akin to itself, not in the realm of fleeting
phenomena but in the Eternal Presence beyond. An
internal adjustment of ideas was achieved in correspondence with an unseen world." "And . . . Religion, thus ushered upon the scene, coeval with the
birth of Humanity, has played such a dominant part
in the subsequent evolution of human society that
what history would be without it is quite beyond
imagination." Such are the facts to be interpreted.

Fiske interprets them thus: "Now if the relation
thus established . . . between the human soul and a
world invisible and immaterial is a relation in which
only the subjective term is real and the objective term
is non-existent, then, I say, it is something utterly
without precedent in the whole history of creation.
. . . To suppose that during countless ages . . . the

progress of life was achieved through adjustments to external realities, but that then the method was all at once changed and throughout a vast province of evolution the end was secured through adjustments to external non-realities, is to do sheer violence to logic and common sense." He punctuates this contention by pointing out that such a supposition would imply that, whereas all previous progress — during the ages when it was least intelligent — was by means of true steps, now, when the advance is most intelligent, it proceeds by false steps! "All analogies of Nature fairly shout against the assumption of such a breach of continuity between the evolution of Man and all previous evolution."

Thus one of the most eminent of evolutionary thinkers is led by his investigations to emphasize the reality that called forth the cry of St. Augustine, "The heart is restless until it find rest in Thee, O God;" [1] and to throw new light on the teaching of Christ that life eternal consists in knowing God.[2]

§ 9. In considering the teaching of the moral argu-

[1] *Confessions*, I. i.

[2] "And this is life eternal, that they should know Thee the only true God, and Him whom Thou didst send, even Jesus Christ." St. John xvii. 3. To "know" here means personal acquaintance and contact. Life in the spiritual realm exemplifies the law which Spencer formulates with reference to physical life. It consists in correspondence with environment (*Prins. of Biol.*, pp. 58–81), and is non-existent unless the environment is real.

On the argument from religious aspirations, see Driscoll, *God*, pp. 91–94; Clarke, *Outline of Christ. Theol.*, pp. 118–120; Calderwood, *Moral Philos.*, pp. 231, 232.

ments we should bear in mind that they presuppose the cosmological and teleological arguments, being specific applications of their logic. Their teaching is not difficult to recognize and is of peculiarly practical importance.[1]

(a) Every force which makes for righteousness in the world has God for its ultimate and true Cause; and the notion that a universe wherein righteousness is the mightiest and most significant factor of development has been created by an unrighteous or imperfectly righteous God is irrational. The righteousness of God is of His essence, and is complete and unalterable. Every element of moral perfection is found in Him as its ultimate source and standard. Coming to details, so far as things are divinely caused they are good, and to the heart of enlightened men the enjoyment of God is the highest good, the *summum bonum* and their chief end. God is therefore good, and His goodness is as essential and characteristic as is His righteousness at large. All truth and beauty come also from Him and must exist in Him in their absolute perfection.[2]

(b) Difficult as it is to understand the place and full meaning of evil in God's world, the moral argument teaches us that evil must be interpreted in harmony with the perfect righteousness and goodness of

[1] On the teaching of the moral argument, see Martineau, *Religion*, Vol. II. pp. 39–48.

[2] The moral attributes of God are considered systematically in ch. xii. Pt. II, below.

God. In short, the evil of things may not be taken to express the divine will and purpose, but what is thus to be interpreted is the overruling of evil for the furtherance of good and holy ends. Evil wills and purposes are to be attributed exclusively to creatures, and the divine allowance of evil should be interpreted in relation to probation and discipline, issuing ultimately in a perfect kingdom of righteousness.

(c) The teleology of the universe is moral throughout, and should be construed in terms of moral personality. Its goal is personal, and its controlling principles have to do with personal relations in the kingdom of God. The universe was made for persons, and its highest utility is found when it is subjected to the control of the persons who dwell therein. Apart from persons it has no meaning, and its highest and truest value is found in its subserving the development of perfect persons, that is, of moral perfection.

(d) The "Power not ourselves that makes for righteousness" is the sovereign force in human history, and signifies the will of God. To be on the winning side, to fulfil one's will perfectly, and therefore to enjoy true liberty, means to conform our wills to the divine will. No contrary will can permanently hold its own, but must, like a machine which is out of gear, come to disaster and destruction.[1]

[1] Liberty is only preserved when the end in view can, in due season, be realized. The hedonistic ends of the wicked are never adequately realized. The glory of Christian liberty lies in the spontaneous enthusiasm with which ends are pursued that cannot be defeated so long as the soul is faithful to Christian ideals.

(e) Since the will of God is both righteous and sovereign, it is the ultimate standard of human righteousness, as well as the controlling force in history. To be righteous is to conform to the divine will, and to contend against that will constitutes unrighteousness. It is true that our information concerning the divine will is not complete; but our knowledge that the righteousness of God is perfect warrants the conviction that He will make His will manifest to us sufficiently for our advance in righteousness and our attainment of the end for which we were made.

(f) Finally, the argument from religious aspiration teaches us that our relations with God are of primary moment. To seek after God, and to enter into worshipful communion with Him, may not be regarded merely from a utilitarian point of view, but is a vital part of human righteousness. If it is the fool that saith in his heart, There is no God;[1] it should be added that men are without excuse who glorify Him not as God, and fail to make adoring knowledge of Him a matter of lifelong concern. Such is the clear teaching of nature to those who exercise their spiritual faculties normally and who do not "hold down the truth in unrighteousness."[2]

[1] Psa. liii. 1.

[2] Rom. i. 18–23. The fact that so many in our day refuse to participate in public worship, who none the less recognize the importance of righteousness, is largely due to the purely utilitarian view of such worship which now prevails.

CHAPTER VIII

THE ONTOLOGICAL ARGUMENT

§ 1. As has been shown, the argument for the existence and nature of God is primarily and properly *a posteriori* and inductive. The being of God is the implicit premise of all reason, and cannot therefore be deduced from *a priori* premises without begging the question at the outset.[1] But, as has also been acknowledged, even *a posteriori* arguments derive their validity from the idea of God as necessarily existing, an idea which is natural to the human mind, and which enables us to discern the theistic bearing of the phenomena of experience.[2] What is called the ontological argument is an attempt to employ this necessary idea of God as the premise of a formal and *a priori* theistic argument.

For the reason above given, no such argument, in its purely formal aspects, can escape logical fallacy. Yet the ontological argument brings to light in a forcible manner the fact that the validity of theistic arguments in general cannot be denied without a repudiation of reason in its fundamental postulates being also logically involved. It is this circumstance, no doubt, which accounts for the fact that the ontological argu-

[1] See ch. iii. §§ 5, 6, above. Cf. J. Orr, *Christian View*, pp. 112–115. [2] See pp. 57, 58, above.

ment continues, in spite of its formal defects, to be given an important place in theistic discussions.[1]

§ 2. The most important forms of the ontological argument are those of St. Anselm and Descartes. It will be convenient first to consider the argument of Descartes.

(a) His argument proceeds as follows: "We possess the idea of an infinitely perfect Being. As we are finite, this idea could not have originated with us. As we are conversant only with the finite, it could not have originated from anything around us. It must, therefore, have come from God, whose existence is thus a necessary assumption." The argument proceeds by exclusion of all possible explanations of the origin of the idea except the theistic hypothesis. A little further on he says, "Our ideas, *notiones*, are either adventitious, or factitious, or innate. The idea of God is not adventitious, for God is not to be discovered within our experience; nor is it factitious, for it has not been voluntarily created by us. Therefore, it is innate, that is, it has been imparted to us by God Himself."[2]

[1] On the ontological argument in general, see J. G. Cazenove, *Historic Aspects of the a priori Arguments;* Martin Rule, *Life of St. Anselm,* Vol. I. pp. 195 *et seq.* (historical); Caldecott, *Philos. of Relig.,* pp. 27–29; Baldwin, *Dic. of Philos.,* s. v. "Ontol. Argument"; Flint, *Theism,* Lec. ix; *Cath. Encyc.,* s. v. "Anselm" (historical); Dorner, *Christian Doctrine,* §§ 18, 19; Pfleiderer, *Philos. of Relig.,* Vol. III. pp. 271–276; J. Caird, *Philos. of Relig.,* pp. 145–150; Fraser, *Philos. of Theism,* pp. 221–231; Illingworth, *Personality,* pp. 100–103, 257–260; J. Orr, *Christian View,* pp. 103–108.

[2] *Medit.,* pp. ii–iv.

The argument is not really *a priori*, for it treats the idea of God as a fact of experience to be accounted for. But it presupposes, none the less, that the idea is as truly valid as it is subjectively necessary. The task of proving the objective validity of the idea was not faced, nor can it be achieved successfully. The fundamental postulates of the reason lie beyond demonstration.[1]

§ 3. (*b*) While Descartes infers the existence of God to account for the idea of God, St. Anselm takes a more daring flight and supposes the existence of God to be directly involved in, and made certain by, our idea of Him.

St. Anselm says, "Even the fool is convinced that something exists, in the understanding, at least, than which nothing greater can be conceived. For when he hears of this he understands it; and whatever is understood exists in the understanding. And assuredly that, than which nothing greater can be conceived, cannot exist in the understanding only. For, suppose it exists in the understanding only: then it can be conceived to exist in reality; which is greater." [2] Such force as this argument possesses depends upon the subjective necessity of the idea of God, and upon its unique supereminence and relation to all other ideas. St. Thomas, who rejects the argument, gives it as follows: "As soon as the meaning of the name God

[1] Descartes' argument is discussed by Dorner, *Christian Doctrine*, Vol. I. pp. 218-221; Bowen, *Modern Philos.*, pp. 27 *et seq.*; Flint, *Theism*, pp. 280-284; Knight, *Aspects of Theism*, pp. 43-46.

[2] *Proslogium*, i–iii.   Cf. St. Augustine, *De Trin.*, VIII. iii.

is understood, it is immediately held that He exists. For by this name is signified that than which no greater can be conceived.[1] But that which exists in reality as well as in the intellect is greater than that which exists in the intellect only," etc.[2]

We may put the argument this way. The idea of God is potentially universal; and, when once suggested to the mind, is seen to be necessary and to be related to all other ideas, as well as to all reasoning, as their fundamental implicate and postulate. No one can deny his possession of it without stultifying himself by the very denial. But the idea is really meaningless unless objectively valid, that is, unless it has a correlative in actual existence. This is so because, if God does not exist, there is no conceivable basis of the idea, and also because, if it is not objectively valid, human reason itself is invalid in its most fundamental postulate. In brief, unless the idea of God is objectively valid, that is, unless God exists, we are confronted by an universal and unavoidable aberration in human reason, a consequence calculated to make cautious reasoners hesitate to reject the argument merely because of its formal defects.[3]

[1] St. Augustine says, *De Doc. Christ.*, i. 6, 7, that the thought of God "takes the form of an endeavour to reach the conception of a nature than which nothing more excellent or more exalted exists."

[2] *Summa Theol.*, I. ii. 1. For expositions and discussions of St. Anselm's argument, see Dornèr, *Christian Doctrine*, Vol. I. pp. 217–219; Flint, *Theism*, p. 279; Knight, *Aspects of Theism*, ch. iv; Ladd, *Philos. of Relig.*, Vol. II. pp. 46–50.

[3] Other forms of the *a priori* argument have appeared: *e.g.* those

§ 4. The objections which have been made against the ontological argument have very unequal value.[1]

(a) Guanilo's *reductio ad absurdum* is futile — that, if the existence of God can be inferred from our idea of Him, so can the existence of a perfect island be proved from our idea of it.[2] The ontological argument is not concerned with the perfection of any particular species of being, but with the Reality involved in the idea of perfection itself. If there be no most perfect being, to speak of perfection is to deal with illusory abstractions.[3]

(b) It is also futile to object that the idea of God is neither innate nor actually universal. The point. is that no one can deny the existence of God without

of Scotus, Leibnitz, Malebranche, Clarke, Gillespie, and others. See Flint, *Theism*, App. xxxviii; Driscoll, *God*, pp. 65–67.

Hegel restated the argument of St. Anselm in the terms of transcendental idealism, and his argument is adopted by J. Caird, *Philos. of Relig.*, pp. 144–150; E. Caird, *Journal of Theol. Studies*, Oct., 1899; and others. Hegelians emphasize the priority of thought. Necessary thought and reality are one. There is no gulf between the two to be bridged. Cf. Caldecott, *Philos. of Relig.*, pp. 32–35; Pfleiderer, *Philos. of Relig.*, Vol. III. pp. 272–276; Jas. Orr., *Christian View*, pp. 103–108; Fraser, *Philos. of Theism*, pp. 226–230.

[1] For adverse criticisms in general, see St. Thomas, *Summa Theol.*, I. ii. 1; Kant, *Critique of Pure Reason* (translated *in re* in Caldecott and Mackintosh, *Selections*, pp. 190–200, 207–210); W. Knight, *Aspects of Theism*, pp. 39–53; Boedder, *Natural Theol.*, pp. 24–29; Driscoll, *God*, pp. 64–70.

[2] Guanilo was a contemporary. His reply to St. Anselm is entitled, *In Behalf of the Fool*. It is translated, and St. Anselm's rejoinder, by S. N. Deane, in *Religion and Science Library*, No. 54, Kegan Paul.

[3] Cf. Flint, *Theism*, p. 279.

15

having the idea of God. The idea is innate in this sense: that the native constitution of the mind causes it to arise inevitably and spontaneously under the conditions of normal experience and reflection. And, when once acquired, the idea is perceived to include necessarily the thought of actual existence.[1]

(c) A more subtle objection is that existence is not, properly speaking, an attribute or predicate at all. The nature of an *idea* is the same whether it is thought of as purely idea or as something actually existing. We may not infer, therefore, that if God did not exist our idea of Him would be reduced in perfection.[2] It was this difficulty that led Descartes to resort to the *a posteriori* argument that the existence of God must be acknowledged in order to account for the origin of the idea.

(d) Granting for argument's sake that the idea of God as actually existing is more perfect than if we conceive of God as an abstract idea only, two further objections may be urged. The first of these is that our idea of God is utterly inadequate and finite, so that it proves, if it proves anything, only the existence of a finite being, whereas God is infinite if real.[3]   There

[1] See Flint, *Theism*, pp. 278, 279; Fleming, *Vocab. of Philos.*, and Baldwin, *Dic. of Philos.*, s. v. "Innate Ideas"; Fairbairn, *Philos. of the Christ. Relig.*, pp. 210, 211.   Cf. p. 10, above.

[2] Knight, *Aspects of Theism*, p. 45; Kant, given in Caldecott and Mackintosh, *Selections*, pp. 192–195. Flint discusses the objection, *Theism*, pp. 279, 280.

[3] This is an agnostic objection, which is anticipated and discussed, with references, in ch. ii. §§ 6, 7, above.

is no force in this objection. It is possible to have a finite idea of an infinite being. That is, we can distinguish the infinite from the finite, in spite of our inability to form positively an adequate conception of it. In fact, unless we possessed the idea of the infinite, the idea of the finite would be meaningless. It suffices for this argument that we can form an idea of God as the sum of perfection, and it is not necessary that we should be able to define such perfection in its positive content.

(e) The other objection is really unanswerable, that is, so far as it concerns the logical completeness and formal validity of the ontological argument. Briefly stated it is that the necessity of conceiving God as really existing does not prove that He really exists, except on the undemonstrable supposition that the fundamental ideas of the reason have their correlatives in the world of reality, of actual existence. This supposition is indeed beyond demonstration, for it is presupposed in all demonstration. The ontological argument, therefore, cannot be reckoned as one of the formal proofs of God's existence.[1]

§ 5. The theistic value of the ontological argument is none the less genuine because of its formal deficiencies. What it really accomplishes is to show how inextricably our belief in God's existence and nature is bound up with our dependence upon human reason. In showing this it also establishes the conclusion that

[1] This objection is urged by every adverse critic of the argument. Cf. refs. given in p. 209, note 1.

there is no other logical alternative to theistic belief than blank scepticism, or a denial that our reason can be trusted in any of its assumptions or conclusions.[1] As has been pointed out elsewhere, such a position is self-destructive, for it nullifies the validity of the reasoning by which it is itself supported.[2]

This conclusion of the matter is the more important and reassuring because every theistic argument depends in its ultimate analysis upon the assumption which immediately characterizes the ontological argument — the assumption that the fundamental laws of human reason which manifest themselves in the idea of God and in the theistic hypothesis with which our arguments begin, can be implicitly trusted.

§ 6. On the basis of such trust — a basis which is essential to all reasoning, to all science, and to all philosophy — we conclude that the lines of verification of the theistic hypothesis which are generalized and formulated in the arguments which we have discussed, are amply sufficient in their cumulative effect to establish beyond reasonable doubt the belief in God.[3]   And, if they establish the truth of God's existence, they accomplish more.   Every argument for the existence of God necessarily implies somewhat as to His nature. Theistic argument not only convinces men that they

[1] See Moberly, *Reason and Relig.*, pp. 141, 142; Calderwood, *Philos. of the Infin.*, pp. 51–56; Flint, *Theism*, pp. 285–288; Pfleiderer, *op. cit.*, Vol. III. p. 274; Jas. Orr, *Christian View*, pp. 103–106; Fraser, *Philos. of Theism*, pp. 226–230.

[2] Cf. ch. ii. § 9, above.

[3] See Flint, *Theism*, pp. 62–75; Illingworth, *Personality*, pp. 81, 82.

are right in believing that God exists, but also immensely enlarges their knowledge as to what He is.[1] All things, when theistically considered, make manifest in their several manners and degrees the nature of their Creator; and the knowledge of God which natural revelation affords, in spite of its confessed inadequacy, is more abundant and more significant than any other knowledge which we can acquire.[2]

[1] St. Thomas, *Summa Theol.*, I. ii. 2; Calderwood, *Philos. of the Infin.*, pp. 148–153; Royce, in *The Conception of God*, pp. 6, 7; Pfleiderer, *Philos. of Relig.*, Vol. III. pp. 276–278; Gwatkin, *Knowl. of God*, Vol. I. p. 40; Dorner, *Christian Doctrine*, Vol. I. pp. 189–191.

[2] Cf. Ch. ii. § 12 (*e*), above.

CHAPTER IX

ANTI-THEISTIC THEORIES

§ 1. Our belief in God articulates the implicit consensus of every race and every age, and is based upon spiritual experience. It does not owe its origin to theistic argument, although it is abundantly confirmed and enriched thereby.

So far as we can see, there are but three imaginable methods of evading the conclusion that the theistic hypothesis is true and essential to sound philosophy and to a rightly ordered life. The first way is the sceptical, which accepts the alternative of repudiating the validity of reason, and thus, as we have shown in discussing agnosticism,[1] destroys itself. The second method is the atheistic, or a direct denial that God exists. As has also been shown,[2] such a denial, in view of the fact that theism holds the field, and apparently has always held it, cannot justify itself without proving that God does not exist. This is to prove the universal negative that no part of the universe of matter and mind contains the slightest trace of divine causation and handiwork — a task quite beyond human capacity to achieve.

The only method which remains is to displace the

[1] See ch. ii, above.   [2] In ch. iv. § 11, above.

theistic hypothesis by some other theory capable of accounting for the phenomena which have been theistically explained. Such a theory must be at least as rational and credible as theistic doctrine, and must be capable of satisfying the imperative demands and requirements of human nature at its best. If it does not meet these conditions, it must be regarded as inferior to theism and, therefore, as untenable by reasonable men. Mere plausibility, or the ability of such a theory to hold its own under conditions peculiar to limited spheres of human life and thought, cannot avail against a doctrine so catholic as theism has shown itself to be in its appeal to human reason and instinct and in its adaptability to human experience.[1]

§ 2. *Materialism* is the most radical of anti-theistic theories, in that it excludes altogether any explanation of the physical order except that order itself. In fact, the dividing line between materialism and atheism is so fine that it is often crossed by materialists.[2]

Materialism repudiates the distinction of substance usually made between matter and mind, and interprets all phenomena, whether physical, vital, or mental, in mechanical terms. In its most common modern form

[1] Cf. N. K. Davis, *Elem. of Ethics*, pp. 22, 23.

[2] On materialism, see Christlieb, *Modern Doubt*, pp. 145–161; Flint, *Anti-Theistic Theories*, Lecs. ii–iv and App., notes v–xix; Liddon, *Some Elements*, pp. 43–48; S. Harris, *Self-Revel. of God*, pp. 201–206; J. Orr, *Christian View*, pp. 141–150; Lange, *Hist. of Materialism;* Baldwin, *Dic. of Philos.*, *s. v.* "Materialism"; H. C. Sheldon, *Unbelief in the Nineteenth Century*, chh. ii, iii; Fisher, *Grounds of Belief*, pp. 68–72; Fraser, *Philos. of Theism*, pp. 43–61; Bruce, *Apologetics*, Bk. I. ch. iv.

it is often called naturalism, and professes to account for all reality by the inherent and eternal laws of matter and force, the results of these laws being capable of precise mechanical measure.[1] Positivism, formulated by Auguste Comte (1798–1857 A.D.), although primarily an epistemological theory which confines knowledge to sensible phenomena and their sequences, is materialistic in its interpretation of phenomena. In thus interpreting phenomena it transgresses the limitations imposed by its theory of knowledge.[2]

Obviously the phenomena of life, mind, conscience, and volition cannot be interpreted truly in mechanical terms,[3] nor can materialists disprove the rational-

---

[1] Baldwin, *Dic. of Philos.*, *s. v.* "Naturalism," distinguishes three uses of the word — as signifying (*a*) the theory that all can be accounted for by the methods of physical science; (*b*) equivalent to materialism; (*c*) a rejection of the supernatural and mystical. J. Ward's *Naturalism and Agnosticism* is the most elaborate and crushing attack on (*a*). Cf. also Balfour's *Foundations of Belief*, which attacks the philosophical basis of naturalism.

[2] On Positivism, see Flint, *op. cit.*, Lec. v. and App., notes xx–xxii; Martineau, *The Positive Philos. of Comte*, 2 vols.; *Types of Ethical Theory*, Vol. I. pp. 394 *et seq.*; H. C. Sheldon, *op. cit.*, ch. iii; Liddon, *op. cit.*, pp. 46–48; Fisher, *op. cit.*, 67–68; Tulloch, *Modern Theories*, pp. 3–88.

[3] It has often been pointed out that by the requirements of the law of conservation of energy the physical forces operative in the human organism constitute a closed circle, and are fully accounted for, without taking note of spiritual activities. On this subject see Lodge, *Life and Matter*; J. Orr, *op. cit.*, pp. 146, 147; Fairbairn, *Philos. of the Christ. Relig.*, pp. 37–55; V. F. Storr, *Devel. and Divine Purpose*, ch. viii; Profeit, *Creation of Matter*, vii, ix; Fisher, *Grounds of Belief*, pp. 70–72; Flint, *op. cit.*, pp. 163–172, 488–504; J. Ward, *op. cit.*, Lecs. ix, xi, xii.

ity of the argument by which we infer intelligence from the phenomena of order, co-ordination and progress upward in the evolution of the universe. Materialism, in brief, fails to explain what it professes to explain, and does not satisfy the requirements of reason, of the moral sense and of religious instinct. The theory is wholly inadequate, and is at the present time fighting a losing battle all along the line. Even those, among contemporary leaders of thought, who refuse to accept theistic doctrine are taking refuge in pantheistic idealism. The human heart can be trusted to recoil from a theory which nullifies every spiritual ideal and aspiration and reduces all to blind and fatalistic process.[1]

§ 3. It is the common weakness of all other anti-theistic theories that they are in reality either perversions of theism, or imperfect approximations thereof which disappear when brought into conflict with full theistic doctrine — that is, with monotheism.

Polytheism has prevailed chiefly among races of backward development in civilization, and among those who divorce religion and morality. It is not, strictly speaking, a theory; but is an unintelligent phase of religion.[2] It represents a failure to realize

[1] As does Haeckel's *Riddle of the Universe.*

[2] The forms which polytheism has taken can be studied in the various works on comparative religion: *e.g.* Hardwick, *Christ and Other Masters;* De La Saussaye, *Handbook of the Hist. of Relig.*; Jevons, *Introd. to the Hist. of Relig.*; Jordan, *Comparative Religion* (where extensive bibliographies can be found). See also, on the general subject of polytheism among ancient races, R. Flint, in *En-*

that a god whose power and operations are limited in degree and range is not really God at all. A real God is necessarily supreme over all. Otherwise He is merely one of the effects which require a supreme Cause and Ruler to account for and order them. The scientific mind demands unity in causation, and the religious instinct is never fully satisfied except by communion with, and worship of, one supreme God over all.[1]

§ 4. *Dualism* is a halting place on the road between polytheism and monotheism. The cause of this halt is partly an exaggerated estimate of the amount and power of evil in the world, and partly belief in the eternity of matter. Thus it is pessimistic and materialistic in its philosophy, sharing in the difficulties of both of these positions.[2]

cyc. Brit. (9th ed.), *s. v.* "Theism," pp. 236–239. The doctrine of divine unity is considered in ch. x. § 9, below, and references are there given. The ancient Christian apologists devoted some attention to the absurdities of polytheism. Cf. p. 245, note 2, below, for examples.

Some of these writers were able to cite pagan testimonies to an undercurrent of belief, never fully extirpated, in one supreme God. Cf. Athenagoras, *Plea for Christians*, chh. v, vi; Justin M., *Exhort.*, chh. xv–xx; *Sole Government*, ch. ii. Cf. also, among modern writers, Macculloch, *Compar. Theol.*, ch. ii.

[1] Christlieb, *Modern Doubt*, p. 162, notes an affinity between polytheism and pantheism, these two being "but a higher and a lower form of one and the same view of the world."

[2] On dualism, see Baldwin, *Dic. of Philos.*, *s. vv.* "Dualism" and "Manichæism"; Liddon, *Some Elements*, pp. 142–148; Hardwick, *Christ and Other Masters*, Pt. IV. chh. iii (esp. pp. 529–543), ch. iv (esp. pp. 554–558); Macculloch, *Compar. Theol.*, pp. 84, 85, 156;

Its characteristic doctrines are two: (a) that two rival Gods or ultimate principles, one good and the other evil, are contending for the mastery in the universe;[1] (b) that matter is intrinsically evil, or at least under the control of evil. It troubled the ancient Church in the forms of Gnosticism[2] and Manichæism,[3] and the Manichæan disparagement of matter makes itself felt in every age.[4]

As has been shown already, we cannot formulate a final theodicy or philosophy of evil.[5] But we have given reasons for the conviction that if the problem of evil cannot be solved in the abstract, it is being solved practically by every sincere Christian theist. For this reason the existence of evil does not shake his faith. No other hypothesis can solve the problem,

A. V. W. Jackson, in Hastings' *Encyc. of Relig.*, *s. v.* "Ahriman"; Ueberweg, *Hist. of Philos.*, Vol. I. pp. 17, 290, 327, 330, 343; St. Augustine, *De Civ. Dei*, xii. 6 *et seq.*

[1] The biblical and Christian doctrine of evil angels is quite different. Satan is not a second God, but a fallen creature, permitted to work for a time, but doomed to defeat. Cf. Hagenbach, *Hist. of Doctrines*, §§ 51, 127; C. Harris, *Pro Fide*, pp. 220-224; Jewett, *Diabolology.*

[2] On Gnosticism, see J. F. Bethune-Baker, *Early Hist. of Christ. Doc.*, pp. 72-93; L. Pullan, *Hist. of Early Christianity*, ch. x.

[3] On Manichæism, see J. F. Bethune-Baker, *op. cit.*, pp. 93-95; W. Bright, *Lessons from the Lives of Three Great Fathers*, pp. 140-148; Smith and Wace, *Dic. of Christ. Biog.*, *s. v.* "Manichæans."

[4] *E.g.*, in the notion that to believe in the grace-imparting value of sacraments, and in the resurrection of the flesh, is unspiritual. So-called Christian Science is an unintelligent but inevitable recoil from the disparagement of the body, considered as a part of what Christ died to save.

[5] See ch. vii. § 5, above.

either in the abstract or practically. The theist alone triumphs over evil, and to the Christian theist matter becomes a useful handmaid of spirit — good because intended and constituted by its Creator for the fulfilment of holy and spiritual ends.[1]

The human mind instinctively seeks the simplest philosophy of things, as most likely to be true in every sphere of thought. Theism is much simpler than either polytheism or dualism, and has nothing to fear from them when their claims to acceptance are rationally weighed.

§ 5. *Pantheism* identifies God and the universe, or at least nullifies any real distinction between them.[2] It is the most plausible of anti-theistic theories, and the most influential among moderns. It enjoys a special popularity at the present time; partly as the result of reaction from the perverted, attenuated, and remote form of theism called deism, and partly because of the peculiar emphasis upon divine immanence which the evolutionary philosophy has brought

[1] On the usefulness of matter for spirit, and the uselessness of spirit for matter, proving that matter is created to be subject to the spirit, see Illingworth, *Divine Immanence*, chh. i, ii.

[2] On pantheism, see S. Harris, *Self-Revel. of God*, Pt. III. ch. ix; Baldwin, *Dic. of Philos.*, *s. v.* "Pantheism"; Boedder, *Natural Theol.*, pp. 112–117, 200–208; Flint, *Anti-Theistic Theories*, Lecs. ix, x; Fraser, *Philos. of Theism*, pp. 76–103; J. Caird, *Fundamental Ideas of Christianity*, Vol. I. pp. 85–113; Martineau, *Religion*, Bk. III. ch. i (Cf. *Types of Ethical Theory*, Bk. I. ch. iii); Liddon, *Some Elements*, pp. 59–66; Christlieb, *Modern Doubt*, pp. 161–190; Martensen, *Christian Dogma*, §§ 39–43. Spinoza's *Ethica* is the most important work in behalf of pantheism.

about, an emphasis which is often excessive and one-sided.

Pantheism has had many forms, ranging from positions closely akin to materialism up to spiritual systems that appear almost theistic — are in fact so regarded by those who fail to grasp the real nature of the distinction between theism and pantheism. Genuine theism insists upon the closely related truths that God is personal; and that He is other than the universe in which He is immanent, transcending it altogether. Pantheism in all its forms fails to acknowledge any genuine personality in God; and is fatal to the doctrine of creation in the proper sense of that term, and to the doctrine of divine transcendence.

Coming to details, pantheists have maintained the following theories: (a) All substance is one and eternal, exhibiting itself in many modes; (b) God is the immanent principle of the world, and does not transcend it. He is often called the *anima mundi*, and the reality of things; (c) He is impersonal, and without consciousness or will. Sometimes He is conceived of as realizing Himself through the evolution of the world, especially in man, in whom He becomes personal. This is a hybrid form of pantheism; (d) There is no creation, but an unending and necessary process in universal substance; (e) Human persons are not individual moral agents, but moments in the life of Deity, doomed to pass away forever; (f) Human acts are divine and the manifestation of predetermining law. Consequently evil is also divine — really good, if good and evil mean anything; (g) Man is the highest mode of divine life. The Incarnation is sometimes accepted in terms, but only as a revelation of this alleged truth.[1]

Such a system is attractive and plausible to many: (a) It is thought to satisfy the requirement of causation, and the philosophical demand for unity; (b) It seems to be in line with the idealistic recoil from materialism; (c) It removes the nightmare of evil by explaining that phenomenon into unreality; (d) It glorifies all things by deifying them, and thus appears to give the highest of all values to what each class of thinkers is inclined to emphasize; (e) No absolute logical demonstration of its falsity has ever been made.

Pantheism shares this last characteristic with theism, but suffers immensely when the arguments for its truth are compared with theistic arguments. The fact is that no positive arguments for pantheism can be formulated which, if valid, are not equally valid for theism; and the arguments which verify the truth of the theistic hypothesis are far more abundant and comprehensive than any which pantheists can form-

[1] The historical forms of pantheism are chiefly found in (a) East Indian Brahmanism; (b) Eleatic metaphysics of Greece; (c) Stoic metaphysics; (d) Alexandrian Neo-Platonism; (e) Gnostic emanationism; (f) the cosmological speculations of John Scotus Erigena; (g) and of Giordano Bruno; (h) Spinoza's philosophy of substance; (i) Hegel's idealism; (j) contemporary exaggerations of the truth of divine immanence, connected with evolutionary forms of thought. Cf. Fleming, Vocab. of Philos., s. v. "Pantheism"; J. Orr, Christian View, p. 368; S. Harris, Self-Revel. of God, pp. 198, 199.

ulate. The whole range of teleology and morality makes for theism and against pantheism.[1]

The tests, however, which are most fatal to the truth of pantheism have to do with its ability, as compared with theism, to satisfy all the elements of the world problem, and with its practical working value. En-lightened experience, as interpreted upon the basis of the postulates which are fundamental to science and to any philosophy which rises above the level of self-stultifying scepticism, teaches the reality of per-sonality and freedom, and of moral responsibility and evil. Pantheism does not satisfy these conditions of the problem, but seeks to explain them away. But they constitute fundamental presuppositions of any life that is worth living. No theory can work which makes personality a vanishing bubble on the ocean of impersonal being; which reduces morality to the working of blind law, over which we can exercise no control; which disguises evil by deifying it; and which reduces the religious instinct to a meaningless illusion.

There have been many noble-minded pantheists, but their noble-mindedness has not been created by pantheism. The noble-minded ones referred to have merely taken refuge in pantheism out of recoil from other positions more obviously immoral, without

[1] Pantheism appears to be the logical outcome of exclusively metaphysical attempts to discover the "world-ground." Its inade-quacy and untruth appear when concrete experience is done justice to. Cf. Bowen, *Modern Philos.*, p. 51.

perceiving that the ideal aspects of pantheism are not the ones which exhibit its real moral logic. Pantheism has never been consistently applied to life; but has either been held simply as an abstract theory, or has degenerated into polytheism.

Theism must always prove conqueror among enlightened and seriously righteous men in any conflict with rival systems. It responds to and justifies their deepest instincts; is justified by the largest inductions; satisfies the conditions of the world problem as no other doctrine can satisfy them; and is the only philosophy that imparts to human life a truly rational meaning and value. To reject theistic doctrine is to embrace unintelligence, illusion, and moral defeat.

CHAPTER X

I. *Its Formal Development*

§ 1. The doctrine of God, so far as we have discussed it, is derived from nature's teaching, that is, from what is called natural revelation. And our method of treatment has been determined by a desire to conform the order of theological exposition, so far as is practicable, to the order of God's self-manifestation to us. Catholic theology recognizes that natural revelation is the preparation for and the presupposition of, supernatural revelation; and also that he who has to some extent assimilated the theistic and spiritual teaching of nature is best able to understand and appreciate the truths of supernatural revelation.

We need both forms of revelation. The natural prepares us for the supernatural, and cannot be violated or stultified by it, but remains true forever. On the other hand, natural revelation is partial and unsatisfying apart from supernatural revelation, and affords insufficient guidance in the fulfilment by men of the divine purpose for which they were made. Moreover, it is only in the light of supernatural revelation, whether this light be properly ours or unwittingly borrowed from others, that we are able to acquire anything approaching an adequate understanding of what nature teaches. Yet the teaching of nature is amply sufficient to convince genuine truth-seekers that God exists, and that He is their supreme Guide, and sovereign Object of adoring service; and it puts men to a real probation of faith and obedience.

Supernatural revelation accomplishes two things in relation to nature's teaching: republishing it in clearer and more definite terms; and supplementing it by truths which could not otherwise be known by us, but which we need to know in order to come into right personal relations with God and advance intelligently to our divinely appointed destiny.[1]

We have reached the point where we can take direct account of supernatural revelation, and exhibit the full Christian doctrine of God in the logical order of its contents, and in the light of God's final self-manifestation in flesh. We shall find that theism takes on fuller meaning, deeper internal rationality, and more impregnable strength, when irradiated and completed by Christian doctrine.

§ 2. However necessary it may be to employ abstract thought in interpreting God's self-manifestation

---

[1] See St. Thomas, *Summa Theol.*, I. i. 1; Butler, *Analogy*, Pt. II. ch. i; Illingworth, *Reason and Revel.*, pp. 143–151, 252–256; and ch. ix; Wilhelm and Scannell, *Manual*, Vol. I. pp. 6–15; Liddon, *Some Elements*, pp. 72, 73; Flint, *Theism*, Lec. x; J. H. Bernard, in Hastings' *Dic. of Christ*, *s. v.* "Revelation"; Newman, *Univ. Serms.*, ii; J. Caird, *Fundamental Ideas of Christianity*, Vol. I. pp. 6–24; V. H. Stanton, *Place of Authority*, pp. 33–38; Hooker, *Eccles. Polity*, I. xi.

theologically, that self-manifestation itself has been through, and in the terms of, concrete experience. The first and most spontaneous formulation of what men learn of God is also concrete, and is to be found in the names which have been applied to God.[1]

(a) Our English *God*, and the German *Gott*, are cognate with the Gothic *gheu*, (1) to invoke; (2) to sacrifice. Thus God is described as the One to whom sacrifice is offered.[2]

(b) The Latin *Deus* and the Greek Θεός are said to be cognate with the Sanscrit *div*, to give light; or from *thes* in *thessasthai*, to implore. In the latter case the name signifies One to whom we pray.[3]

(c) *El* is the original Semitic name for God, and signifies the Mighty One. This becomes *Elohim* (plural) in the Old Testament, where it is more frequently employed than any other name of God. Some have regarded this use of the plural as indicating the existence of polytheism among the Hebrews. But, whatever may have been its history, the name is clearly

[1] On the divine names, see Hastings, *Dic. of the Bible, s. v.* "God (in O T)," by A. B. Davidson; St. Jerome, Epis. 25 *al* 136, *ad Marcellam;* St. Thomas, *Summa Theol.*, I. xiii; Petavius, *De Deo*, Lib. VIII. capp. vi–ix; Suarez, *Summa*, Tr. I. Lib. II. ch. xxxii; R. Owen, *Dog. Theol.*, ch. ii. § 14; Wilhelm and Scannell, *Manual*, § 58; Driscoll, *God*, pp. 42–44; S. J. Hunter, *Outlines of Dog. Theol.*, Vol. II, § 353. Cf. Max Müller, *Science of Religion*, pp. 74 *et seq.*; Keary, *Outlines of Prim. Belief*, pp. 41–48.

[2] Cf. Murray, *New Dictionary.*

[3] Cf. Max Müller, *Science of Lang.*, 2d Series, pp. 405, 449; *Science of Relig.*, p. 269; *Chips from a German Workshop*, Vol. IV. pp. 227 *et seq.*

employed in a monotheistic sense in Genesis and other portions of the Old Testament.[1] It may be interpreted as a plural of majesty, indicating the manifold greatness of God,[2] or as foreshadowing the later revelation of the Trinity.[3]

(d) *Jehovah*, more critically pronounced *Jahweh*, יהוה, has traditionally been translated as the present of the verb *to be*, and as signifying *I am*, the self-existent and eternal One. Some recent writers, however, consider it to be future, I *will be*. In any case, the thought of enduring existence lies near the surface. This was reckoned as the most sacred of divine names by the Jews. It was never pronounced, but read as *Adonai*, Lord.[4]

(e) *Father*, אב, Πατήρ, signifies nourisher and producer, and implies personal relations with men. In Holy Scripture God is described as Father of all things by creation,[5] and of men as their personal Governor and Protector;[6] but as peculiarly the Father of bap-

---

[1] Liddon, *Divinity of our Lord*, pp. 49–51.

[2] Driver, *Genesis*, pp. 202–204; S. J. Hunter, *op. cit.*, Vol. II. pp. 40–42; A. B. Davidson, *op. cit.*

[3] Liddon, *op. cit.* It is not to be believed, of course, that the Old Testament writers were conscious of any such foreshadowing.

[4] Driver, *Genesis*, pp. 407–409; A. B. Davidson, *op. cit.*; Baldwin, *Dic. of Philos.*, *s. v.* "Jave, Yahveh, Jehovah"; Tanquerey, *De Deo Uno*, cap. i. pp. 100, 101; S. J. Hunter, *op. cit.*, Vol. II. pp. 43–49. Cf. Exod. iii. 13–15; vi. 2, 3. The rendering "I will be," is defended by Burney, in *Journal of Theol. Studies*, Apr., 1908; Cf. *Expos. Times*, July, 1908, pp. 438–442.

[5] Gen. ii. 4; Job. xxxviii. 28, 29; St. Jas. i. 17. Cf. Gen. i. 1; 1 Cor. viii. 6.

[6] Isa. lxiii. 16; lxiv. 8; Mal. ii. 10; Acts xvii. 28.

tized members of the Body of Christ, who have become His children by adoption and grace.[1] The doctrine of the Trinity shows that the name Father is especially to be applied to the first of the three Divine Persons, as being the one of whom the Son is begotten.[2]

(f) The most perfect name of God is that of the Blessed Trinity [3] — *The Father, the Son and the Holy Ghost* — a name which is at once singular in number, and threefold in articulation. It signifies the eternal and personal distinctions within the indivisible divine essence, and the internal relations involved in them. It also indicates the relations in which we stand to God as our Creator, Redeemer, and Sanctifier.

§ 3. The names of God indicate some of the more obvious characteristics by which ordinary men distinguish Him practically from all other beings. The divine attributes [4] constitute a series of predicates by which we summarize all our knowledge of the divine

---

[1] St. Matt. vi. 9 (Cf. St. Luke xi. 2); St. John iii. 3–8; xiv. 6; Rom. viii. 15; Gal. iv. 5–7; 1 St. John ii. 23, 24; iii. 1; 2 St. John 9. Cf. the passages in which Israel is described as peculiarly God's child: *e.g.*, Exod. iv. 22; 1 Chron. xxix. 10; Hos. xi. 1.

[2] St. Matt. iii. 17; St. Luke ii. 49; St. John i. 14; v. 17, 18; x. 36; Rom. i. 4; Heb. i. 5. Cf. Pearson, *Apostles' Creed*, Art. I. pp. 45–74; Thayer, *Greek-Eng. Lex. of the N. Test.*, *s. v.* πατήρ.

[3] St. Matt. xxviii. 19. Cf. Mason, *Faith of the Gospel*, ch. ii. § 2; Sparrow-Simpson, *Christian Doc. of God*, pp. 22–26; Wilhelm and Scannell, *Manual*, Vol. I. pp. 266, 267; Franzelin, *De Deo Trino*, Thes. iii.

[4] On the whole subject of the divine attributes, cf. bibliography given in ch. i. § 4 *fin.*, above.

nature; whether this knowledge is obtained (a) by natural experience; (b) by supernatural revelation;[1] or (c) by considering the necessary implications seen to be involved in infinity and absolute perfection.

All divine names and attributes are analogical and symbolical, for they describe the Infinite in human and finite terms.[2] Such terms are necessarily inadequate; and, when pressed in their ordinary and finite connotations, take on the appearance of mutual contradiction and unreality. But to understand them thus in theology is to misinterpret them.[3] They should be interpreted as indicating the manners in which the supereminent Cause and Principle of all things transcends every finite being and conception. When they are thus understood they can be seen to be true in spite of their inadequacy. They describe beginnings of true thoughts concerning God, thoughts which we are unable fully to complete, but which are necessary and are sufficient for the correct guidance of our minds in apprehending the infinite God.[4] Taken

[1] The nature of God is revealed in Holy Scripture by (a) His names; (b) works ascribed to Him; (c) attributes predicated of Him; (d) worship of Him which is prescribed; (e) His self-manifestation in the Word-Incarnate.

[2] Cf. ch. ii. §§ 6, 12 (c), above; and § 4 of this chapter. See also St. Thomas, Summa Theol., I. xiii. 1–3; G. C. Joyce, in Hastings' Encyc. of Relig., s. v. "Analogy," esp. 5.

[3] St. Thomas, op. cit., I. xiii. 5; Boedder, Natural Theol., pp. 101–106; Wilhelm and Scannell, Manual, Vol. I. pp. 164, 165.

[4] Cf. Mozley's remarks on incipient truths, Predestination, ch. ii. init.; and Thos. Richey, Truth and Counter Truth, Introd.

in this way they are neither misleading nor purely metaphorical, but describe a real knowledge of God — such knowledge as the self-manifestation of God has made possible for finite minds.[1]

This knowledge of God, as we have seen, is formulated in three ways: (*a*) of causation, inferring the nature of His attributes from the nature of His works; (*b*) of negation, excluding the idea of external or finite limitation; (*c*) of eminence, ascribing every perfection to God which is consistent with His infinity, to the exclusion of all quantitative· and temporal measures and comparisons.[2]

§ 4. The sense in which God is inscrutable, or mentally incomprehensible, ought clearly to be understood. Divine inscrutability does not mean that God

---

[1] See St. Thomas, *Summa Theol.*, I. xiii. 4–6; *Catholic Encyc.*, *s. v.* "Attributes (Divine)"; *Jewish Encyc.*, *s. v.* "Attributes"; R. Owen, *Dog. Theol.*, ch. iv. § 2; Darwell Stone, *Outlines of Christ. Dogma*, ch. ii; Bp. Pearson, *De Deo*, Lec. iv. pp. 37–41; Lacey, *Elem. of Doctrine*, pp. 85–92; Schouppe, *Elementa Theol. Dog.*, Tr. V. §§ 61–84; Dorner, *Christian Doctrine*, Vol. I. pp. 194–201.

[2] Cf. ch. i. § 9, above. This threefold method has been accepted by theologians of all types. It is derived from scholastic writers. See Pseudo-Dionysius, *Divine Names*, cap. i. § v; St. Thomas, *Summa Theol.*, I. xii. 12; xiii. 1, *et passim; c. Gent.*, III. 49; *Catholic Encyc.*, *s. v.* "Analogy"; Boedder, *Natural Theol.*, pp. 234–237 (Cf. pp. 101–108); Wilhelm and Scannell, *Manual*, § 56, iv; Gratry, *Knowl. of God*, pp. 170–172; C. Hodge, *Syst. Theol.*, Vol. I. p. 339; Clarke, *Outline of Christ. Theol.*, pp. 77, 78. Dorner, *Christian Doctrine*, Vol. I. pp. 202, 203, says that this method presupposes knowledge of what God is. This is true. It is not a method of discovery, but one of accurate definition of what we learn about God from the teaching of nature — a method designed to exclude false anthropomorphism. Cf. Thos. Jackson, *Works*, Vol. V. p. 36.

is wholly unknowable, but that we are unable to know Him fully or adequately.[1]

The inadequacy of our knowledge appears in the following limitations. (a) God is invisible to our physical senses because He is pure Spirit and infinite.[2] Even the beatific vision hereafter will be intellectual;[3] and mystical contemplations do not have the divine essence itself for their visible object, but symbols only.[4]

(b) God is also unimaginable, and for the same reason that He is invisible. Having no form or like-ness, He cannot be pictured either by art or by the mind.[5] Christian imagination is not concerned with God as He is in eternity, but with God-Incarnate.[6]

(c) Our knowledge of God is indirect, being de-

---

[1] On divine inscrutability, see St. Thomas, Summa Theol., I. xii; Hooker, Eccles. Polity, I. ii. 2; Pearson, De Deo, xiii. pp. 128–136; Petavius, De Deo, VII. iii, iv; Wilhelm and Scannell, Manual, Vol. I. pp. 197–202; Flint, Agnosticism, pp. 578–585; Dorner, Christian Doctrine, Vol. I. pp. 206–212. Cf. Job. xi. 7–9; xxxvi. 26; Psa. lxxvii. 19; cxxxix. 6; Prov. xxx. 4; Isa. xlv. 15; lv. 8, 9; Rom. xi. 33, 34; 1 Cor. ii. 11.

[2] Exod. xxxiii. 20; Job. ix. 11; St. John i. 18; v. 37; 1 Tim. vi. 16; Heb. xi. 1. Cf. St. Thomas, op. cit., I. xii. 3. God is visible in Christ only in His Manhood.

[3] St. Thomas, op. cit., I. xii. 9. The beatific vision is also super-natural, and belongs to the order of grace.

[4] Récéjac, Essay on the Basis of the Mystic Knowledge, treats at large on this.

[5] We have shown that to be unimaginable is not necessarily to be inconceivable. Cf. pp. 19, 33, 34, above.

[6] This is illustrated by the fact that the Father and the Holy Spirit are represented in sacred art by symbols rather than by portraitures. Exceptions to this rule have always been considered in the Church to be objectionable.

rived from the consideration of finite things. Even the knowledge which is made available by supernatural revelation, and by the manifestation of God in Christ, is one that involves the translation of what is revealed into human and finite terms. We see through a mirror — not face to face.[1]

(d) The relativity which characterizes human knowledge in general conditions and limits our knowledge of God.[2] We know Him only so far as He manifests Himself to our minds, and the finite capacity of our minds limits the possibilities of His self-manifestation to us.

(e) Our mental conceptions do not cease to be finite when concerned with the Infinite. Consequently, although we can arrive at a true conception of God, our conception can never be an adequate one. The Christian idea of God grows continually more full and significant, and enlists in its development the combined labours of countless minds. But this development can never reach its goal. We must ever be falling short of perfect and absolute knowledge.[3]

(f) God is ineffable. That is, no language can adequately describe His infinite nature and attributes.[4]

[1] i Cor. xiii. 12. When St. Paul speaks of hereafter seeing God face to face, the words "face to face" are, of course, not to be pressed in a physical sense. Our vision of God is in any case intellectual and not physical.

[2] On the relativity of human knowledge, see ch. ii. § 5, above.

[3] Cf. a suggestive passage in Knight, *Aspects of Theism*, pp. 114–118, on the progressiveness of theistic knowledge. On anthropomorphism, see ch. ii. § 6, above.

[4] On divine ineffability, see Wilhelm and Scannell, *Manual*, Vol. I. § 71. Cf. Eccles. v. 2.

Theological terms are necessarily symbolical;[1] and, when this is forgotten, they become misleading. Yet they are true, so far as they go, and are necessary means for protecting and clarifying our knowledge of God.[2]

The counter truth to divine inscrutability is the certainty that we can rightly, although but partially, apprehend and conceive of God.[3] Were this not the case we could not serve Him; nor could we enter into any relations with Him, or justly be held accountable to Him. Such knowledge as we have of Him, inadequate to reality though it be, is the most significant and illuminative of all knowledge available to us. It is the knowledge which alone makes life worth living.[4]

[1] Cf. ch. ii. §§ 6, 12 (c), above.

[2] Cf. *Authority Eccles. and Biblical*, ch. iv. § 3, and the refs. there given.

[3] Cf. ch. ii. § 12, above. See also, St. Thomas, *Summa Theol.*, I. xii; Wilhelm and Scannell, *Manual*, § 69, iii; Dorner, *Christian Doctrine*, Vol. I. pp. 206–212. "Only he who knows God, knows His unfathomableness." The Fathers commit themselves to the opposite statements that we cannot know what God is, but only what He is not; and that we know Him truly. The contradiction is not a real one, but corresponds to an assertion of the inscrutability of God, on the one hand, and of His apprehensibility, on the other hand. Cf. Petavius, *De Deo*, lib. I. cap. v; and Hagenbach, *Hist. of Doctrines*, Vol. II. pp. 26 *et seq.*, for illustrations.

[4] Our Lord identifies eternal life itself with the knowledge of God: St. John xvii. 3. Cf. Jerem. ix. 24; xxix. 13; Rom. i. 19–22. Every part of Scripture implies the knowability of God, and our obligation to know Him. On the scriptural teaching on this point, see Calderwood, *Philos. of the Infin.*, ch. x.

The late Dr. Bright distinguishes helpfully between the Christian doctrine of divine inscrutability and the agnostic theory, in *Lessons from the Lives of Three Great Fathers*, app. vi. Thompson, in *Prins. of Natural Theol.*, pp. 70–98, shows how close an analogy exists

II. *Primary Attributes*

§ 5. In discussing the cosmological argument we
have seen that God manifests Himself to us as the
real Cause of all things, whether we consider Him
in relation to phenomenal events or to the substantial
contents of the universe. We have seen further that
the idea of universal causation cannot be satisfied
unless we assume that the Cause of all things is infinite, absolute, personal, and singular.

The terms "infinite" and "absolute" have been
taken in abstract meanings, and as signifying the exclusion of all limitations whatsoever, and of all relations. In brief, the infinite has been defined as the
unlimited, and the absolute as the unrelated. Agnostic writers have succeeded to their own satisfaction
in proving that such an infinite is really a negation
of thought, and that such an absolute cannot be the
Cause of the universe. The truth is that, if God is
infinite in the sense above defined, He is not real; for
a real being must be a determinate something, and
this constitutes a limitation.[1]

The thought that in calling God infinite and absolute we are describing a real Being, and One who is
related to finite things as their creative and sustaining

between our knowledge of God, and that of the external world.
Both are relative and inadequate. Flint shows that the same analogy
exists in relation to our knowledge of other human persons. We
never apprehend them directly: *Theism*, pp. 76–78. Cf. Ladd, *Philos.
of Relig.*, Vol. II. pp. 119–121.

[1] Cf. ch. ii, above, esp. § 7.

Cause, shows that "infinite" and "absolute" must be defined differently when applied to Him. The Infinite is the Being whose limitations are wholly within Himself. He is limited by what He is, but is not externally limited.[1] The term "infinite" is the correlative of "finite." Finite things are what they are by virtue of external relations and limitations. The Infinite is what He is independently of all else.[2]

God is absolute in the sense that He is self-sufficient and not dependent for His fulness upon relations to other realities. He is not incapable of entering into

[1] That is by other things. The word "externally" is, of course, not used in a spatial sense.

[2] On divine infinity, see St. Thomas, *Summa Theol.*, I. vii; Pearson, *De Deo*, vi, pp. 60–64; Boedder, *Natural Theol.*, pp. 98–101; Porter, *Human Intellect*, Pt. IV. ch. viii; Baldwin, *Dic. of Philos.*, s. vv. "Finite"; "Infinite (the) and the Finite"; "Infinite (notion of) and Infinity"; Max Müller, *Origin of Religion*, pp. 26–36; Wilhelm and Scannell, *Manual*, § 64; Dorner, *Christian Doctrine*, Vol. I. pp. 237, 238. Dorner says "God has no limits, although He has preciseness (ὅρους) in Himself. By the fact that God is something defined, a logical, further, a moral, limitation is of course placed upon His idea." Gore says, *The New Theology*, p. 57, note, "It is often said, and may be truly said, that God is infinite, or 'unlimited.' But it is more exact to say that God is self-limited: limited by nothing except the eternal law and character of His own being." When Christian writers speak of God as unlimited, they may, usually at least, be understood to imply the qualifying phrase "in His perfection." Calderwood, *Philos. of the Infin.*, pp. 76, 77, says (his italics), "*The term Infinite is not a mere form of expression to indicate our inability to think in a certain manner; but on the contrary, is exclusively applicable to one great Being, whom we adore as supreme.*" Obviously the meaning of a term, whatever may be its etymology, is determined by its actual application.

external relations; but these relations are unnecessary for His self-sufficiency. They are voluntary. God brought the universe into being by His will; and, although no finite being can exist except in relation to God, the fact that such beings exist at all is due to the divine will, and not to any dependence of God upon either the act or the results of creation to complete the fulness of His being and life.[1] If we call God the Cause of finite things, we do not by using the term "Cause" seek to describe His essential nature. We do indeed imply that God possesses a nature which makes all possibilities of causation reside ultimately in Him; so that, if finite things exist at all, they must owe their existence to Him. But that actually to be a Cause is essential to God is a supposition which is neither required by any necessities of thought concerning Him nor consistent with revealed doctrine.

§ 6. We have, in appropriate connections, endeavoured to show that theistic arguments, in so far as they are valid to confirm our belief in the existence of God, also justify our belief in His personality.[2] The

---

[1] On the absolute, see Baldwin, *Dic. of Philos.*, *s. v.* "Absolute"; "Relative (and absolute)"; *Catholic Encyc.*, *s. v.* "Absolute"; S. Harris, *Self-Revel. of God*, ch. viii; Ladd, *Philos. of Relig.*, ch. xxx; Porter, *Human Intellect*, pp. 650–655; J. B. Baillie, in Hastings' *Encyc. of Relig.*, *s. v.* "Absolute."

[2] On the personality of God, as taught by nature and reason, see Illingworth, *Personality Human and Divine;* R. C. Moberly, *Reason and Relig.*, pp. 140–156; Sparrow-Simpson, *Christ. Doctrine of God*, Lec. iii; Iverach, *Is God Knowable?* pp. 7–12, 37, 223, 233; Pfleiderer, *Philos. of Relig.*, Vol. III. pp. 284–290; Lotze, *Outlines of the Philos. of Relig.*, ch. iv; Boedder, *Natural Theol.*, pp. 35–46, 227–232; Clarke,

arguments which we have given for divine personality may be epitomized as follows: We infer that God is personal by reason of (a) His being the true and ultimate Cause of finite things, since causation involves intelligence and will;[1] (b) the evidences in nature of intelligent purpose on the part of its Maker and Governor;[2] (c) the impossibility that a universe containing persons should have an impersonal Creator;[3] (d) the futility of any other explanation of our sense of moral responsibility, and of our religious instincts;[4] (e) the thought that if God were impersonal He would not be supreme, for He would at least be inferior to finite persons. These arguments are based upon the teaching of nature, and they enable us to see that belief in a personal God is demanded alike by our reason, our conscience, our heart, and our religious nature, in short, by every requirement of our own personality. This conclusion is confirmed by many clear intimations and implications in supernatural revelation, which cannot be understood except as the self-manifestation to us of a personal God, the Father and Saviour of mankind.[5]

Can I Believe in God the Father? Lec. ii (untechnical); S. Harris, *Self-Revel. of God*, pp. 212–221; ch. xii; Iverach, *Theism*, ch. vii.

[1] See ch. v. §§ 10, 11.

[2] Ch. vi.

[3] Ch. v. § 10.

[4] Ch. vii. § 9.

[5] The personality of God is shown in Holy Scripture by (a) the attributes predicated of Him; (b) the operations ascribed to Him; (c) the relations in which we are said to stand to Him, and the services which we are declared to owe Him; (d) the names which are

§ 7. When we call God a personal being we imply that He is possessed of intelligence and will.[1] That is, we describe Him in terms of human personality, although without meaning that His personality can be measured by ours, or by any finite measures.

(a) It is objected that such a description of God is anthropomorphic, and this objection is made to seem plausible by the fact that many have regarded God in the light of a magnified human being.[2] The significance of such an objection lies in the charge that we fall into the mistake of measuring the higher by the lower, and of thinking that the personal life and activity of God can be adequately described in human terms.

given Him; (e) the revelation of Christ, who is declared to be "the very image of His substance": Heb. i. 3. (A. V. reads, "express image of His person"). Cf. St. John xiv. 9; 2 Cor. iv. 4; Col. i. 15.

[1] The scholastic definition of *persona*, formulated by Boethius, is *animae rationalis individua substantia*, which may be paraphrased in modern terms, "the indivisible subject, self, or ego, of a rational nature." St. Thomas, *Summa Theol.*, I. xxix; F. J. Hall, *Kenotic Theory*, pp. 49–51; *Doctrine of God*, pp. 133–137; Illingworth, *Personality*, Lec. iii.

We are here treating of personality in relation to monotheistic doctrine. We shall consider the subject in relation to the divine Trinity and the Incarnation in subsequent volumes. It is enough, at present, to say that *persona, ὑπόστασις*, as applied to God in catholic theology, is determined in its meaning by (a) the existence of three Persons in the indivisible Godhead; (b) the subsistence in Christ of one Person in two natures. Heresy has caused the Church also to repudiate any interpretation of the term which either reduces the three divine Persons to mere aspects or manifestations of God (Sabellianism), or separates them, as if they were so many individual beings (tritheism). On the theological history of the term, see Newman, *Arians*, ch. v. § i. 3; Powell, *Principle of the Incarnation*, pp. 145–169.

[2] Cf. ch. ii. § 6 and the references there given.

No doubt there have been those who have made such a mistake, but it is not a necessary result of belief in the personality of God, nor is it found in reputable theological literature. That the term person, when applied to the Infinite, is symbolical, and does not adequately describe Him, is a theological truism.[1] The reason why the term is none the less insisted upon is that it is more adequate and less misleading than any other term that is available.[2] So long, of course, as men fail to realize that God is infinite, they will apply the term person to Him in a misleading sense; but the difficulty lies in their initial ignorance of God rather than in their choice of the term person.

The idea of personality, when carefully considered, can be seen to transcend its embodiment in human persons. Moreover the finitude of human personality does not arise from any *a priori* or essential requirements of personality, but from the fact that human beings, whether personal or not, are finite. It is

[1] Cf. St. Thomas, *Summa Theol.*, I. xiii. 5. Cf. pp. 230–231, above.

[2] Martineau says, *Religion*, Vol. I. p. 316, "There are but three forms under which it is possible to think of the ultimate or immanent principle of the universe, — Mind, Life, Matter." The inference suggested is obvious, the highest form, provided it is regarded as a symbol of what is still higher, is the truest. The fact is that "Personality is . . . the gateway through which all knowledge must pass": Illingworth, *Personality*, p. 25. St. Thomas, *Summa Theol.*, I. xxix, 3, says that person signifies that which is most perfect in all nature. Therefore, since perfection is in every respect to be attributed to God, the name person is conveniently given to Him, although not in the manner in which it is given to creatures, but in a more excellent mode.

because in us personality is human that it is also finite and externally limited and conditioned.

We can see more than this. We can see that the idea of personality cannot be adequately actualized in any finite embodiments, but requires an infinite subject for its full realization. This appears when we note that personality involves the requirement of self-determination. Finite persons are externally conditioned and determined, and cannot be self-determining in the full and absolute sense of that phrase. There is but one Being who can be said to be self-determining without qualification. That Being is the Infinite and Absolute.

The truth is that the idea of personality, when rightly understood, so far from involving finitude, requires infinity for its full embodiment. Our knowledge of divine personality is indeed made possible by our experience of personality in human persons; but when personality is analysed we are led to the inference, corroborated by revelation, that all other personality owes its possibility to divine personality, and is patterned after it. Human beings, in brief, are personal because, and only so far as, they are made in the image of God. But inasmuch as human beings are finite, they are unable to participate in personality except in an imperfect manner and under finite limitations and conditions.[1]

---

[1] It is as erroneous to regard finiteness as of the essence of personality as it is to consider it to be of the essence of power. Cf. S. Harris, *Self-Revel. of God*, pp. 215, 216.

17

God is more truly personal than we are; and this remains true in spite of the fact that we are unable entirely to eliminate human and finite connotations in calling Him personal.   This inability of ours makes the term person symbolical and inadequate; but we are able to perceive wherein the inadequacy lies, so that our incapacity to imagine an infinite person does not cause our acknowledgment of divine personality to mislead us.[1]

Some writers have preferred to call God suprapersonal.   Their desire to avoid anthropomorphism is commendable; but, in so far as they obscure the truth which is really signified by the assertion that God is personal, they defeat their own purpose.   The question demanding an unambiguous reply is this: "Is God personal or impersonal?"   He is one or the other.   There can be no third alternative.   If He is impersonal, He is inferior to man.   Only by believing in His personality can we obtain a rational standpoint for belief in His supereminent infinitude.[2]

[1] That divine personality is the only complete and perfect personality, and that our own personality depends for possibility upon participation in the divine, see Lotze, *Microcosmus*, Vol. II. pp. 659–688; *Outline of the Philos. of Relig.*, p. 69; Schultz, *Apologetics*, pp. 42–45; Illingworth, *Personality*, pp. 243–246, who quotes R. C. Moberly as saying, "It is not that human personality is a realized completeness to which we desire to make our conceptions of Divine Being correspond, but rather that human experience gives us indications of what Personality, in its fuller realization, would mean."

[2] Illingworth, *Divine Immanence*, pp. 188, 189.   On the anthropomorphic objection in general, see S. Harris, *Self-Revel. of God*, pp. 433–440.   Martineau, *Religion*, Vol. I. pp. 313–329; Flint, *Theism*,

§ 8. (*b*) Another objection is based upon the supposed requirements of personal life and activity. The characteristic activities of a person include self-consciousness, love, and will. Self-consciousness involves distinguishing between self and not-self, ego and non-ego. Love can only be exercised between persons, and involves the same contra-position of ego and non-ego. Will requires an objective sphere of exercise — a non-ego. Such considerations, it is alleged, establish the conclusion that personal activity involves the necessity of external relations. A person cannot therefore be himself except as conditioned and externally limited, that is, finite. If God is personal He is finite.[1]

Such an objection is really anthropomorphic in the bad sense of that term. That is, it is based upon the assumption that the limitations of personality which are observed in finite persons, and which emerge in finite definitions, are essential and do not disappear in divine personality. It is impossible for our finite minds to justify such an assumption. The modes of activity in an infinite being transcend all modes with which we are sufficiently acquainted to employ as the basis of such precise inferences.[2] The most

pp. 87–95; Ladd, *Philos. of Relig.*, ch. xiv; E. R. Conder, *Basis of Faith*, pp. 68–72; J. Caird, *Philos. of Relig.*, pp. 171–176, 228–246; Boedder, *Natural Theol.*, pp. 106–108. As Boedder hints, no careful reader of St. Thomas, *Summa Theol.*, I. xiii, would feel justified in charging catholic theology with forgetting the infinite transcendence of God in regarding Him as personal.

[1] Mansel, *Limits of Religious Thought*, Lec. III. pp. 93–97.

[2] Lotze, *Microcosmus*, Bk. IX. ch. iv; S. Harris, *Self-Revel. of*

that can be said is that all the analogies of our experience *suggest* that personality, which is real only as active in intelligence, love and will, requires for its existence and activity the contra-position of ego and non-ego.

This fact accounts for the difficulty which bald unitarians of every type experience in retaining a firm and living hold upon the truth of divine personality. That God is infinite is an axiomatic proposition with all genuine theists, but it is difficult to discover any point of view which justifies one in believing that the God of unitarian conceptions is at once infinite, absolute, and personal. Thus it is that pantheism is peculiarly successful in undermining unitarian theology, for pantheism is the natural refuge to those who lose their hold upon the doctrine of divine personality.

The case is altogether different with trinitarians, whose fuller knowledge of divine personality enables them to find a sphere of full personal activity within the divine essence. The divine Persons are non-egos to each other without mutual externality being involved. The divine Persons exist in one indivisible essence and in each other. The Father is not the Son, for example, and yet the Son is in the Father, and co-sharer of His indivisible essence, and *vice versa*. Between these two Persons, who are co-equal

God, pp. 174 *et seq.* and 210 *et seq.*; Pfleiderer, *Philos. of Relig.*, Vol. III. pp. 280–284; Knight, *Aspects of Theism*, ch. xi, esp. p. 163; Iverach, *Theism*, pp. 208, 209.

and co-eternal, every form of activity which is necessary for the realization of personality is actualized, and that independently of any conditions or relations that are external to either of the Persons concerned.[1]

The truth of the doctrine of the Trinity cannot be considered argumentatively at this point. We content ourselves with two remarks. (*a*) The fact that trinitarian theism can hold its own more easily than any other monotheistic doctrine against pantheistic perversion shows that it constitutes the best working form of theistic doctrine; (*b*) The acceptance of Christianity in any adequate sense, which involves the acceptance of the divine claim of Christ, depends for validity upon the truth that God subsists in more than one Person, although the divine Persons possess but one indivisible essence and are one God. *We worship one God in Trinity, and Trinity in Unity; neither confounding the Persons, nor dividing the Substance.*

§ 9. If God is infinite and absolute, He must be one and unique, *unus et solus.*[2] If there were two

---

[1] Illingworth, *Personality*, p. 244; *Doctrine of the Trinity*, pp. 136–144, 254–256 and ch. x; R. C. Moberly, *Reason and Relig.*, pp. 152–155; Gore, *Creed of the Christian*, pp. 18–25; R. Flint, in *Encyc. Brit.* (9th ed.), *s.v.* "Theism," pp. 248, 249.

[2] On divine unity, cf. ch. v. § 12, above; and see St. Thomas, *Summa Theol.*, I. xi; *c. Gent.*, I. xlii; R. Owen, *Dogmatic Theol.*, ch. iv. § 6; Forbes, *Nicene Creed*, pp. 25–38; Pearson, *Apostles' Creed*, pp. 40–44; Franzelin, *De Deo Uno*, Thes. xxv, xxvi; F. J. Hall, *Doctrine of God*, Quest. 46; Boedder, *Natural Theol.*, pp. 85–92; Medd, *One Mediator*, § 8; Dorner, *Christian Doctrine*, Vol. I. pp. 230–234.

The early Christian writers had frequent occasion to argue for

infinites, they would limit each other externally — a self-contradictory supposition. If God transcends every external limitation of His essence, this must be because all other beings are dependent upon Him and owe their existence to His will. Similarly the absoluteness of God requires that all reality shall be summed up in Him and proceed from Him.

This *a priori* necessity is confirmed by *a posteriori* evidence: (*a*) by the causal and teleological unity of the universe; (*b*) by divine supremacy in the moral sphere; and (*c*) by supernatural revelation. Whatever conclusions may be adopted as to the antiquity and development of monotheism among the Hebrews, or as to the gradualness of God's revelation of His unity to Israel, the monotheistic significance of that revelation is apparent at every stage to those who are in a position to interpret the process in the light of its final result.[1] The signs and wonders which the Israelites witnessed were designed from the outset to show "that the Lord He is God; there is none else beside Him."[2] The first commandment of the decalogue forbids the acknowledgment of other gods than Jahveh;[3] and the

monotheism as against the polytheism prevailing around them. Some examples are Athenagoras, *Plea for Christians*, iv–ix; St. Justin, *Exhort. to the Greeks*, xv–xx; *Sole Govt. of God*, ii; St. Irenaeus *adv. Haer.*, III. iv *et seq.*; Tertul., *Adv. Hermog.*, iv; Novatian, *De Trin.*, iv; St. Athanasius, *c. Gent.*, xxxviii, xxxix.

[1] On the progress of the doctrine of God in the Old Testament, see A. B. Davidson, in Hastings' *Dic. of the Bible*, *s. v.* "God (in O T)," iv. Cf. p. 2, above, on primitive monotheism; and W. P. Paterson, in Hastings' *Dic. of the Bible*, *s. v.* "Idolatry."

[2] Deut. iv. 35.   [3] Exod. xx. 3. Cf. Deut. v. 7.

proclamation, "The Lord our God is one Lord," [1] received increasing emphasis in succeeding generations as the first article of Israel's faith.[2] This doctrine was reiterated and enriched by the teaching of the new Covenant,[3] and protected by its enrichment from deistic impoverishment, and from pantheistic degeneration as well.[4] The Christian doctrine of the Trinity is in no sense a qualification of Old Testament teaching that God is one, unique, and indivisible, but a revelation of the manner of divine unity.[5]

(a) Three truths are involved in the unity of God: His numerical oneness, His uniqueness, and His indivisibility. The first of these truths means that there is and can be but one divine Being. Henotheism falls short of this; for although it confines national or tribal allegiance to one God, it does not deny either the reality or the divine rank of the gods of other peoples. Monotheism declares that God is *solus* in all the realm of being. "All the gods of the nations are idols." [6]

---

[1] Deut. vi. 4. Cf. also 1 Kings viii. 60; Isa. xlii. 8; xliv. 6, 8 *et seq.*

[2] A doctrine which became the chief inspiration of the Jews in their wars against the Syrians under the leadership of the Maccabees.

[3] Cf. St. Mark xii. 29; St. John xvii. 3; Rom. iii. 29, 30; 1 Cor. viii. 4–6; Gal. iii. 20; 1 Tim. i. 17; ii. 5; St. Jas. ii. 19. No series of isolated texts, however, can be made to exhibit the richness of New Testament evidence for divine unity. Cf. A. S. Geden, in Hastings' *Dic. of Christ*, *s. v.* "Monotheism."

[4] Cf. Liddon, *Divinity of our Lord*, pp. 452–459.

[5] The bearing of the doctrine of the Trinity on the doctrine of divine unity will be considered in our next volume.

[6] Psa. xcvi. 5. Cf. 1 Cor. viii. 4, 5. The term "henotheism" was

(b) God is unique; which means that there is none like Him,[1] except so far as derivatively, partially and finitely participating in His attributes by reason of His creative will.[2] No other being can be classed as divine, for God cannot be comprehended in any class or genus or species.[3] He is indeed the presupposed Cause of genera and species, and is absolutely differentiated by His infinitude from all else.

(c) Finally, God is indivisible. He must be so, if He is truly infinite. Division must result either in parts or in plurality. If God were divided into parts, the parts would be dependent upon the whole and thus would be externally limited, that is, finite. God would consist, therefore, of a totality of finites; and finites cannot be added up to make a true infinite. If, on the other hand, God were divided so as to become two beings, each of these beings would shorten the absolute fulness and supremacy of the other.

coined by Max Müller. He held that henotheism historically precedes both polytheism and monotheism. Cf. Baldwin, *Dic. of Philos.*, *s. v.* "Henotheism."

[1] Exod. ix. 14; Deut. xxxiii. 26; 2 Sam. vii. 22; Isa. xl. 18–25; xlvi. 5–9; Jerem. x. 6, 7.

[2] By reason of this participation man is said to be created in the image of God: Gen. i. 26, 27. Cf. Bp. Bull, *Discourse on the Primitive State*, pp. 112–121; T. B. Strong, *Manual of Theol.*, pp. 238–240. A higher participation is secured by the Incarnation: Cf. 2 St. Pet. i. 4. From the nature of the case, this partaking of the divine nature is finite, and cannot destroy the infinite difference between God and man. Even the glorified Manhood of the Word is finite.

[3] St. Thomas, *Summa Theol.* I. iii. 5; Petavius, *De Deo*, lib. II. cap. v. (who gives patristic references); Boedder, *Natural Theol.*, pp. 104, 105; Thos. Jackson, *Works*, Vol. v. pp. 24, 25.

There can be but one infinite God.[1] The doctrine of the Trinity is consistent with this conclusion. The three divine Persons are not parts of God, nor do they constitute a plurality of beings, or separate individuals.

§ 10. The attributes which we have been considering — infinity, absoluteness, personality, and unity — must occupy a central and determinative place in any true theological conception of God. That is, the meaning of each and every divine attribute is determined by the truth that it is the attribute of an infinite absolute and unique Person. Nothing can be said truly of God the meaning of which is really inconsistent with this fundamental proposition. The practical application of this principle involves abstract thought and subtle distinctions, and has brought upon theology the charge that it is metaphysical, and to that extent inconsistent with true religion.[2]

Such an objection has no force against a theology which is faithful to the aim of correctly expounding the truths upon which religion depends. To do this is the one purpose of sound theologians, and such a purpose warrants the employment of any and every manner of thinking and expounding which will enable us to enter truly and as deeply as possible into the knowledge of God.

Metaphysics is not necessarily anti-religious or inconsistent with sincere truth-seeking and trustworthy

[1] Novatian, *De Trin.*, iv.
[2] The forms of this objection and their fallacies are admirably set forth by Liddon, *Divinity of our Lord*, Lec. i. IV.

conclusions. Metaphysical thought is indeed largely speculative; and we may not allow speculative conclusions to determine theological doctrine. But a sound metaphysic deals also with certainties, although with such as transcend the capacity of untrained minds to investigate; and many of its distinctions are as valid as are the distinctions which are recognized by men of ordinary intelligence. Metaphysical thought is concerned with the fundamental and unifying principles of being and life.[1] Theology is concerned, from a different point of view, no doubt, with the most fundamental principle of all, the supreme God and Cause of all things. It follows, therefore, that a sound metaphysic is to some extent theological, and a sound theology is to some extent metaphysical, without being controlled by any metaphysical conclusions except those which are seen to be true and undeniable.[2]

The requirement to be borne in mind is this: that

[1] Its problems transcend empirical methods of solution. Cf. Ueberweg, *Hist. of Philos.*, Vol. I. p. 145; Baldwin, *Dic. of Philos.*, *s. v.* "Metaphysics"; Fleming, *Vocab. of Philos.*, ibid.

[2] On scholastic terms, see Signoriello, *Lexicon Peripateticum Philosophico-Theologicum*; Baldwin, *Dic. of Philos.*, *s.v.* "Latin and Scholastic Terminology."

On the use of metaphysical terms in dogma and theology, see Liddon, *op. cit.*, pp. 3-5, 34-43; *Inspiration of Selection*, pp. 14, 15; Illingworth, *Divine Immanence*, 181-190; *Reason and Revel.*, pp. 121-132; T. B. Strong, *Place of Authority*, ch. vi; R. C. Moberly, in *Lux Mundi*, pp. 243, 244 (cf. pp. 217-220); Fairbairn, *Philos. of the Christ. Relig.*, pp. 3-5. The Church resorted to the use of extra-scriptural terms only when driven to do so in order to set forth the real teaching of Scripture as against heretical interpretations. So St. Augustine, *De Trin.*, VII. ix. Cf. Newman, *Arians*, ch. II. i. 3.

truth shall be supreme; and truth is that which can stand the test of comparison with the contents of human knowledge. An immediate application of this principle is that we should begin our treatment of the divine attributes with a correct understanding of the truth that God is one infinite and absolute Person. The terms involved have had a long history in metaphysical thought, but their theological use is determined by their being employed to describe the true idea of God in its primary elements.[1]

Accordingly, when we insist that every divine attribute is infinite and absolute, we do not mean abstractedly unlimited and unrelated, but free from *undivine* limitations and necessities. We have to mean this, if we believe God to be real and personal. But, when we insist that every divine attribute is a personal attribute, we do not mean that any one of them is adequately described in terms of human personality, but that they all pertain to a Being who exhibits a supreme fulness of life and action, along the lines of intelligence, love, and volition.

[1] Cf. *Authority, Eccles. and Biblical*, pp. 108, 112–114.

CHAPTER XI

QUIESCENT ATTRIBUTES

I. Self-existent and Eternal

§ 1. God is *self-existent*. This means that He is without origin, and is Himself the ground of His being. He simply is.[1] This is a most obvious truth. If God were not self-existent, He would not be infinite; for He would be determined and limited by His cause and dependent upon it. Divine self-existence is also involved in the cosmological argument. That argument teaches that God is the real and ultimate Cause of all things which are caused. But a being who is himself caused to be is not a cause at all, except in a derivative and secondary sense. He is an effect or link in the chain of causation. A true and ultimate cause must be uncaused, that is, self-existent.[2]

We may not speak of God as self-caused, for His being is not a product of His will but a fact of His

---

[1] Self-existence is also called aseity, *aseitas*. On divine self-existence, see St. Thomas, *Summa Theol.*, I. iii. 4; St. Anselm, *Monologium*, v, vi; Bp. Pearson, *De Deo*, Lec. V. p. 47; Wilhelm and Scannell, *Manual*, Vol. I. pp. 176, 177; Petavius, *De Deo*, I. vii; Baldwin, *Dic. of Philos.*, *s.v.* "Aseitas"; *Catholic Encyc.*, *s.v.* "Aseity"; Franzelin, *De Deo Uno*, Thes. xxii. Boedder, *Natural Theol.*, Bk. II. ch. vii. Cf. Exod. iii. 14; St. John v. 26; viii. 58; Acts xvii. 24, 25. [2] See ch. v. § 9, above.

essence.[1] The same must be acknowledged as to the essential mode of His subsistence. The tri-personal subsistence has no cause. It is an eternal necessity, characterizing God as He is in Himself.

§ 2. If God is self-existent, He is *eternal*. That is, He utterly transcends in essence, life, and action the relations of time.[2] If He were a temporal being He would have a beginning, even though His origin coincided with the origin of time.[3] Such a being cannot be uncaused or self-existent. Moreover, if He were temporal, whether in essence or in action, He would be conditioned externally and limited by temporal relations and sequences, and His self-realization would at each moment be partial and imperfect.

Time is a relation of finite things and events, and has no existence except as the measure of finite duration and change. There is no such thing as infinite time. If we speak of time as endless, we mean simply

[1] St. Thomas, *Summa Theol.*, I. iii. 4.

[2] On divine eternity, see St. Augustine, *Confess.*, XI, x–xxxi; St. Anselm, *Proslogium*, xix–xxii; *Monologium*, xviii–xxv; St. Thomas, *Summa Theol.*, I. x; Thos. Jackson, *Works*, Vol. V. pp. 60–78; Pearson, *De Deo*, Lec. x. pp. 96–98; Petavius, *De Deo*, III. iii–vi; Wilhelm and Scannell, *Manual*, Vol. I. pp. 195–197; Smith and Cheetham, *Dic. of Christian Biog.*, s. v. "Eternity"; Boedder, *Natural Theol.*, Bk. II. ch. ii; Baldwin, *Dic. of Philos.*, s. vv. "Eternity"; "Eternity of God"; "Time"; Mason, *Faith of the Gospel*, ch. i. § 11; F. J. Hall, *Doctrine of God*, Quest. 49. Cf. Exod. iii. 14; Deut. xxxiii. 27; Job. xxxvi. 26; Psa. xc. 2–4; xciii. 2; Isa. xli. 4; xliii. 13; xlviii. 12; lvii. 15; Mic. v. 2; Rom. i. 20; Ephes. iii. 11; 1 Tim. i. 17; 2 St. Pet. iii. 8; Rev. i. 8; xxii. 13.

[3] Clement Alex. says, *Strom.*, V. xxv., that God, Himself without beginning, produces beginning.

this: that prior to time, or subsequent to it, no time can exist. There is no time outside of time. But the only possible idea that can be formed of time is an abstraction from the measure of finite duration, succession, and change. It has no reality apart from the concrete things and events from which we abstract the idea, and these are finite.

The word eternal is often used to describe finite duration, conceived of as having no limit within the divisions of time. For example, eternal life is the life of the saints, which endures throughout all time. But such duration is finite, in that it is divisible into parts and is dependent upon the will of God — that is, it is contingent. We must not mistake the impossibility of imagining the end of time for proof that time is infinite. This impossibility arises from our inability to escape temporal forms of imagination and thus to contemplate time from a non-temporal standpoint.[1]

Real eternity is infinite and non-temporal. It is not, in particular, an indefinite expansion of temporal duration, but is that attribute of God which, although timeless, is conceived when we contemplate the infinity of God from the point of view of the temporal. Temporal forms of thought constitute the only possible window, so to speak, through which we can contemplate the Eternal; but we are not compelled for this reason to confuse eternity with the temporal window through which we contemplate it. We can

[1] Origen, *De Princip.* I., iii. 4.

conceive and mentally distinguish the eternal, but cannot imagine or picture it. If we could, it would not be what we know it to be — an infinite attribute — but finite and temporal.

Such are some of the necessities of thought concerning the Infinite, when considered in relation to time. They are recognized in Scripture, which plainly indicates (a) that God altogether transcends the conditions of time;[1] so that (b) He neither began to be, nor can cease to exist;[2] (c) Neither contingency nor any of the limitations of time sequence may be ascribed to His life or operations.[3] These teachings are tersely summarized by the well-known scholastic definition of eternity as the "simultaneous and perfect possession of interminable life."[4]

There can be no adequate illustration of what transcends imagination; but the figure of the circle

[1] Exod. iii. 14; Psa. xc. 2; St. John viii. 58; 2 St. Pet. iii. 8.

[2] Gen. i. 1; Isa. xli. 4; Psa. cii. 25–27; Revel. i. 4, 8; xxii. 13. Cf. Deut. xxxiii. 27; Job. xxvi. 26; Isa. xlviii. 12; Lam. v. 19; Rom. i. 20.

[3] That is, there is neither "before" nor "after" as between His operations; and none of His acts may be said to be either past or future, prospective or incomplete, in themselves. If they are thus described, it is in relation to their temporal effects. No interval of time can separate any event from God's present. St. John viii. 58. Cf. Isa. xliii. 13.

[4] *Aeternitas est interminibilis vitae tota simul et perfecta possessio.* Boëthius. *De Consol. Phil.*, lib. V. prop. 6. Cf. St. Augustine, *De Vera Relig.*, cap. 49, "Aeternitas tantummodo *est*, nec fuit, quasi jam non sit, nec erit, quasi adhuc non sit." Also the antithesis, of Boethius, "Nunc fluens facit tempus, nunc stans facit aeternitatem." Royce gives some thoughts on the contrast between an eternal and a temporal present in *Conception of Immortality*, note 6, pp. 84 *et seq.*

is helpful in comparing time and eternity. The circumference is subject to division and measure and yet endless to those who pursue its path. It is a fit symbol of time. The centre, being a point, has no measure, and yet is abreast of every part of the circumference, however vast that may be. It symbolizes eternity. The radii occupy various positions, and are drawn in different directions. But while these divergences produce different points of contact with the circumference, their points of contact at the centre coincide under all circumstances. They symbolize the relations between the temporal and the eternal. Like the radii these relations are diverse and changeable, but the region of change lies in the temporal alone. When, therefore, we describe the relations of the eternal mind and will of God to the temporal effects of His operations in terms of temporal change and sequence, we are describing truly, if we remember that we are not describing the eternal centre itself, which is immutable.[1]

§ 3. Divine *immutability* is the entire freedom of God from the vicissitudes of change and contingency.[2] Rightly understood it does not constitute a restriction

---

[1] This illustration is found in many treatises. The sum of the matter is that although we attribute temporal *relations* to God we may not ascribe temporal *attributes* to Him.

[2] On divine immutability, see St. Thomas, *Summa Theol.*, I. x; Hooker, *Eccles. Polity*, I. v. 1; Thos. Jackson, *Works*, Vol. V. pp. 105–116; Martensen, *Christian Dogmatics*, § 48; R. Owen, *Dogmatic Theol.*, ch. iv. § 7; Pearson, *De Deo*, Lec. ix. pp. 87–95; Wilhelm and Scannell, *Manual*, § 65; Boedder, *Natural Theol.*, Bk. II. ch. i.

of His personal life and operations, but characterizes their transcendent perfection and fulness. The very infinitude from which divine immutability is deduced forbids all external limitation.

We know that God is immutable (a) because of His infinity and eternity, and (b) because the very quality of change which we observe in finite and temporal things presupposes an immovable and immutable Cause and Ground.[1] (c) The Scriptures teach the same truth. As a vesture God changes the works of His hands, but remains Himself the same.[2] "Whatsoever He doeth it shall be forever."[3] "I am the Lord, I change not."[4] "The gifts and calling of God are without repentance."[5] As sharing in the divine essence Jesus Christ is described as "the same yesterday and to-day, yea and forever."[6] With "the Father of lights" "can be no variation, neither shadow that is cast by turning."[7] All that immutability here signifies is wrapped up in the thought that God is the great "I am,"[8] for if all events are *now* to God, there can be no temporal movement or transition from one state to another within His essence. (d) This truth has often come to the surface in the Church's conflicts with error — especially in the Arian conflict, which led the Council of Nicea to decree an anathema

[1] Cf. Aristotle's argument from change and motion to an immovable first principle: *Metaph.*, XI. vi–viii. See ch. v. § 1 (a), above.

[2] Psa. cii. 26, 27; Heb. i. 12.

[3] Eccles. iii. 14.

[4] Mal. iii. 6.

[5] Rom. xi. 29.

[6] Heb. xiii. 8.

[7] St. James i. 17.

[8] Exod. iii. 14 and elsewhere.

against those who say that "the Son of God is variable or changeable."[1] The underlying principle which
determined the Church's attitude is that, if God were
to change in essence or attribute, He would cease to
be God.[2]

Chiefly, perhaps, because this truth has been pressed
in isolation, and in such wise as to seem to nullify the
reality and fulness of the divine life and operations,
but also in the interests of an exclusively humanita-
rian view of Christ's earthly life, it has been much
criticised and disparaged in our time. To discuss
kenoticism at this point would take us too far afield.[3]
It is enough now to say that the truth of divine immutability is caricatured when formulated without reference to the counter-truths of divine personality and
action. If we are unable to expound fully the relations

---

[1] Appendix to the Creed adopted by that Council: — " "Τοὺς δὲ
λέγοντας· . . . ἀλλοιωτὸν, ἢ τρεπτὸν τὸν υἱὸν τοῦ Θεοῦ· τούτους ἀνα-
θεματίζει ἡ καθολικὴ καὶ, ἀποστολικὴ ἐκκλησία." Divine immutability was also vindicated against the Gnostic and Manichæan
theory of emanations, and against those who considered the Incarnation to involve either a conversion of the Godhead into human finitude
or an absorption of human nature into the Godhead. The former
of these last two errors has been revived in the modern kenotic theory.
See the author's *Kenotic Theory*, pp. 99–101, 233, 234; and Powell,
Prin. of the Incarn., pp. 265–270.

[2] As Novatian says, *De Trin.*, iv., "Whatever it be in Him which
constitutes divinity, must necessarily exist always, maintaining itself
by its own powers, so that He should always be God . . . for whatever at any time is changed is shown to be mortal in that very particular which is changed. For it ceases to be what it had been, and
consequently begins to be what it was not."

[3] For full discussion see the author's *Kenotic Theory*, Longmans,
Green, & Co.

between divine immutability and divine action, this is because we cannot describe any action except in the terms of our own temporal and changing experience. Yet the proposition, that the actions of an infinite being transcend the conditions of time and change, can be seen to be necessarily true. The doctrine of divine immutability is too well established and too vitally connected with the fundamental idea of God to be rejected or even to be neglected by Christian believers.

Divine immutability involves (a) that no change, whether of accretion or subtraction, of growth or corruption, or of alteration in manner of existence and internal relation, can take place in the divine essence or attributes;[1] (b) that the operations of God, which may not be evaporated of reality by the manner in which we hold this truth, are eternal in themselves, and involve no transition or mutation in God. They may have changes for their effects, but an eternal operation cannot itself be changed;[2] (c) that the changes which occur in the relations between God and creaturely things and events are not changes in God or in His actions, although we do not err neces-

[1] On the distinction between absolute and relative attributes, and the immutability of the latter, see below, p. 289; and the author's *Kenotic Theory*, ch. vii.

[2] It is truly said that God can will a change, but cannot change His will. St. Augustine, *Confess.*, I. iv., says, "Thou changest Thy works without changing Thy plans." Boethius says, " . . . immotusque manens dat cuncta moveri." Cf. St. Augustine, *De Civ. Dei*, x. 12; xiv. 11; xvii. 7.

sarily in symbolically describing His actions in temporal terms — terms which, strictly speaking, apply only to their effects in history.[1]

The truth of divine immutability, however abstract it may be in its theological explication, has practical value: (a) It affords a guarantee that science will never be stultified in assuming that the fundamental principles by which natural phenomena are governed will never cease to control them;[2] (b) It assures us of the inviolabilty of the laws of the moral order,[3] and of the principles that lie behind the mystery of the Cross and the future dispensation of mercy and justice;[4] (c) It enables us to rely with confidence upon the promises of God, and upon the eternal purposes which they reveal.[5]

II. *Transcendent Spirit and Life*

§ 4. From the point of view of substance, or essence, God is *absolutely simplex.*[6] The term substance is

[1] St. Augustine, *De Trin.*, v. 17; *De Civ. Dei*, xii. 17; xvi. 29; St. Anselm, *Monologium*, xxv.

[2] Cf. Fraser, *Philos. of Theism*, Pt. II. Lec. viii; and our *Introd. to Dog. Theol.*, ch. ii. § 4. See Psa. cxviii. 89–91 (cf. Gen. ix. 8–17; Jerem. xxxi. 35, 36; xxxiii. 20, 21).

[3] Psa. xxxi. 4; St. Jas. i. 13.

[4] Acts ii. 23; Rom. viii. 29, 30; Ephes. i. 4–11; 1 St. Pet. i. 2, 20.

[5] Deut. vii. 9; 2 Cor. i. 20; 2 Tim. ii. 13; 2 St. Pet. iii. 9; Num. xxiii. 19.

[6] On divine simplicity, see St. Thomas, *Summa Theol.*, I. iii; St. Anselm, *Monologium*, xvi, xvii; Boedder, *Natural Theol.*, pp. 92–98; Wilhelm and Scannell, *Manual*, Vol. I. pp. 182–185; Forbes, *Nicene Creed*, pp. 40, 41; R. Owen, *Dogmatic Theol.*, ch. iv. § 4; Petavius, *De Deo*, II. i, ii; W. Humphrey, *His Divine Majesty*, pp. 75–85. Cf. Deut. iv. 16; St. John iv. 24.

too well established in the theology of the divine attributes to be set aside. But, although metaphysical,
its theological meaning is not determined by metaphysical theories. It signifies that in God which
we contemplate from the point of view of concrete
things. In other words, to describe divine attributes
in terms of substance represents an effort to describe
God as a real Being, in opposition to any reduction of
His essence and attributes to the level of mere abstractions. The idea of infinite substance, however, does
not connote materiality, composition, divisibility, or
any external limitation.[1]

Composition has been distinguished as physical and
metaphysical.[2] Even finite spirits are without physical composition, but freedom from metaphysical
composition is peculiar to God. In particular, the

[1] The two terms essence and substance are closely related in theology. Essence, *essentia*, οὐσία, is that which constitutes a thing
what it is, and is signified by the definition of a thing. Substance is
either (*a*) the same as essence; (*b*) that which underlies accidents
(there are no accidents in God); or (*c*) that which exists *per se*, and
needs no subject in which to inhere. St. Anselm, *Monologium*, xxvi,
xxvii; Ottley, *Incarnation*, Vol. II. pp. 255–258; Rickaby, *Metaphysics*, Pt. I. ch. iii; Schouppe, *Elem. Theol. Dog*. Tr. VI. §§ 6–9,
17–24; Boedder, *Natural Theol.*, pp. 325–329; St. Thomas, *Summa
Theol.*, I. iii. 3, 5; xxix. 2; Baldwin, *Dic. of Philos.*, *s. vv.* "Substance"; "Substance (in Theology)."

[2] A thing is physically composite when it consists of parts — *e.g.*
man consists of body and soul. It is metaphysically composite
when we can form true conceptions in relation to it which do not
connote the same complete reality. Thus the concept man includes
the concepts animal and rational, which are capable of reference to
diverse realities. See Boedder, *Natural Theol.*, pp. 92–98.

distinction between the divine essence and existence is purely notional, for the essence of God is to exist. There is also no composition of essence and personal characters, or of the divine Persons. These Persons are eternal modes of subsistence of an indivisible essence. Again, we may not employ the distinction between substance and accident in describing the divine essence; and whatever can be said truly of God has reference to an indivisible essence in which there is nothing which is not eternal and necessary.[1]

In brief, the simplicity of God must determine our use of the term substance in relation to Him. This principle is asserted when God is said to be *pure form*.[2] What is meant is that there is no "can be" in God, for whatever He can be He *is* eternally and *in toto*. The phrase comes from the Aristotelic distinction between matter and form.[3] The matter of a thing is its relation of potentiality, whereas its form is its actuality. God is wholly actual, and there can be no

---

[1] Each divine attribute is identical *in esse* with the divine essence. The attributes have indeed a distinct truth and meaning, but they do not differ *in re*. St. Thomas, *op. cit.*, I. iii. 3, 4, 6, 7; Thos. Jackson, *Works*, Vol. V. pp. 38–42; Wilhelm and Scannell, *op. cit.*, pp. 184, 185; Schouppe, *Elem. Theol. Dog.*, Tr. V. §§ 64–82.

[2] St. Thomas, *op. cit.*, I. iii. 2; Wilhelm and Scannell, *op. cit.*, p. 183. Cf. Baldwin, *Dic. of Philos.*, *s. v.* "Matter and Form." This distinction is not equivalent to substance and its shape. There is, of course, no shape in God.

[3] ὕλη and εἶδος. This and the corresponding distinction between δύναμις and ἐνέργεια are discussed in Aristotle's *Metaph.*, Bks. vi–viii. Cf. Ueberweg, *Hist. of Philos.*, § 48; Wallace, *Outlines of the Philos. of Aristotle*, §§ 35, 36.

process of actualization or self-realization in Him.[1] This is but a metaphysical way of insisting upon the scriptural teaching that God is the "I am."

§ 5. It is from the point of view of substance and space that God is said to be immense.[2] Divine *immensity* is that in God of which spatial relations are the shadow, or divine infinity as regarded from a spatial standpoint.[3] It signifies that God transcends all spatial relations;[4] although He is their Cause and the immanent ground of their reality. That is, divine immensity comprehends in its implications both the immanence and the transcendence of God.[5] By reason of it His presence penetrates all space and substance, but cannot be circumscribed, measured, or divided by any spatial relations. "His centre is everywhere, His circumference nowhere."[6]

---

[1] God is said to be *purus actus*. Cf. § 8, below.

[2] The Athanasian Symbol says, *Immensus Pater, immensus Filius, immensus Spiritus Sanctus . . . nec tres immensi; sed . . . unus Immensus*. The word *immensus* is translated in the English Prayer Book "incomprehensible."

[3] On divine immensity, see Thos. Jackson, *Works*, Vol. V. pp. 42–59; Pearson, *De Deo*, Lec. VIII. pp. 78–86; Forbes, *Nicene Creed*, pp. 50, 51; Suarez, *Summa*, Tr. I. lib. ii. ch. 2; St. Anselm, *Proslogium*, xiii; Boedder, *Natural Theol.*, Bk. II. ch. iii; Wilhelm and Scannell, *Manual*, § 67; W. Humphrey, *His Divine Majesty*, pp. 124–130. Cf. 1 Kings viii. 27; Psa. cxxxix. 7–10; Jerem. xxiii. 23, 24.

[4] This is signified when He is said to be *illocal*.

[5] Cf. Deut. iv. 39 with 1 Kings viii. 27. See Gore, *The New Theology*, Lec. iii, for a discriminating exposition of divine immanence and its counter-truth of transcendence.

[6] Attributed to St. Bonaventura.

Like time, space is a generalized abstraction from relations of finite things. Spatial relations are real,[1] but necessarily presuppose and pertain to spatial substances. Space is quantitative, and therefore not truly infinite. There is indeed no beyond space, but that means nothing more than that "beyond" is itself spatial. Space is transcended by the Infinite, but in a manner which makes the phrase "beyond" or "outside" inapplicable, except as a metaphor.

When, therefore, we speak of God as "near" and "far off," we do not signify any finite localizing of God, but we symbolically describe relations between the Infinite and the spatial in terms of space.

> "Super cuncta, subtus cuncta, extra cuncta, intra cuncta:
> Intra cuncta nec inclusus, extra cuncta nec exclusus,
> Subter cuncta nec subtractus, super cuncta nec elatus;
> Super totus possidendo, subter totus sustinendo,
> Extra totus complectendo, intra totus es implendo;
> Intra nusquam coarctaris, extra numquam dilataris,
> Subtus nullo fatigaris, super nullo sustentaris."[2]

[1] Therefore real to God, but not as attributes of Himself. They are products of His will and attributes of His creatures. Cf. Dorner, *Christian Doctrine*, Vol. I. p. 239, note; Baldwin, *Dic. of Philos.*, *s. v.* "Space."

[2] Abelard, *Rythm. De Trin.*, v. 3 *et seq.*, being a versification of St. Greg. Mag., *Moral. in Job*, l. ii. c. 8.

St. Clement, Rom., describes God as one who is in and around all things, using the expressive word ἐμπεριέχοντος: *Ad Cor.* xxviii. 4. Hermas, *Pastor*, Bk. II. Com. i, says that God contains all but is not contained: Cf. St. Irenæus, *adv. Haer.*, IV. xx. 2. Tertullian says that in God is every place, but that He is in no place: *adv. Prax.*, xvi. Cf. also Novatian, *De Trin.* ii, xvii; St. John Damasc., *Orth. Fid.*, i. 13; St. Hilary, *De Trin.* I. i.

On divine omnipresence, see ch. xii. § 4, below.

§ 6. The truths of divine simplicity and immensity are included in, and completed by, the proposition that God is *pure Spirit*.[1] The spiritual quality of the divine essence signifies (*a*) that He is incorporeal, without materiality and invisible; (*b*) that He has no extension, no spatial circumscription, and no parts; (*c*) that, being infinite, He is illocal. We indeed speak of God as present in places, but the relation thus described does not localize His essence; (*d*) that His essence is life and the source of life; (*e*) that He is immortal, and not subject either to growth or to corruption; (*f*) that He is essentially unpicturable.

The spirituality of God is a necessary consequence of His simplicity and immensity, that is, of His infinity. If He were corporeal He would be subject to measure, and division, which signifies and involves external limitation. Spirituality has also been inferred from His supreme eminence.[2] Matter everywhere appears as inferior to spirit, and as made for spirit.[3] The teaching of Scripture is unmistakable, although there is but one direct assertion that "God is Spirit,"[4] for it contains truths from which His spirituality is to be inferred — such as infinity, self-

---

[1] On the spiritual essence of God, see the references given for divine simplicity, § 4 *init.*, above. Also Franzelin, *De Deo Uno*, Thes. xxxv; Mason, *Faith of the Gospel*, ch. i. § 8; Pearson, *De Deo*, Lec. V. pp. 47–51; Hastings, *Dic. of the Bible*, *s. v.* "Spirit." Cf. Origen, *De Princip.*, I. i. 1–7; St. Augustine, *De Trin.*, viii. 3.

[2] St. Thomas, *op. cit.*, I. iii. 1.

[3] Illingworth, *Divine Immanence*, ch. i.

[4] St. John iv. 24. Cf. Acts xvii. 29; Deut. iv. 15, 16.

existent life, omnipresence, invisibility, etc. There has never been any serious difference of opinion on this subject among genuine and intelligent believers in monotheism, and the passages in Scripture which speak of God's hand, eye, and the like are obviously to be taken, and have always been understood, metaphorically.[1]

The second commandment of the decalogue forbade the making of material images of God, ostensibly in order to shut out every approach to the worship of false gods, which among the neighbours of the Israelites took the form of image worship. But the principle that no image of man's device can truly represent the supreme Spirit was seen by the prophets to be involved.[2] Our Lord revealed to the woman of Samaria that because "God is a Spirit, . . . they that worship Him must worship in spirit and truth."[3] Wherein such worship consists He did not fully explain, except that it is not to be regarded as confined to particular places like Jerusalem and Mount Gerizim.[4]

God is essentially unimaginable; although, as has been shown in other connections, He is mentally conceivable and knowable.[5] But this is quite consistent

---

[1] St. Thomas, *Summa Theol.*, I. i. 9; A. B. Davidson, in Hastings' *Dic. of the Bible*, "God (in O T)," ii.

[2] Cf. Isa. xl. 18, 19.

[3] St. John iv. 24.

[4] *vv.* 20, 21. Our Lord deduces the superiority of Jewish worship from the fact that the Jews knew whom they worshipped — not from the locality of the temple.

[5] Cf. pp. 19, 33, 34, above.

with the fact that the Son of God, coessential with the Father, has voluntarily condescended to assume our flesh, and to make it his own personal property forever. It is necessary, however, to remember that in doing this the Son did not alter His divine essence, or impart to it fleshly attributes. The divine and human natures remain forever distinct in His Person. Yet the consequence is involved that the human nature of Christ becomes an image and medium through which our worship is directed to Him. In such worship the *terminus ad quem* is Himself, and is truly divine; because the human nature of Christ is the human nature of a divine Person, and altogether inseparable from Him. At our altars God is worshipped "through Jesus Christ our Lord." [1]

§ 7. Spirit and life are inseparable ideas; and neither can exist, so far as we can conceive, apart from the other. If God is Spirit, He is also *Life*.[2] We say "Life," rather than "living," [3] because of His infinity, and because all life flows from Him as from its primary seat and necessary source. The principle of biology that life comes from life would remain,[4] even

[1] See F. J. Hall's *Doctrine of the Church*, p. 114, and references there given.

[2] Acts xvii. 22 *et seq.*; St. John v. 26; 1 St. John v. 20. On this subject, see St. Thomas, *Summa Theol.*, I. xviii; R. Owen, *Dogmatic Theol.*, ch. iv. § 10; Dorner, *Christian Doctrine*, § 21; Wilhelm and Scannell, *Manual*, § 78; Hastings, *Dic. of Christ*, *s. v.* "Living," 2; Pearson, *De Deo*, Lec. xiv. pp. 137–143.

[3] The Old Testament speaks of God as living, and the New calls Him Life. Both, of course, are true.

[4] This principle is called "biogenesis": *omne vivum a vivo*. Spon-

if what is called spontaneous generation of life from, or rather in, dead matter were established. That is, dead matter cannot be the real source or cause of life. Spontaneous generation, if it be a fact, can only mean that the conditions are sometimes present in dead matter under which life is caused to appear by some living cause. If the cause of life is not discoverable in the matter itself in which life emerges, we are constrained to infer that an invisible cause is working which transcends in nature the medium in which it operates.[1] The demand for an adequate cause of

taneous generation is termed "abiogenesis." See Baldwin, *Dic. of Philos.*, *s. v.* "Biogenesis." The term was proposed by Huxley in 1870. Pasteur, Tyndall, Roberts, and Dallinger have helped to establish biogenesis. See Huxley, *Essays*, viii; *Encyc. Brit.*, *s. v.* "Biology," iii; Tait, *Recent Advances in Physical Science*, Lec. vii; Knight, *Aspects of Theism*, pp. 87–92; Porter, *Human Intellect*, pp. 29–40. F. R. Tennant gives an interesting account of attempts to prove abiogenesis in *The Expository Times*, May, 1908, pp. 352–355. Sir Oliver Lodge's *Life and Matter* throws much light on the subject. Belief in spontaneous generation was common among the ancients, and even Christian fathers did not shrink from it: Origen, *c. Celsus*, iv. 57; St. Augustine, *De Civ.* Dei, xvi. 7. Cf. St. Thos., *Summa Theol.*, lxxi. 1, *ad primum; Catholic Encyc.*, *s. v.* "Biogenesis and abiogenesis"; Hastings, *Encyc. of Relig.*, *s. v.* "Abiogenesis."

[1] Lodge says, "So far . . . all effort at spontaneous generation has been a failure . . . But suppose it was successful; what then? We should then be reproducing in the laboratory a process that must at some past age have occurred on the earth; for at one time the earth was certainly hot and molten and inorganic, whereas now it swarms with life. Does that show that the earth generated the life? By no means . . . Life may be something not only ultra-terrestrial, but even immaterial, something outside our present categories of matter and energy; as real as they are, but different, and utilizing them for its own purpose." *Life and Matter*, pp. 172–175.

life is not satisfied except by postulating a living cause.
The cosmological argument justifies the doctrine that
the ultimate Cause and immanent principle of all life
is God.[1]

If God is infinite and self-existent, the ground of
every divine attribute is internal to Himself. Accordingly Holy Scripture teaches us that God has life in
Himself; and that "as the Father hath life in Himself,
even so gave He to the Son also to have life in Himself." [2] The same may, of course, be asserted in relation to the Holy Spirit, whose economic function it
is to be the "Giver of life." [3]

God is also the source of life to His creatures, whether
we speak of physical life or of life everlasting.[4] The
New Testament expounds this more particularly in
relation to the latter. Thus we are told that our life
is in the Son,[5] so that the Spirit imparts life to us as
from Him; [6] "He that hath the Son hath the life; he
that hath not the Son of God hath not the life." [7]
The manner in which the Spirit imparts this life is by
engrafting us into the body of Christ.[8]

It remains to consider, What is life? We can only
describe life phenomenally, in terms derived from its

[1] Cf. pp. 148, 149, above.
[2] St. John v. 26. Cf. Acts xvii. 25, 28.
[3] *Nicene Creed.* St. John, iii. 5, 6; vi. 63; Rom. viii. 14. Cf. Job.
xxxiii. 4; Ezek. xxxvii. 9, 14.
[4] Gen. ii. 17; Acts xvii. 25, 28; Rom. iv. 17; 1 St. John v. 11.
[5] St. John i. 4; xiv. 6; 1 St. John v. 11.
[6] Cf. St. John vi. 57 with verse 63.
[7] 1 St. John v. 12.
[8] 1 Cor. xii. 13.

effects within our experience. It exhibits itself in physical organisms as a capacity of self-adjustment to appropriate environments.[1] Personal life in its distinctive aspects transcends physical life, and is spiritual. But the two are analogous in their capacity of adjustment to appropriate environment. The environment of personal and spiritual life is personal and spiritual; and the manner of self-adjustment thereto is also personal and self-conscious. The life of a person actualizes and realizes itself through conscious communion and fellowship with other personal spirits. The possibilities of such life are found in the triune God, and eternal life consists for us in conscious communion and fellowship with God.[2] The basic truth of all this, that God is life, is also realized in self-conscious personal relations — the mutual and eternal relations of the divine Persons. It is because these mutual relations are wholly internal to the indivisible essence of God, and independent of all else, that God possesses the fulness of life in Himself.[3] This life,

---

[1] See Baldwin, *Dic. of Philos.*, *s. vv.* "Life"; "Living Matter"; Fleming, *Vocab. of Philos.*, *s. v.* "Life"; Herbert Spencer, *Prins. of Biology*, Vol. I. pp. 59–81. Spencer describes physical life as "The continuous adjustment of internal relations to external relations." By internal relations he means "definite combinations of simultaneous and successive changes"; and by external relations "co-existences and sequences." Their connection is expressed by the term "correspondence." A living organism is one which continuously adjusts itself so as to correspond uninterruptedly with its environment.

[2] St. John xvii. 3.

[3] We cannot correctly describe God's own life as requiring either

however, is caused by the divine will to flow forth into created things, in manners appropriate to their several natures, whether merely physical or personal. In brief, life has its source in God; and, in its highest creaturely forms, exhibits itself through personal relations with Him, through Jesus Christ our Life.[1]

Because He has life in Himself, is essentially eternal, and is the source of all life in others, God is said alone to have immortality. Human immortality is not intrinsic, but wholly derivative, and dependent upon the will of God. God is subject neither to growth nor to corruption.[2]

§ 8. Life cannot realize itself in a state of passivity, and He who is Life must be characterized by activity. But divine activity cannot in its own nature be inconsistent with divine infinity, eternity, immutability, and simplicity, even though its external effects and its manifestations to us are finite, temporal, mutable, and multiplex. We are compelled in practice to describe divine operations in the terms of their finite and temporal effects, as if they were in themselves events in the life of God and contingent. Yet we are able to perceive that such descriptions of divine action are only relatively true. They are not applicable to infinite action as it is in itself, but describe relations

adjustment or external relations. But it does undoubtedly exhibit itself in "correspondence" of the divine Persons with each other — these Persons being, however, internal to each other.

[1] Cf. Acts xvii. 28 with Col. i. 15–19; and with St. John xvii. 3.

[2] Deut. xxxii. 40; 1 Tim. i. 17; vi. 16; Rev. iv. 9; x. 6. See Martensen, *Christian Dogmatics*, § 48.

between the eternal and the temporal in terms of the temporal.

This is signified by the scholastic proposition that God is *purus actus*, pure act.[1] The Aristotelic distinction between power and energy is employed.[2] The point is that in God power is never a latent capacity but always an active energy, for divine actions are eternal. They cannot be initiated, as if previously unactualized; nor can they cease, so as to be over with. Whatever God does He does from eternity, so that there never was a time previous to His doing it, nor will His doing it be ended in any future time. This does not mean that divine actions are incomplete at any time, or that temporal process is a condition of their perfection; for incompleteness and temporal process cannot pertain to the infinite and eternal. It means simply that such descriptions have truth and validity only in relation to the effects of divine action and to their manifestation in finite events.

The activity of God is not wholly, nor even primarily, external. If it were so, He would be externally conditioned and finite. His external operations proceed entirely from His will of good pleasure. The doctrine of the Trinity shows us that the necessary activity of God — that which makes Him *purus actus* independently of all else than Himself — consists in

[1] This phrase applies to actuality of essence as well as to that of operation. See *Catholic Encyc.*, *s. vv.* "Actus et Potentia"; "Actus Purus"; St. Thomas, *Summa Theol.*, I. iii. 1, 2; *c. Gent.*, I. xiii, xvi.

[2] δύναμις and ἐνέργεια. Aristotle, *Metaph.*, Bks. vi–viii. Cf. Wallace, *Outlines of the Philos. of Aristotle*, § 36.

the eternal generation of the Son and the spiration of the Holy Spirit.[1]

But, voluntary though they be, the external operations of God are also eternal in themselves, and without beginning, end, or change, since the will from which they proceed is eternal. Holy Scripture bears witness to this truth by the twofold manner in which it describes the death of Christ. Concerned chiefly as its pages are with the historical aspects of divine redemption, it describes that mystery at length in the temporal aspects of its manifestation and its effects in history. But the eternal aspect is not overlooked; and the death of Christ is described not only as achieved once for all, but as a living fact in all time. The Lamb was slain from an eternal standpoint, and is offered in the heavenly Holy Place by an eternal Priest.[2]

The same eternal nature of all divine action accounts for the puzzle which emerges when the truth of creation is closely examined. The creature is temporal by nature, and began to be with the inception of time. Time is itself nothing more than a relation and attribute of created things and events. Yet, if the universe of creatures began to be in the beginning of time, it is

[1] On the so-called internal and external operations of God, see Schouppe, *Elem. Theol. Dog.*, Tr. V. §§ 134, 135, 164, 165. As has been noted elsewhere, nothing is external to God in the sense of being outside of Him. Divine operations are called external only in the sense that they have relation to things *other than* God.

[2] W. Milligan, *Ascension and Heavenly Priesthood*, pp. 97–103; Medd., *One Mediator*, §§ 10–14. Heb. vii. 1–3, 21–28; viii. 3; Rev. v. 6; xiii. 8.

everlasting. There never was a time when it was not. The divine act of creation, being eternal, never began; but its substantial effect, having a temporal nature, did begin to be, and is everlasting only in the sense of coinciding in duration with the duration of time. It does not, properly speaking, coincide in duration with eternity. We cannot indeed imagine eternity, or define the manner in which it transcends time. We speak of God as existing *prior* to creation, but we do not speak correctly, if we mean that eternity is really "prior" to or "after" anything.[1] "From everlasting to everlasting thou *art* God."

The puzzle arises from the non-picturable nature of eternity, and our consequent inability to imagine any act as real which is eternal and immutable. But God is not God if He changes in action, and He is not a living Person if He cannot act. Both truths must be held together, each with the proviso that the other is true.[2]   Similarly, our inability to picture time and eternity together must not induce us to sacrifice the truth expressed in the phrase, God is *purus actus*, to the reality of the temporal effects of divine action; nor may we regard the events of history as illusory, in the interests of the eternal.   The eternal is the causal

---

[1] There can be no temporal sequence or interval between divine acts and their effects in time. This bears on the so-called infinite regress of causation associated in some minds with the cosmological argument. Such a regress, if temporal, would be absolutely meaningless, for time is finite.

[2] Cf. *Introd. to Dog. Theol.*, pp. 170, 171; Richey, *Truth and Counter Truth*, Introd.; Mozley, *Predestination*, ch. ii. *init.*

ground of the temporal, and temporal events are true manifestations of an activity which in its own nature transcends all that we experience or imagine. This transcendence is an element in its perfection. Divine action would not be absolute in its fulness and freedom, if it were conditioned otherwise than voluntarily by the laws of time and change.

The significance of our emphasis upon the truth that God is eternal in act, even when acting with reference to temporal effects, will appear more fully when we consider the divine will and knowledge. The sum of the matter is that, while God can cause temporal, mutable, and contingent events, He would not be God if He could initiate, modify, or bring to an end His causal action itself.

CHAPTER XII

ACTIVE AND MORAL ATTRIBUTES

I. *Active Attributes*

§ 1. We have seen that, if God is the ultimate and sovereign Cause of all realities and of all events, He must be the Source and Controller of all power, the *Omnipotent* or Almighty.[1] If He is indeed infinite, this conclusion is inevitable; and we may not measure divine power by the external effects of divine operations. The nature of these effects is due to the will of God, and they may not be regarded as limitations of His power, which cannot be reduced or abandoned.[2] The teaching of nature and reason as to the infinite power of God is confirmed both directly and indirectly by many portions of Scripture.[3]

---

[1] Ch. v. § 10, above.

[2] Only in the impersonal and purely physical sphere are effects to be regarded as necessarily adequate to their causal antecedents. The power of a personal cause is one thing, the determination of effects to be produced thereby is another. A depotentiated God is not really God, nor could such a being resume omnipotence. To do this, if it meant anything, would be to exercise an omnipotence already in one's possession. Cf. the author's *Kenotic Theory*, pp. 107–109; Fairbairn, *Philos. of the Christ. Relig.*, p. 90.

[3] Cf. Gen. i. 17; xviii. 14; Job xlii. 2; Psa. lxii. 11; lxvi. 7; St. Matt. xix. 26; St. Luke i. 37; Revel. iv. 8; xv. 3; Eph. iii. 20. Cf. also the Nicene and Apostles' Creeds, "I believe in . . . the Father Al-

Divine omnipotence [1] signifies such power as necessarily pertains to the Infinite and Eternal, who cannot
be limited in any of His attributes by anything but
Himself. In particular, therefore, (a) He is the Seat
and Source of all power, so that no power either exists
or can exist which has any other ultimate ground than
Himself; (b) The limits of His power are determined
by the nature of power itself, which is equivalent to
saying that they are wholly internal to the divine
essence; (c) The power of God cannot rightly be said
to be externally limited by His employment of means,
for these very means are created by His will, as elements in a system of His own choice. And, if in
particular instances God cannot achieve His purpose
without the use of means, this necessity does not arise
from a lack of power in Him, but from the nature
both of the end and of power itself, which does not
pertain to what is essentially impossible.[2]

mighty"; and the Athanasian Symbol, "The Father Almighty, the
Son Almighty . . . Yet not three Almighties, but one Almighty."

[1] Patristic teaching on the subject of divine omnipotence is gathered
in Petavius, *De Deo.*, Bk. V. chh. v–xi. For later treatments see St.
Thomas, *Summa Theol.*, I. xxv; Pearson, *Apostles' Creed*, art. I;
Forbes, *Nicene Creed*, pp. 48, 49, 91–93; Suarez, *Summa*, Pt. I, Tr.
V, l. 3, cap. 9; Schouppe, *Elem. Theol. Dogm.*, Tr. V. §§ 161 *et seq.*;
Wilhelm and Scannell, *Manual*, Vol. I. § 76; Mason, *Faith of the
Gospel*, ch. i. § 12; Franzelin, *De Deo Uno*, Thes. xxxiv; Boedder,
Natural Theol., Bk. II. ch. vi; Baldwin, *Dic. of Philos.*, *s. v.* "Om-
nipotence"; Hastings, *Dic. of the Bible*, *s. v.* "Power"; Ladd, *Philos.
of Religion*, Vol. II. pp. 124–126. Cf. ch. v. § 10, above.

[2] To create a world suited for man's employment of means to ends,
which contains no adaptations of means to ends, is obviously impossible. Cf. ch. vi. § 9, above. See St. Anselm, *Proslogium*, vii.

Power has intrinsic limits: (*a*) The absurd does not pertain to power; for example, to make a square triangle; (*b*) Power cannot violate itself; and for God to violate His own essence and holiness would mean this, since power has its seat in the divine essence; (*c*) If God were to change His will, which is essentially eternal, the same violation of the essence of power would be involved. The impossibility, therefore, that God should achieve the absurd, or do evil, or change His will, is not a proof of divine weakness, but pertains to His perfection.

Divine power does not depend for its exercise upon the existence of an extraneous sphere, but energizes within the divine essence through the eternal generation of the Son and the spiration of the Spirit. Every so-called external operation of God is voluntary. In a sense, creation may be regarded as inevitable. That is, its motive is to be found in the very essence of God, which is goodness; and the will to create beings capable of sharing in His goodness is an eternal and unalterable will. But, eternal though it be, the will of God is a true *will*, and creation is an effect of His will — not a necessity of His essence.

To create is possible only for infinite power, and the existence of creatures constitutes evidence of divine omnipotence. But creation is not an event which has come within human observation; and our knowledge of it is obtained by inference and by supernatural revelation. What we observe consists of phenomenal sequences; which, when considered in themselves, are seen to be finite effects. The Almightiness of God is not phenomenally laid bare; nor could it be thus exhibited to us, for phenomena are necessarily limited externally and finite.

The truth of divine omnipotence assures us that God is able to perform whatsoever He determines and promises. In particular, it guarantees the triumph of righteousness, goodness, and love, and the final establishment of a kingdom from which every thing that offends will be forever cast out. In short, the absolute sovereignty of the Holy One constitutes the moral significance of divine omnipotence; and this determines the point of view from which the problem of evil is to be considered.

§ 2. *The Divine Will* [1] is a phrase employed in three meanings: (*a*) the power of God to determine absolutely His own operations and purposes, and their effects; (*b*) what He determines; (*c*) the manifestations of His will as to human conduct — the will of signs.

(*a*) The power of God to determine His own operations and purposes is involved in His personality; and is not only the unvarying teaching of Scripture,[2]

[1] On the divine will, see St. Thomas, *Summa Theol.*, I. xix; Pearson, *De Deo*, Lecs. xx, xxi, pp. 206–231; Thos. Jackson, *Works*, Vol. V. pp. 292–373; R. Owen, *Dogmatic* Theol., ch. iv. § 13; Forbes, *Nicene Creed*, pp. 47, 56–61; Liddon, *Some Elements*, pp. 56, 57, 184–190; Wilhelm and Scannell, *Manual*, Vol. I. pp. 227–233; Petavius, *De Deo*, V. i–iv; Franzelin, *De Deo Uno*, Thes. xliv–xlvi; Hastings, *Dic. of the Bible*, *s. v.* "Will," iii.

[2] Deut. xxxii. 39; 1 Sam. ii. 6–8; Job ix. 12; Psa. lxvi. 7; cxxxv. 5, 6; Jerem. xxvii. 5; Ephes. i. 11; Revel. iv. 11.

but is implied in the causal relation between Him and the universe.[1] This power is absolute, if, as we have seen, God is almighty. The freedom of the Infinite cannot be limited by anything which is not essential to the idea of freedom in a perfect Being. His will is, in short, His essence; and its motives are eternal and internal to Himself. He cannot, therefore, will anything inconsistent with His holy nature; and this constitutes a quality of His perfection, not a lack of freedom.

(b) The divine will in its second sense is called His "will of good pleasure," or what He wills from eternity, to bring to pass. It is in itself essentially eternal and immutable, but manifests itself to us in temporal and contingent effects; and we are obliged to describe it in relation to these effects, that is, in terms of temporal sequence and of contingency. We do not err in doing so, if we remember that we are describing the divine will relatively only. The relations which we describe are objectively real, but their temporal and contingent aspects are derived from the nature of the effects willed by God, not from the nature of the divine will itself, which is eternal and absolute. God can will changes and contingencies, and these changes and contingencies are real to Him; but He cannot change His will or make it contingent in itself.[2]

These considerations determine the sense in which we speak of the will of God as antecedent and conse-

[1] Cf. ch. v. § 10, above.
[2] St. Augustine, *De Civ. Dei*, xxii. 2.   Cf. p. 259, above.

quent, and as absolute and conditioned.[1]   In so speaking we are describing the divine will in its effects. (1) God is said to will anything *antecedently*, *secundum se*, when He wills it without reference to other particular circumstances. He thus wills the salvation of mankind. (2) He is said to will by His *consequent* will, when He wills in view of foreseen events; for example, when He wills the future punishment of the wicked. (3) He is said to will *absolutely* when no external conditions attend the event; for example, His will to create the universe. (4) Finally, His will is called *conditional*, when it concerns conditional effects in time. Thus He wills the future blessedness of the elect, if they make their calling and election sure. The antithesis between the essential eternity and absoluteness of the divine will and the temporal and contingent nature of its effects is one that transcends human capacity to rationalize. Yet its reality is not beyond our ability to perceive and allow for in interpreting the phraseology with which we are here concerned.

This same antithesis determines the interpretation of scriptural and theological language concerning divine predestination and fore-ordination. The "pre" and the "fore" may not be understood to mean that there is a temporal sequence as between the divine

[1] On these distinctions, see Franzelin, *De Deo Uno*, Thes. xlix; C. Hodge, *Syst. Theol.*, Vol. I. pp. 404, 405; Schouppe, *Elem. Theol. Dog.*, Tr. V. § 157; Tanquerey, *De Deo*, §§ 107, 108; Thos. Jackson, *Works*, pp. 331–336.

will and the events with which it is concerned. An eternal will is coincident with all time, and with every temporal event and effect. What is meant, therefore, is that the divine will, being eternal, does not date from any moment in time, but constitutes the causal *prius* of the entire range of temporal events.

Two truths have to be held together in this connection: — the eternal, immutable and all-controlling quality of the divine will, without which nothing ever happens; and the reality of temporal contingency and human freedom within its appointed limits. We cannot harmonize them by mere human reason; but we can perceive that each is true, and, therefore, that they are not in fact mutually contradictory. To neglect the former is to embrace the Pelagian standpoint, and to neglect the latter is to reduce moral responsibility of human agents to unreality.[1]

(c) The will of signs, or the manifestation of God's will as to our conduct, is usually divided into five branches: (1) commands; (2) prohibitions; (3) permissions; (4) counsels; (5) example. Its particulars are to be ascertained chiefly, although not exclusively, from supernatural revelation; and their treatment pertains to moral theology.[2]

§ 3. Personality involves knowledge as well as will,

---

[1] See Mozley, *Predestination*, ch. ii, *init.*; Thos. Jackson, *Works*, Vol. V. pp. 292–300. The subject of predestination will be considered in a future volume, in connection with the doctrine of grace.

[2] St. Thomas, *Summa Theol.*, I. xix. 11, 12; Bp. Sanderson, *Conscience and Law*, Lec. iv. §20; Schouppe, *Elem. Theol. Dog.*, Tr. V. §158. Cf. St. Matt. vii. 21.

and the Creator of mind cannot but possess intelligence. God is said to be *omniscient*,[1] which means that His knowledge, like Himself, is infinite and eternal. The Infinity of divine knowledge appears (*a*) in its range, for God knows all things which can in the nature of things be objects of knowledge; (*b*) in its method, transcending every temporal process and condition. In brief, divine knowledge has no limits or conditions except such as pertain to the essential nature of knowledge in its perfection.

Four characteristics of divine knowledge may be mentioned: (*a*) Since God is *purus actus*, His knowledge is eternally actual in all its range, never beginning or increasing, and never ceasing or decreasing. God neither learns nor forgets, and He is oblivious to nothing.

(*b*) Divine knowledge cannot be conditioned by mental processes, or by any temporal relations or physical *media*, but is purely intellectual, direct, and immediate; that is, intuitive.

---

[1] On divine omniscience, see St. Thomas, *Summa Theol.*, I. xiv; Petavius, *De Deo*, lib. iv; Pearson, *De Deo*, Lecs. xv–xix. pp. 149–205; Powell, *Prin. of the Incarn.*, pp. 126–132; Forbes, *Nicene Creed*, pp. 52–56; R. Owen, *Dogmatic Theol.*, ch. iv. § 11; Baldwin, *Dic. of Philos.*, *s. v.* "Omniscience"; Royce, in *Conception of God*, pp. 7–15; Martensen, *Christian Dogmatics*, § 49; Pfleiderer, *Philos. of Relig.*, Vol. III. pp. 297, 298; Ladd, *Philos. of Relig.*, pp. 134–153; Dorner, *Christian Doctrine*, § 27; Wilhelm and Scannell, *Manual*, Vol. I. pp. 214–224; Franzelin, *De Deo Uno*, Thes. xxxvi–xlvi. St. Augustine refers to the subject frequently: *e.g. De Trin.* xv. 22; *De Civ. Dei*, xii. 18. Cf. Psa. xciv. 9–11; cxxxix. 1–24; cxlvii. 4, 5; Isa. xlvi. 9, 10; Jerem. xxiii. 24; Ezek. xi. 5; St. Matt. vi. 8; Acts viii. 18; Rom. xi. 33; Heb. iv. 12, 13; 1 St. John iii. 20.

(c) Temporal and spatial relations are real objects of divine knowledge. But God contemplates them in their true nature, as properties of finite things and events. They cannot separate God or His act of knowing from the things and events which He contemplates. The Infinite and Eternal is necessarily at the centre of every place and time. If we speak of divine foreknowledge or of divine remembering, we ought not to mean that the divine act referred to is in itself previous to, or later than, the event. We should mean this: that since eternal knowledge transcends every time relation, the relations of "fore" and "after" cannot come between God and finite events, or alter His immediate contemplation and knowledge of them.[1]

(d) The grounds of knowledge, and the light in which God knows all things, are to be found in God Himself and in His eternal will.

All that we have been saying is based upon the absolute and indisputable transcendence of eternity over time. It should be remembered, however, that no event is determined beforehand, or deprived of its contingency, by what is called the foreknowledge

[1] St. Augustine, De Civ. Dei, xi. 21. Cf. Clarke, Outline of Christ. Theol., pp. 81, 82. On divine foreknowledge, see St. Thomas, op. cit., I. xiv. 13; St. Augustine, De Civ. Dei, v. 9, 10; x. 12; Thos. Jackson, Works, Vol. V. pp. 93–105; Franzelin, De Deo Uno, Thes. xlii–xlvi; Baldwin, Dic. of Philos., s. v "Forenowledge"; A. Stewart, in Hastings' Dic. of the Bible, ibid; Wilhelm and Scannell, Manual, Vol. I. pp. 219–224. Cf. Isa. xlii. 9; xlvi. 10; Jerem. i. 5; Acts xv. 18; Rom. viii. 29.

of God. The principle which determines the course of events is the divine will; and, as we have seen in the previous section, the absoluteness of God's will does not preclude contingency in its effects. God knows whatever is to happen, but what He foreknows is determined by what will happen and not *vice versa*.[1]

Inasmuch as divine knowledge comprehends all the determinative secondary causes at work in the universe, God knows not only what really happens but also what would happen under any possible conditions. He comprehends the hypothetical as perfectly as the actual.[2]

The knowledge of God with which men are primarily concerned is His knowledge of finite things and events; and it is of such knowledge that we have chiefly been speaking. But the omniscience of God is not dependent upon the existence of finite things, or upon the occurrence of finite events. It is an eternal attribute of the divine essence. God is self-conscious by reason of His eternal and personal nature; and the relations subsisting in the divine essence itself between the divine Persons afford an infinite sphere for the activity of His contemplating mind.

Divine immutability forbids the supposition that God can abandon His omniscience, or that this attribute can be shortened by any relation between God

[1] St. Augustine, *De Civ. Dei*, v. 9, 10; St. Thomas, *op. cit.*, I. xiv. 8; Wilhelm and Scannell, *op. cit.*, § 80; Franzelin, *op. cit.*, Thes. xliv; Hastings, *Dic. of the Bible*, *s. v.* "Foreknowledge."

[2] This is called by scholastic writers "scientia media." See Schouppe, *Elem. Theol. Dog.*, Tr. V. § 144.

and His creatures. The Incarnation did not deprive the Son of His possession of the Godhead, and therefore did not shorten His divine knowledge. The nature and mind which He assumed was indeed finite, and *in that nature and mind* His knowledge was, and still is, finite. Moreover, the only mind of Christ which has come within earthly observation is His human mind. But the Incarnate subsists in two distinct natures; and we may not attribute the limitations of His human nature to His divine essence, or think that one nature displaces the other.[1]

§ 4. God is present in all things and in all places with a perfection of presence which is peculiar to Himself. This is the meaning of His *omnipresence*.[2] Presence signifies immediacy of contact, whether we view such contact from the standpoint of spatial substance, of knowledge, or of operation. Finite presence is always imperfect, and cannot wholly remove the relation of externality between things. It signifies no

[1] Cf. the writer's *Kenotic Theory*, chh. x–xii.

[2] On divine omnipresence cf. ch. xi. 5 (on divine immensity), above, and the references there given. See also St. Thomas, *Summa Theol.*, I. viii; Petavius, *De Deo*, III. vii–x; St. Augustine, *De Civ. Dei*, xxii. 29; Novatian, *De Trin.*, vi; St. Anselm, *Monologium*, xx–xxiv; R. Owen, *Dogmatic Theol.*, ch. iv. § 9; Pearson, *De Deo*, Lec. viii. pp. 76–86; Hastings, *Dic. of Christ*, s.v. "Omnipresence"; Ladd, *Philos. of Relig.*, pp. 126–130; Pfleiderer, *Philos. of Relig.*, Vol. III. pp. 295–297; Dorner, *Christian Doctrine*, Vol. I. pp. 239–247; Wilhelm and Scannell, *Manual*, Vol. I. pp. 211–213; Franzelin, *De Deo Uno*, Thes. xxxiv. Cf. 1 Kings viii. 27; Psa. cxxxix. 7–12; Job. xii. 10; Acts xvii. 24, 27, 28; Ephes. i. 23; Col. i. 16, 17; iii. 11; Heb. iv. 12, 13.

more than a relative nearness. The presence of God is not thus external, but He is in His infinite entirety at the centre of all, without being divided, extended, or circumscribed.

Omnipresence is a necessary inference from divine immensity; for if, from the point of view of substance, God transcends every spatial relation and limitation, His essence cannot be excluded from any thing or place, nor can it be present in part at one place and in part at another.[1] It is also to be inferred from divine omniscience, for, as we have seen, no manner of separation can divide God knowing from what He knows, and He knows all things and events whatsoever.[2] Finally, it is to be inferred from divine causation of all things, since God does not operate as an external Cause, but as the immanent principle of being and movement in all things. The notion of separation between cause and effect is in its ultimate analysis really unthinkable.[3] Such is the unavoidable teaching of reason, which is confirmed by the Scriptures and by the consent of catholic theologians.

The peculiarities of divine omnipresence can be very briefly summarized. That presence is (*a*) voluntary in relation to creatures, since it presupposes their coming into existence by the will of God; (*b*) necessarily actual in every existing sphere of reality, for nothing in God can be merely potential; (*c*) penetrating the

---

[1] Cf. ch. xi. § 5, above. [2] Cf. § 3, above.
[3] See St. Athanasius, *c. Gent.*, xli–xliv; St. Thomas, *op. cit.*, I. viii. I, 3.

innermost essence of all things, but not as from without, nor either by extension or division, for infinite essence can neither be excluded, extended, nor divided; (d) conscious and infinitely discerning from within; (e) effectual, creative, and sustaining; (f) without possibility of motion, for the Cause of all motion cannot be moved; (g) transcending all unaided creaturely observation by reason of divine invisibility and infinitude.

As the presence of God does not come within our direct experience in its infinite essence, if we are to enter into divine communion and fellowship, it is necessary that God should manifest Himself to us in special and limited modes of presence.[1] Such presence is relative. Thus God vouchsafes (a) a presence in glory to the hosts of heaven;[2] (b) a presence of efficiency in nature;[3] (c) a providential presence in human affairs;[4] (d) an attentive presence to His worshippers and petitioners;[5] (e) a judicial presence in our consciences;[6] (f) a bodily presence in the Incarnate Son;[7] (g) a mystical presence in the Church and her means of grace;[8] (h) an official presence with His ministers;[9] (i) a sacramental presence in the Holy Eucharist.[10]

[1] See Martensen, *Christian Dogmatics*, p. 87; Illingworth, *Divine Immanence*, p. 157.

[2] Isa. vi. 1–3; St. Matt. xviii. 10; Rev. vii. 9–12.

[3] Nah. i. 3–5.   [4] Psa. lxviii. 7, 8.

[5] St. Matt. xviii. 19, 20; Acts xvii. 27.

[6] Gen. iii. 8; Psa. lxviii. 1, 2.

[7] St. John i. 14; Col. ii. 9: 1 St. John i. 1–3.

[8] Ephes. ii. 12–22.

[9] St. Matt. xxviii. 19, 20.   [10] St. John vi. 56; 1 Cor. xi. 29.

Divine omnipotence, omniscience, and omnipresence are called *relative attributes* because exhibited to us in relation to the created universe. But they are none the less essential and eternal attributes of the Godhead. We have seen this to be so with omnipotence and omniscience, by virtue of the internal relations of the divine Persons. Similarly, divine presence in its essential nature is actualized eternally by the existence of the divine Persons in each other — a presence which is unconditioned by anything external to the divine essence. It is to be added that even in their relative aspects, these attributes are incapable of abandonment by God. The existence of creatures being presupposed, God would not be infinite — would not be God — if He were to cease from being almighty, omniscient, and omnipresent in relation to them.[1]

The truths of divine presence and knowledge are closely connected in their practical bearing; and a continual remembrance of them is required for our warning and comfort. We can never escape the contemplation of our eternal Judge, who discerns our innermost thoughts and designs; and our recollection of the unvarying watchfulness of our heavenly Father also assures us that divine love is effectual in all that we may be called upon to endure.

§ 5. God is *infinitely wise;* that is, He is absolutely infallible in judgment, whether in relation to His own operations or to creaturely actions, or in relation to past,

---

[1] We have discussed this subject more fully in *Kenotic Theory*, ch. vii. Cf. Dorner, *Christian Doctrine*, Vol. I. pp. 193, 194.

present, or future events.   Divine wisdom is the omniscience of God in its teleological and judicial aspects.[1]

That God is wise, we may infer from the indications of wisdom which are discovered in the effects of
His operations.[2]   That He is all-wise, appears from the
fact that no wisdom exists, or can exist, which is not
found in Him as its ultimate Ground and Cause.   A
wisdom which has no limits except such as arise from
the nature and possibilities of wisdom itself is necessarily infinite; and if any wisdom is to be attributed
to an infinite Being, such wisdom cannot be either
finite or unactualized within the divine mind.[3]   No
problems can be too great for God; or, rather, nothing
can be problematical to Him.   Discerning all things
eternally in the light of His own will and causation,
He sees the end in the beginning and the beginning
in the end, without possibility of any obscuration of
His judgment by the relations of futurity and contingency.   All possible grounds of judgment lie bare and
clear to the infinite and eternal mind, which both
designs and judges all things without process of thinking or mental effort.

[1] Divine wisdom is usually not discussed separately from divine
omniscience. The references on that subject in the first note of
§ 3, above, will be found serviceable. See also Schouppe, *Elem.
Theol. Dog.*, Tr. V. §§ 167–170; Martensen, *Christian Dogmatics*,
§ 50; Van Oosterzee, *Christian Dogmatics*, § xlix. 3; Wilhelm and
Scannell, *Manual*, § 81; Thos. Jackson, *Works*, Vol. V. pp. 83 *et seq.*;
Tanquerey, *De Deo Uno*, §§ 46–50. Cf. Psa. civ. 24; Prov. iii. 11–31;
viii; Rom. xi. 33; 1 Cor. i. 18–30; St. Jas. i. 5; Wisd. vii, viii.

[2] Cf. ch. vi, above, on the teleological argument.

[3] Cf. ch. vi. §13, above, on the infinite nature of divine wisdom.

The wisdom of God appears especially in *divine providence*,[1] or the teleological government of finite events and human history. It is distinguished as (*a*) general, having reference to the world at large;[2] (*b*) particular, concerned with details, and with the exigencies of individual human lives.[3] These two are in reality but one providence; for God orders all things in a teleological unity for the furtherance of His eternal purpose.[4] Yet the distinction is based upon truth, for God is as truly and as directly ordering the minutest details of history as He is overruling all things to one end.

The baffling mystery of the relation between divine sovereignty and creaturely freedom attends any adequate consideration of divine providence. As has been seen elsewhere, neither factor of the mystery may be disregarded. We know this much, that God

---

[1] On divine providence, see St. Thomas, *Summa Theol.*, I. xxii; Petavius, *De Deo*, VIII. i–v; Novatian, *De Trin.*, viii; Pearson, *De Deo*, Lec. xxii. pp. 232–242; Forbes, *Nicene Creed*, pp. 61–63; Hooker, *Eccles. Polity*, I. iii. 4; Wilhelm and Scannell, *Manual*, Vol. I. pp. 372–375; Clarke, *Outline of Theol.*, pp. 147–153; Schouppe, *Elem. Theol. Dog.*, Tr. V. §§ 135, 195–201; A. E. Garvie, in Hastings' *Dic. of the Bible*, *s. v.* "Providence"; J. C. Lambert, in Hastings' *Dic. of Christ*, *s. v.* "Providence."

[2] Cf. Gen. viii. 22; 1 Chron. xxix. 12, 14, 16; Job xxxvii. 6–24; Psa. cxxxv. 5–7; Prov. xix. 21; Jerem. x. 23; Rom. xi. 32–36; Ephes. ii. 10; Philip. ii. 13.

[3] Cf. Deut. ii. 7; 1 Sam. ii. 7, 8; Job xxxiii. 14–30; Psa. xxiii. 1–6; xxxiv. 7–10; St. Matt. vi. 31–33; x. 29, 30; St. Jas. iv. 15; Rev. xvii. 17; and many other passages in every part of Scripture.

[4] That purpose is the coming of His Kingdom of saints. Cf. Rom. viii. 28.

fulfils His purposes in part by the agency of creaturely
wills; and that these wills react upon Him, although
without ever changing or defeating His eternal design.
Somehow His design leaves room for, and makes use
of, other wills — wills capable of evil; and the evil
which creatures do is done by means of power supplied
by God. But God is not the Author of the evil, which,
in spite of creaturely malice, is overruled by Him to
the furtherance of holy ends.[1]

The prayers of men constitute forces allowed for and
employed by God in the fulfilment of His eternal plan.
They are moral forces, and their working is moral; but
their effect is not less real, and is in harmony with the
principle that all causation is ultimately grounded in
will. It is clear that the power of prayer depends upon
the spiritual energy behind it, and upon its conforming in purpose to the divine will. The will of God
is never changed, but many changes are willed from
eternity to be achieved by our prayers.[2]

II. *Moral Attributes*

§ 6. The ultimate standard of morality, if theism
be true, is the will of God, and, since that will is deter-

[1] St. Augustine writes, *De Civ. Dei*, i. 7; "Sic Deus res quas con-
didit administrat, ut eas agere proprius motus sinat." Cf. St.
Thomas, *op. cit.*, I. xxii. 4.

[2] Cf. Liddon, *Some Elements*, pp. 184–190; Bp. Gore, in *Oxford
House Papers*, 2d Series, vi. St. Augustine says, *De Civ. Dei*, v.
10, "Prayers also are of avail to procure those things which He fore-
knew that He would grant to those who offered them." See St.
Thomas, *op. cit.*, II. II. lxxxiii. Cf. Psa. x. 17; lxv. 2; xcix. 9; Isa.
lviii. 9; St. John xi. 42; xv. 7; St. Jas. iv. 3; v. 16.

mined by nothing external to Himself, the source and basis of morality is the divine essence.[1] Whatever, therefore, is in harmony with that essence is holy and righteous, and whatever is contrary thereto is by reason of that fact unholy and unrighteous. In brief, the moral character of God is absolutely perfect.[2] An imperfect being would not be infinite — would not be God.

The *moral perfection* of God involves (a) that each and every virtue proper to One who is the Supreme Being is to be found in Him; (b) that no limit can be placed upon the perfection of any divine virtue; (c) that divine virtues are mutually harmonious, so as to constitute a morally consistent character.

It is impossible for the moral perfection of God to be made fully manifest in the terms of our finite experience. The consequence is that, although both the reality and the necessity of such perfection in the Supreme Being seem obvious to intelligent theists, no one is able adequately to explain the harmony which we must assume to lie behind the various and opposite manifestations to us of His moral attributes. The problem of evil, in particular, is only explainable in

[1] Calderwood, *Moral Philos.*, ch. v. Div. I; Elmendorf, *Moral Theol.*, I. iii. pp. 35, 36; Porter, *Moral Science*, §§ 128, 129; Davis, *Elem. of Ethics*, pp. 202–204.

[2] On the moral perfection of God, see Wilhelm and Scannell, *Manual*, § 85. The majority of writers treat of this under the heading of holiness: *e.g.* Mason, *Faith of the Gospel*, ch. i. § 13; Schouppe, *Elem. Theol. Dog.*, Tr. V. §§ 174–176; Boedder, *Natural Theol.*, p. 306; Tanquerey, *De Deo Uno*, §§ 55–58; Pfleiderer, *Philos. of Religion*, Vol. III. pp. 300–306.

the terms of a larger knowledge than we possess.[1] We can perceive, however, that the moral perfection of God must differ in certain important respects from that of creatures. (a) God is absolutely supreme, and virtues which especially pertain to a creaturely status and to the moral accountability of creatures are foreign to His perfection;[2] (b) He is Himself the governing principle of righteousness, so that His perfection does not involve any *external* principle or rule of action;[3] (c) God is the final as well as the efficient Cause of all things. His perfection, therefore, is self-centred, and requires that His own will of good pleasure should absolutely determine His operations. This would be a mark of imperfection in us.

These considerations help us to interpret the scriptural principle that our moral perfection consists in imitating God;[4] that is, in appropriating divine perfection. To become perfect as our Father in heaven is perfect[5] requires that we should translate divine virtues into the terms of our finite conditions and of our relations to God as our Creator, Ruler and Judge.[6]

---

[1] On the problem of evil, see ch. vii. § 5, above.

[2] The virtues of obedience and humility pertain exclusively to creatures. It is not vain-glory on the part of God that He should glorify Himself.

[3] This does not mean that no moral principles control Him, but that the seat of these principles is Himself. His will is neither constrained nor capricious.

[4] Gal. v. 1.

[5] St. Matt. v. 48.

[6] Our Lord, by His example, has shown us how to do this. Cf. Gal. v. 2.

§ 7. The difference between divine and creaturely moral perfection appears clearly in the attribute of *holiness*.[1] Holiness, in its biblical use, includes the thought of separation.[2] God is holy because separate from creatures, that is, in the moral sphere. He is their God, and they are His creatures and subjects. Thus the holiness of God often signifies His Divinity, and is treated as the basis of what is called "holy fear," of reverence and of adoration.

Translated into human terms, holiness becomes consecration, or separation from mundane things in order to draw near to God. It is, in short, the characteristic mark of the practice of religion, and becomes accentuated in special religious vocations.[3] The Jewish priests, for example, were holy because set apart for divine service.

[1] Many writers fail to distinguish between the moral perfection and the holiness of God. But see Martensen, *Christian Dogmatics*, § 51; A. H. Strong, *Syst. Theol.*, Vol. I. pp. 268–275; J. Skinner, in Hastings' *Dic. of the Bible*, *s. v.* "Holiness, — in the Old Testament," II; G. B. Stevens, in same work, *s. v.* "Holiness in N T." The following among many scriptural passages imply the idea of holiness here defined: Exod. iii. 5; xv. 11; xix. 10–16; Isa. vi. 3, 5–7; Psa. xcix. 9; Ezek. xxxvi. 22, 23; 2 Cor. vii. 1; 1 Thess. iii. 13; iv. 7; Heb. xii. 29; Rev. xv. 4.

[2] See Brown, *et al.*, *Heb.-Eng. Lexicon*, *s. v.* קדשׁ; Thayer, *Gk.-Eng. Lexicon of the New Test.*, *s. v.* ἅγιος. J. G. Tasker, in Hastings' *Dic. of Christ*, is inclined to regard separation as a secondary idea. In any case it is a part of the biblical conception of divine holiness, which abundantly justifies us in distinguishing the holiness of God from His moral perfection in general. Cf. Ladd, *Philos. of Relig.*, ch. xxxiv, on the growth of the conception of holiness in various religions.

[3] Cf. St. Thomas, *Summa Theol.*, II. II. lxxxi. 8.

But just in proportion to men's advance in the knowledge of God, they learn to give an ethical significance to the idea of holiness. Divine holiness comes to mean freedom from every form of moral evil; and our holiness, while still based upon religious consecration, is perceived to involve purification from sin and moral conformity to the righteousness of God.

§ 8. The *righteousness* of God is the constant determination of His will and purpose by His moral perfection, and the invariable harmony of His operations with His eternal purpose.[1] The will of God is the unifying and directive principle of all things, so that the right is nothing else in the concrete than that which conforms to His will. The righteousness of God consists, therefore, in the fulfilment of His own will; because that will is determined by His moral perfection, and because all righteousness depends upon the supremacy of His will. It can be seen that two important differences exist between divine righteousness and that of His creatures. (*a*) In God righteousness is determined by His own will, whereas, our righteousness lies in fulfilling Another's will; (*b*) Unrighteousness is impossible with God, but with us righteousness is impossible except by divine assistance.[2]

---

[1] On divine righteousness, see St. Thomas, *Summa Theol.*, I. xix. 9; Martensen, *Christian Dogmatics*, § 50; Hastings, *Dic. of the Bible, s. vv.* "Righteousness in O T," by J. Skinner; and "Righteousness in N T," by G. B. Stevens. Cf. the references on moral perfection, p. 293, note 2, above. Cf. Psa. l. 6; lxxi. 19; cxlv. 7; Rom. iii. 4–6; St. Matt. v. 48.

[2] Cf. Wilhelm and Scannell, *Manual*, Vol. I. pp. 240, 241. We

Divine righteousness is revealed to us in the forms of moral law, of divine judgments and of the distribution of rewards and penalties. *Dispensational justice* is an important branch of the righteousness of God,[1] and consists in His perfect dispensation of happiness to creatures according to the deservings of each.

Our deservings proceed from three sources: (*a*) our divinely created nature — made in the image of God for participation in certain divine blessings;[2] (*b*) the personal characters which we acquire, by reason of which we become fit or unfit recipients of these blessings; (*c*) our good works, or what we do in order to please God. It is obvious that the second source of deserving is essential to give value to the first, for personal unworthiness of character must exclude the favour of a righteous God. It is also clear that unrepented and unexpiated sin is fatal to any form of personal deserving, whether of created nature, of personal character, or of good works. And, even if our good works were not deprived of value by our sins, they would be inadequate in themselves to estab-

are speaking of righteousness of life; the subject of the righteousness which is imputed to those who believe is not here considered.

[1] On divine justice, see St. Thomas, *Summa Theol.*, I. xxi. 1, 2, 4; Schouppe, *Elem. Theol. Dog.*, Tr. V. §§ 208, 210; Wilhelm and Scannell, *op. cit.*, Vol. I. pp. 241–246; A. Bisset, in Hastings' *Dic. of the Bible*, *s. v.* "Justice, the, of God"; Boedder, *Natural Theol.*, pp. 309, 310. Cf. Gen. xviii. 25; Psa. vii. 9–11; xviii. 24; lxxxix. 14; cxix. 37; Jerem. xxiii. 5; Rom. ii. 2–11; 1 St. Pet. i. 17; St. Jas. ii. 12 *et seq.*; Rev. xix. 11; xx. 13.

[2] A stone cannot deserve, nor can a horse — *i.e.*, in the human sense. "A man is a man for a' that."

lish a claim to the priceless blessings which Christ
has earned for us.

These considerations teach us that our deservings
are wholly based upon the merits of Christ, which are
appropriated by faith, imparted by our being made
members of His body, and established by our bringing
forth fruits worthy of repentance — this last being
made possible only by the grace of God.[1]

It is a part of the justice of God that His judgments
are without respect of persons. They are absolutely
impartial, and exhibit the righteousness of God in
the presence of right and wrong.[2] His punitive judgments are not vindictive but vindicative,[3] and have
perfect regard for the unequal knowledge and oppor-
tunities of His creatures. This impartiality of divine
justice is not violated by the fact that God wills to
place particular individuals and races in some respects

[1] The subject of justification is to be considered in a future volume,
in connection with the doctrine of grace.

[2] Cf., in mutual connection, St. Luke xvii. 7–10; Acts x. 34, 35;
Rom. ii. 6–12; Gal. ii. 6; Tit. iii. 4–7; 2 St. John 8.

[3] Scripture speaks of the wrath, the jealousy, and the hatred of
God (cf. Exod. xxii. 24; Num. xi. 1; Deut. xxxii. 21, 22; Judges iii. 8;
Psa. vii. 11; Jerem. xlii. 18; Nah. i. 2; Rom. i. 18; Rev. vi. 17.   Also
Isa. xliii. 4; Mal. i. 8; Rom. ix. 13; xii. 19), but metaphorically.   As
St. Augustine says, such language sets forth the just retribution of
God, and does not signify either perturbation of mind or cessation
of love: *De Trin.*, xiii. 21; xv. 25.   Cf. Hastings, *Dic. of the Bible*,
s. vv. "Anger (Wrath) of God" (by Jas. Orr); "Hatred" (by J. F.
Bethune-Baker); "Jealousy" (by J. S. Banks); Hastings, *Encyc. of
Religion, s. v.* "Anger (Wrath) of God," by T. B. Kilpatrick (who
gives further references); St. Thomas, *Summa Theol.*, I. iii. *2 ad sec.*
See also p. 306, below.

at an advantage over others in this world. Such inequalities are inevitable incidents attendant upon the distribution of vocations and stewardships, and are necessarily allowed for in the ultimate issues of a governmental justice which is really divine. That God is immutably just is involved in His being God.[1]

§ 9. By virtue of His *goodness* [2] God wills to impart life and manifold benefits to His creatures.[3] This goodness is a characteristic of His essence, which is communicative. The Father eternally communicates His self-existent essence and life to the Son, by eternal generation; the Father and the Son in like manner communicate their common essence to the

[1] The righteousness of God involves not only His justice, but also His truthfulness (Num. xxiii. 19; St. Matt. xxiv. 35; St. John iii. 33; Rom. iii. 4), and His faithfulness (Rom. xi. 29; 1 Thess. v. 24; 2 Tim. ii. 13; Heb. vi. 17, 18; x. 23).

[2] The word "good," according to Murray's *New Dictionary*, meant originally fitting, suitable, pleasing. Its derivative meanings are various. As applied to God it has meant either His moral perfection, which we have considered in § 6, above, or His bountifulness, the meaning here. Another use of the word is to signify what is desirable, in particular, morally desirable. This use of the word appears in the proposition, considered in § 13, below, that God is the Summum Bonum.

[3] On divine goodness, see Martensen, *Christian Dogmatics*, §§ 50, 51; Hastings, *Dic. of the Bible, s. v.* "Good," 6; Pearson, *De Deo*, Lec. vii; pp. 73, 74; C. Hodge, *Syst. Theol.*, Vol. I. pp. 427–436; Schouppe, *Elem. Theol. Dog.*, Tr. V. §§ 173, 177, 179–194; Wilhelm and Scannell, *Manual*, Vol. I. pp. 205, 206; St. Augustine, *De Trin.*, viii. 4, 5; Tertullian, *Adv. Marcion*, Bk. II; St. Anselm, *Proslogium*, xxiii–xxv. Cf. Psa. xxxiii. 5; xxxiv. 8; lxviii. 19; cvii. 8, 9, 43; Isa. lxiii. 7; Jerem. xxxi. 12–14; St. Matt. vii. 11; Rom. xi. 22; St. Jas. i. 5, 17. The references given under divine providence, § 5, above, are also pertinent.

Holy Spirit; and the Three eternally communicate of their fulness of life to each other.

God is goodness,[1] and this it is that moves Him to create finite beings in order to impart to them such benefits as they are respectively capable of receiving. Creatures are dependent wholly upon the goodness of God for what they are[2] and enjoy; and, if in any respect their respective needs are not supplied, the reason lies in themselves. The goodness of God has no other limit than the nature of a goodness which is also righteous and just.[3]

Divine goodness includes *benevolence*, or the will of God to communicate happiness.[4] This appears in

---

[1] The divine attributes are His essence. This is especially noted by theologians in connection with the attributes of truth, goodness, love, and beauty. He *is* truth; He *is* goodness; He *is* love; He *is* beauty. Cf. Boedder, *Natural Theol.*, p. 335; St. Thomas, *Summa Theol.*, I. iii. 3.

[2] Because whatever any thing is in itself is due to the creative operation of God, so that all things in their original and positive natures are good — *i.e.* desirable. The evil that is in them is due to creaturely causation, and constitutes a perversion of nature. Cf. Gen. i. 31.

[3] Origen discusses the seeming opposition which sometimes appears between the justice and the goodness of God, in *De Princip.*, II. v. If justice and goodness are both virtuous, he shows, they must involve each other. Cf. Tertullian, *Adv. Marcion*, II. xi, xii.

[4] That is, as was pointed out in discussing divine justice, "according to the deservings of each." God indeed showers many good things upon all alike (cf. St. Matt. v. 45); but the nature of God's creation is such that real happiness comes exclusively to those who worthily receive them. God offers happiness to all, but under conditions which cannot be disregarded by a righteous God. Cf. ch. vii. § 2, above, on the working out of all things for the happiness of the righteous.

the fact that the miseries of this life which are caused
by sin are alleviated by divine providence, and do
not become what they would become in a world really
dominated by the forces of evil. The dispensation
of salvation from sin, and consequent banishment of
the causes of misery, constitutes the highest manifestation of divine goodness. Christian doctrine does
not wholly shut out even the finally impenitent from
the benefits of goodness, and we are permitted to believe
that the misery of the lost will not be absolute, or greater
than the immutable requirements of divine justice
demand. It is God's will of good pleasure to impart
such measures of blessing to all as they are respectively
capable of enjoying, and the limits of enjoyment have
their causes in creatures themselves.

§ 10. The most glorious and significant moral
attribute of God is His *love;* which is His will to embrace in personal fellowship with Himself all who
are capable of enjoying such fellowship or who by
divine mercy can be enabled to enjoy it.[1]

God is love itself, and is the source of all righteous
love in His creatures.[2] Love is essentially concerned

[1] On divine love, see St. Thomas, *Summa Theol.*, I. xx; Mason,
Faith of the Gospel, ch. i. § 14; Pseudo-Dionysius, *Divine Names*,
ch. iv; Martensen, *Christian Dogmatics*, § 51; Clarke, *Outline of
Theol.*, pp. 94–102; Pfleiderer, *Philos. of Religion*, Vol. III. pp. 305,
306; Baldwin, *Dic. of Philos.*, *s. v.* "Love"; Wilhelm and Scannell,
Manual, § 84. Cf. Jerem. xxxi. 3; Hos. xi. 1; St. Luke xv. 11–27;
St. John iii. 16; xvi. 27; xvii. 23, 26; Rom. v. 8; Tit. iii. 4; Heb. xii. 6;
1 St. John iii. 1; iv. 8–19.

[2] St. Augustine, *De Trin.*, vi. 7.   Cf. St. John xvii. 26; Ephes.
ii. 4, 7; 1 St. John iv. 16.

with persons, and with their mutual union and fellow-ship.[1] The conditions of love are found in the eternal Trinity; and love is realized within the divine essence, independently of creatures. Love constitutes the moral basis and expression of divine unity and bles-sedness.[2]

But the goodness of God manifests itself in the crea-tion of a world of persons who are capable of being sanctified and brought within the sphere of divine fellowship. And the participation of men in such fellowship constitutes, apparently, the real purpose of creation. The entire economy of nature is developed and directed to the evolution and equipment of persons and to their participation in the life of God.

Love necessarily requires for its object the lovable, and for its basis mutual congeniality. The condition in creatures which produces such congeniality between God and them is likeness of personal character, or holi-ness. In so far as men are made in the image of God, and are capable, by divine help, of acquiring personal holiness, they are all the objects of divine love. And the love of God for sinners remains because, and in so far as, the possibility of recovery to holiness and divine fellowship remains.[3] Divine love is infinite; and, if any of His creatures should fail to enjoy its blessings, it will be because they have ceased to be possible objects

[1] As Pfleiderer says, *op. cit.*, love is "will directed to community of life."

[2] Cf. A. H. Strong, *Syst. Theol.*, Vol. I. p. 265.

[3] Cf. Rom. v. 8: "But God commendeth His own love toward us, in that, while we were yet sinners, Christ died for us."

of love. In other words, divine love is never shortened, but it is limited by its own essential nature,
and therefore presupposes objects which are at least
capable of being helped to become lovable.

Divine love for creatures is participated in by all
of the divine Persons, for to be divine is to be love.
This appears clearly in the crowning manifestation of
God's love — His dispensation of *mercy* to sinners.[1]
The mercy of God is the form which divine love must
take when sin has intervened. It is necessarily stern,
and is inseparable from conditions which are expia-
tory; but it is also curative, sanctifying, and reconciling. Moreover, man's will has to be enlisted, for the
restoration of personal holiness and congeniality is
otherwise clearly unthinkable. To achieve such restoration the Father spared not his Only-begotten;[2] the
Son willingly died for us;[3] and the Holy Spirit ever
seeks to win our spirits to the labour of accepting and
working out the salvation which the death of Christ
has made possible.[4] It is, to sum up the mystery,

---

[1] On divine mercy and long-suffering, see St. Thomas, *Summa
Theol.*, I. xxi. 3, 4; Schouppe, *Elem. Theol. Dog.*, Tr. V. §§ 207, 209;
Wilhelm and Scannell, *Manual*, pp. 246, 247; Hastings, *Dic. of the
Bible, s. vv.* "Long-suffering" and "Mercy"; *Dic. of Christ, s. v.*
"Mercy of God." Cf. Exod. xx. 6; xxxiv. 6, 7; Isa. xxx. 18; Lam.
iii. 22, 23; Dan. ix. 9; Joel ii. 13; St. Luke i. 50; Ephes. ii. 4–7; Tit.
iii. 5; St. James v. 11; 2 St. Pet. iii. 9. Clement Alex., in *Exhort. to
the Gentiles*, x, gives an eloquent description.

[2] Rom. viii. 32; St. John iii. 16. The notion that the death of
Christ is the cause of the Father's love for sinners is, of course, un-
scriptural.

[3] Gal. ii. 20; Ephes. v. 2.   [4] Cf. Rom. viii. 14–17, 26–27.

God in Christ who is reconciling the world unto Himself.[1]

It is truly said that God declares His almighty power "most chiefly in showing mercy" to sinners;[2] and love is altogether the most powerful force in the spiritual world. But, as we have seen, power is meaningless when we think of it as applied to what is intrinsically impossible. Salvation consists primarily in bringing about a change in our wills and dispositions. To save creatures from sin in spite of obstinate creaturely unwillingness is to achieve the impossible; and to be unable to do this constitutes no defect in either power or love, intelligibly defined. The power and love of God are infinite, but they are power and love — not an unintelligible something else.[3]

III. *Divine Excellence*

§ 11. Any adequate study of the divine attributes, as we have said, involves abstract thought and a resort to subtle and metaphysical distinctions.[4] It is imperatively necessary, however, if we would arrive at true results, that we should repeatedly remind ourselves

---

[1] 2 Cor. v. 19.

[2] Collect for the 11th Sunday after Trinity, English form.

[3] We are not here concerned with the subject of future punishment, which is to be considered in the last volume of this series; and the truth of what is here said is not dependent upon any conclusions as to the number of those who are finally to be saved. On the inviolability of human wills in the mystery of salvation, see Pusey, *What is of Faith as to Everlasting Punishment*, pp. 14–16, 22.

[4] See ch. x. § 10, above.

that we are concerned in all our distinctions with
a real and personal Being. Abstract qualities may
exercise our wits, but they can have no proper value,
except as they are the qualities of reality. The fact
that God is a real and personal Being — the ground of
all reality, — who unites in Himself without discord,
and in absolute perfection, all the attributes which
we have been considering, constitutes Him the adorable
God, our king of Love, and the sum of all blessedness
forever.

The *blessedness* of God in its stricter meaning is the
richness and joy of his life;[1] which arises primarily
from what He is, and from the internal and mutual
relations between the divine Persons. This blessedness is infinite, eternal, and satisfying. God is sufficient unto Himself.[2] If He were not, He would be
dependent upon external relations and would be finite.
But the goodness and love of God have caused His
blessedness to include within its reference the relations
subsisting between Himself and His creatures. God
rejoices from eternity in the historical outpouring of
His goodness and love upon those whom He has made
to be partakers in His blessedness.[3]

[1] On divine blessedness, see St. Thomas, *Summa Theol.*, I. xxvi;
Wilhelm and Scannell, *Manual*, Vol. I. pp. 254–256; Martensen,
Christian Dogmatics, § 51; A. H. Strong, *Syst. Theol.*, Vol. I. pp.
265, 266. See also above, pp. 236, 237, on the absolute, and the
references there given. Cf. 1 Chron. xxix. 11, 12; St. John xvii. 5;
2 Cor. viii. 9; Phil. iv. 19; 1 Tim. vi. 15, 16.

[2] St. Irenaeus, *Adv. Haer.*, iv. 14; Novatian, *De Trin.*, iv; St.
Augustine, *De Civ. Dei*, xi. 11.

[3] Cf. Psa. civ. 31; cxlix. 4; Prov. xv. 8; Isa. lxii. 5; Rev. iv. 11.

21

The sins and shortcomings of men are said meta-phorically to evoke divine grief and anger. But such descriptions are borrowed from human analogies, and when pressed literally signify a temporal point of view. When applied to the eternal they still retain a meaning, for they describe a real relation between God and sinning creatures. But the eternal point of view which God enjoys makes it impossible that rela-tions to the contingent should interrupt or alter divine blessedness. To God the ultimate victory of righteous-ness, and the fruition of His purpose, is as immediately present as is the working out of the drama of sin and its consequences.[1] If sin abounds, grace still more abounds;[2] and in Christ all things redound to the eternal and unchangeable blessedness of their Creator.

The response of mankind to the goodness of God is expressed by worship, and reaches its climax and reward in eternal life. Eternal life consists in our fellowship with God and His saints — an unending participation in divine blessedness.[3]

§ 12. The beauty of creation constitutes a revela-tion of the *glory and beauty* of God. As we have seen elsewhere,[4] beauty is not a subjective illusion merely,

---

[1] Cf. note 3, on p. 298, above, where references are given.

[2] Rom. v. 20.

[3] St. John xvii. 3; 1 St. John i. 3; v. 11–13. Cf. 1 Cor. xii. 12, 13; 2 Cor. vi. 14–18.

[4] On the glory and beauty of God, see ch. vii. § 7, above, and the references there given. See also Hastings, *Dic. of the Bible, s. vv.* "Glory (in O T)," ii; and "Glory (in N T)." Cf. Exod. xxiv. 17; xxxiii. 20, 22, 23; Psa. xix. 1–4; xxiv. 8–10; xxvii. 4; xcvi. 6; Isa.

but a real and objective attribute of things. It is also seen to transcend in significance everything mutable. The standard of reference which is implied in our perception of the glory of a sunset, of the grandeur of an ocean, or of an Alpine peak with its eternal snow, is recognized, when thought on, to be absolute, infinite, and eternal. "The heavens declare the glory of God, and the firmament showeth His handiwork." [1]

The prodigality with which nature has been beautified,[2] and the instinctiveness, so to speak, with which it beautifies itself again when cataclysms or human misuses have marred its glories, have often been noticed. There can be but one rational explanation. The Creator admires beauty, and all His immanent working reflects in its results the beauty which has its primal seat and source within Himself.[3]

Each constituent element is endowed with the form of beauty which is appropriate to itself, and which in combination with the beauty of other elements and

vi. 1-5; xxviii. 5; Ezek. i. 28; iii. 23; viii. 4; Acts vii. 55; Rom. i. 23; Rev. xxi. 23.

[1] Psa. xix. 1.

[2] The poet Gray says, in his *Elegy*,

> "Full many a gem of purest ray serene,
> The dark unfathomed caves of ocean bear:
> Full many a flower is born to blush unseen,
> And waste its sweetness on the desert air."

The word "waste" expresses only the seeming. God never causes waste, in the proper sense of language.

[3] As the handiwork of a true artist is always beautiful, even when the end in view does not require this, so the handiwork of the supreme Architect is necessarily beautiful.

elemental relations makes the whole universe a temple
to its Maker.   There is a hierarchy of beauty, in which
the glory of each member corresponds with its place
in the rising scale of being.   Highest of all is spiritual
beauty, the beauty of persons and characters.[1]   This
beauty also manifests the glory of God.   God is personal, and His beauty must be appropriate to His nature; — a personal glory which transcends our most
glorious thoughts concerning it, and which must bring
rapture to all who obtain glimpses of its synthesis of
sweetness and majesty.   That glimpse is to be had
in the Son of Man, in whom indeed unlovely souls
discern no beauty that they should desire Him,[2] but
who is rightly seen by multitudes which no man can
number to be fair and glorious beyond compare —
"the chiefest among ten thousand." [3]

§ 13.   The good has been defined as that which is
desirable,[4] whether from the point of view of immediate
pleasure, happiness, or virtue.   "Every good gift and
every perfect boon is from above, coming down from
the Father of lights"; [5] and nothing can be rightly
regarded as desirable which cannot also be reckoned
as coming from God.

---

[1] The beauty of a human face transcends the beauty of a graceful
fawn because it reveals personality; and the comparative beauty of
faces depends upon the personal qualities which they exhibit.   Even
those who are too uncultivated in spiritual perception to realize this
are often calmed and subdued, they know not how, by the glory of
a saintly countenance.

[2] Isa. liii. 2.   [3] Song of Sol. v. 9–16.

[4] Cf., on other uses of the word "good," p. 299, note 2, above.

[5] St. Jas. i. 17.

But the most desirable of all blessings is that God should give Himself to us; for He is, in Himself, not only the source but the sum of what is required to satisfy man's ultimate needs. This is so not only because God is what He is, but because He has made us for Himself, so that nothing else can permanently satisfy us. "The heart is restless until it find rest in Thee, O God." [1] All experience teaches this. A man who is kept for a long period in solitary confinement is in danger of becoming insane, because he is by nature a social being, and needs personal fellowship to make life anything else than a nightmare. But human fellowship, necessary as it is for man, even in the life hereafter, is not all that we crave for. There is a limit to what the best merely human friend can give us, and we yearn for contact with one whose resourcefulness and love can never be exhausted. Such a friend we have in God. And "our chief end is to glorify God and enjoy Him forever." [2] To put it in another way, He is our *Summum Bonum*,[3] without whom all else is dust and ashes, but with whom all our life is full of glory and peace.

If we are tempted to look upon God as too remote

[1] St. Augustine, *Confess.*, i. 1. Cf. Martenson, *Christian Dogmatics*, § 50 *fin.*

[2] *Westminster Catechism*, first answer.

[3] On the truth that God is the *Summum Bonum*, see St. Thomas, *c. Gent.*, Bk. III, esp. chh. xvii, xviii, xxxvii, lxi, lxiii; Hooker, *Eccles. Polity*, I. xi. 1, 2; Elmendorf, *Moral Theol.*, I. i; Thos. Slater, *Manual of Moral Theol.*, Vol. I. p. 16; Boedder, *Natural Theol.*, pp. 385-391. Cf. esp. St. John xvii. 3; but also Psa. xxvii. 4; xxxiv. 8; Lam. iii. 25.

in His majesty for us to approach, or too awful for us to enjoy, we know that He has condescended to our weakness, and that in Jesus Christ is revealed the fulness of the Godhead bodily.[1] The perfect Man, who was tempted at all points like as we are, thus showing Himself to be touched with the feeling of our infirmities,[2] He is our God — our Maker, Saviour and Friend. And this is life eternal, that they might know Thee the only God, and Jesus Christ whom Thou has sent."

> "Crown Him the Lord of heaven,
> Enthroned in worlds above;
> Crown Him the King to whom is given,
> The wondrous name of Love."

[1] Col. ii. 9. Cf. Ephes. ii. 13; iii. 12; 1 St. Pet. iii. 18; 1 St. John iv. 7, 13, 15, 16.

[2] Heb. iv. 15.

By the Rev. Francis J. Hall, D.D., Professor of Dogmatic Theology in the General Theological Seminary, New York.

THE LONG DESIRED ANGLICAN SUMMA OF DOCTRINE

A series of ten volumes in Dogmatic Theology, crown
8vo., each complete in itself, designed to constitute a connected treatment of the entire range of Catholic Doctrine.
Price, each volume, $2.00 *net*

LONGMANS, GREEN AND CO.
NEW YORK, LONDON, BOMBAY and CALCUTTA

Occupying a point of view which is Anglican and Catholic, the writer joyfully recognizes the value of modern advances in knowledge and thought, and seeks to coördinate the new with the old. Convinced that the ancient Catholic Faith cannot be imperilled by Truth from any quarter, he also believes that it needs to be exhibited in the terms of modern intelligence, if theology is to retain its place as the queen of sciences.

The volumes which have thus far been published have secured a favorable and encouraging reception on both sides of the Atlantic. The learning, skill in argument and clearness of exposition shown in the work; the author's success in translating ancient doctrines into modern terms, and his sympathetic understanding of new knowledge and contemporary thought, have been acknowledged by reviewers of every type —Roman Catholic, Anglican, and Protestant alike;—and his reverent adherence to Catholic doctrine has also been noticed. The following brief extracts are selected from a considerable number of generally favorable reviews.

Volume I.

INTRODUCTION

Pp. xlii–273.

JOURNAL OF THEOLOGICAL STUDIES, *Oxford and Cambridge:* "The author's learning and wide reading are as conspicuous throughout the book as is his fidelity to the point of view. . . ."

CHURCH UNION GAZETTE, *London:* . . . "is a comparatively small book into which an immense amount of valuable fact and criticism has been compressed . . . there breathes a spirit of large-mindedness, a refusal to be confined within any groove of prejudice."

CHURCH TIMES, *London:* "This admirable treatise should be found very useful on both sides of the Atlantic. . . .The book reaches a high level of excellence."

THE LIVING CHURCH, *Milwaukee:* "It exhibits the qualities which previous books have led us to expect from Dr. Hall, the severely restrained language, the careful accuracy of statement, the equitable judgement, and the background of knowledge. . . .When completed, the series will undoubtedly be a monumental addition to Anglican and indeed to Catholic Theology. It may, indeed, in time be recognized as holding such a place in Anglican theology as is held by the *Summa* of Thomas Aquinas in the Latin communion."

CHURCH STANDARD, *Philadelphia:* "Dr. Hall is not Latin. He is Catholic, to be sure, very much so, but in the true Anglican spirit he continues to bring the modern into his Catholicity, and give us a modern while he is giving a Catholic theology."

EXPOSITORY TIMES: After referring to the writer's briefer outlines, "the fuller scope of the new volume reveals a new writer, a writer with a very extensive knowledge of the litera- ture of his subject, to which he makes continual reference, and one who has manifestly mastered its literature and made his subject a real personal possession."

SCOTTISH CHRONICLE: "Its earnestness and learning are admirable."

IRISH THEOLOGICAL QUARTERLY, *Dublin:* "Dr. Hall is eminently qualified for the task he has undertaken. . . . Not the least of Dr. Hall's qualifications as a theologian is his extensive acquaintance with our Catholic authors . . . his style may be commended as a model of theological writing in English; it is clear; concise, direct, dignified, and elegant."

PAX, *England:* "That Dr. Hall possesses the necessary qualifications for the task will be apparent to those who know his theological monographs and his book on *The Kenotic Theory;* and this volume promises well for the success of his undertaking."

Volume II.

AUTHORITY

ECCLESIASTICAL AND BIBLICAL

Pp. xvi–300.

THE GUARDIAN, *London:* "The present volume, which forms a treatise complete in itself, is even abler than the first, and most opportune. . . .The entire book is marked by caution, balance, and restraint, and deserves to be carefully read.   A noticeable feature of the book is the immense number of modern writers referred to or discussed."

LONDON QUARTERLY REVIEW: "Dr. Hall uses his space well. . .he writes with candor and ability."

CHURCH TIMES, *London:* "Everything that is said in this book about œcumenical authority, the authority of Councils, of National Churches, and so forth, is admirable. . .[Referring to the whole series.]   That is a great enterprise, worthily begun."

RECORD-HERALD, *Chicago:* "It is refreshing to meet such a book, simple and lucid in style, scholarly, thorough, conservative, but not bigoted, marshalling arguments and meeting objections after the manner of the masters of theology."

THE CHURCHMAN, *New York:* "Of special value. . .is the chapter on the Dogmatic Office and Tradition. . . .There is a good analysis of the various theories of inspiration and a cautious discussion of the functions and legitimate scope of Biblical criticism."

SCOTTISH CHRONICLE: "This book. . .will be welcomed by many students of divinity.   It is a well thought-out treatise on the meaning of authority in religion, in which are considered the three factors of spiritual knowledge. . .viz., ecclesiatical authority, biblical authority, and reason."

LIVING CHURCH, *Milwaukee:* "We believe that. . .Dr. Hall states most adequately and most accurately the answer of the Anglican communion to the questions that divide Christians to-day, and that on substantially the lines of his answer must be built up the position that will ultimately prove the factor that will unite Christendom."

SEWANEE REVIEW, *Tennessee:* "Prof. Hall has a very distinct gift for systematizing."

CHURCH UNION GAZETTE, *London:* "Its chief value lies in the way in which he recognizes and emphasizes all the factors which are involved in any true knowledge of Divine things, not minimizing any, nor exalting one at the expense of another; but showing how, by the combination of all, we obtain a certitude which nothing can overthrow."

PAX, *England:* "As a really good compendium with valuable references, this book deserves all praise."

Volume III.
THE BEING AND ATTRIBUTES OF GOD
Pp. xvi–310.

EXPOSITORY TIMES: "It is the book of a student, the book of a thinker, the book of a believer. There is not a loose sentence in it, and there is no trivial rhetoric. It is above all the book of a student. Professor Hall's knowledge of the subject is an amazement."

LIVING CHURCH, *Milwaukee:* "Dr. Hall has produced a noble book."

IRISH THEOLOGICAL QUARTERLY, *Dublin:* "We. . .are glad to be able to praise the third still more unreservedly than its predecessors. It is an excellent manual of systematic theism, the very best of its kind by an Anglican that we know of, and one of the absolutely best. . .the book has to be read in order to be appreciated."

JOURNAL OF THEOLOGICAL STUDIES, *London:* "No argument for the existence of God has escaped his notice, and any one who reads his book must feel that Christian theists have no cause to be ashamed of the intellectual case they can present."

THE GUARDIAN, *London:* ". . .the admirable second volume on Authority led us to expect much from the writer. . . . One of the best things between the covers is the discussion of the Ontological Argument. . . . It should be needless to add that Professor Hall's work is marked throughout by the firm and reverential adherence to the Catholic religion which characterizes all the products of the author's mind."

CHURCH UNION GAZETTE, *London:* "An atmosphere of solid, hard work breathes through this book. The reader is made to feel that every sentence has been deeply weighed, and more than once rewritten. The task. . .is of an intensely difficult nature, but the result. . .can be generally described as successful in the better sense of the word."

CHURCH TIMES, *London:* "His theology is always thoroughly Catholic and scientific. . .preserving the balance and proportion of faith. . .is a compendium of sound and luminous theology, which should be on every student's shelf."

INTERIOR, *Chicago:* "The previous numbers we have heartily commended. . . .Every page bears witness to the learning of the writer and the precision of his mental processes. Such a study so pursued is rare nowadays, but in its matter and its method it justifies itself."

Volume IV.
THE TRINITY
Pp. xix–316.

GUARDIAN, *London:* "The most valuable part of this volume. . .is the chapter on personality and related terms in modern thought. . .we have again to thank him for a learned and useful exposition."

CHURCHMAN, *New York:* "It must be reckoned the most important and valuable of the series so far; indeed, the most noteworthy theological treatise of the year. . .one may hope that many clergy and laity. . .will make themselves masters of this admirable volume. American and English Christianity owes a great debt to the learned and devout scholar."

CHURCH TIMES, *London:* "Professor Hall's excellent and worthy series. . . .But we refer the reader to Dr. Hall's volume, which will be indispensable to every student, elementary or advanced."

RECORD, *London:* "The student. . .will find in this book a useful and comprehensive survey of the history of the doctrine of the Trinity, and its theological significance."

LIVING CHURCH, *Milwaukee:* "The marvel is how Dr. Hall can so exactly treat in such a brief way the many matters he handles. . . .We have said enough to show how valuable and masterly is this volume."

CONTINENT, *Chicago:* "It cannot be said that the able and learned author avoids any real difficulty, although dealing with a most difficult theme. . . .No one can deny that these lectures are able, clearly stated and imbued with the spirit of a true believer."

CHURCH OF IRELAND GAZETTE: "Professor Hall. . .has made a decidedly valuable contribution to Dogmatic Theology by his. . .book on the Trinity. . . .The chapter dealing with 'Difficulties' is exceedingly well written. This is a book which should find a place at an early date on every well appointed book-shelf. Its freshness, the straight, clear presentation of its matter, will appeal to everyone."

Volume V.
CREATION AND MAN
Pp. xviii–353

THE GUARDIAN, *London:* "We heartily commend this book as a very able introduction to the vast subject of which it treats. . . . The subject-matter is admirably arranged and the main arguments are lucid and satisfying. The references to modern literature are extensive and supply a very complete course of reading with Dr. Hall as a competent critic and guide."

LIVING CHURCH: "A large number of difficult problems falling within the domain not merely of the theologian, but also within the domain of the philosopher and metaphysician and scientist, are taken in hand by Dr. Hall in his wonted lucid, calm, and balanced way of treating his subjects. . . . We trust that many will procure and carefully read Dr. Hall's able treatise."

SOUTHERN CHURCHMAN: "As a clear statement of the position of the Catholic faith, the young theologian can find no better help than this."

BIBLICAL WORLD: ". . . The book should be found in all theological libraries. . . . The author has defined with great care his attitude toward the results of modern physical and biological investigation. . . ."

CHURCHMAN: "The author shows in this, as in the previous volumes of the same series, a wide range of reading, logical thought, clear and convenient arrangement of material, and painstaking scholarship. Beside this, abundant and valuable references to many books and treatises, ancient and modern, may well stimulate the reader to a criticism and amplification of the author's own conclusions. Dr. Hall is a theologian of whom our Church may well be proud. Able, sincere, and scholarly theological work, such as this volume exhibits, is of real service to the Church, and is bound to be useful to serious students of all schools of thought."

AMERICAN JOURNAL OF THEOLOGY: "The style is simple, vigorous, eminently readable — one might almost add fascinating. The book is supplied with abundant bibliographical notes. . . ."

Volume VI.
THE INCARNATION
Pp. xix–353.

CHURCH TIMES: "Each volume has increased our admiration for his scholarship, wide learning, and amazing industry."

LIVING CHURCH: "It must be said that no point of modern Christological speculation has escaped his notice, and that he endeavors throughout to preserve a sympathetic and open mind, quite as much as to state his own very positive convictions."

CHURCHMAN, *New York:* "All of Dr. Hall's writing is important, and it is gratifying to have such a work as his presented to the world as the characteristic product of the American Episcopal Church. He is one of our few really distinguished theologians."

EXPOSITORY TIMES: "Now Professor Hall is very capable, and even on such a subject as the Person of our Lord he is entitled to write. He is both ancient and modern."

THE BIBLICAL WORLD: "Dr. Hall's exposition of the traditional orthodox view of the incarnation is admirable. . . . Anyone who will study and not merely read his book will at least respect the traditional view and see that there is still some living thought in bygone controversies."

HOLY CROSS MAGAZINE: "It is . . . not only a spiritual but an intellectual treat, to find Dr. Hall moving with such complete ease amid the Incarnation data, yet appreciating at the same time the theologian's moral obligation at least to attempt to express the Faith in 'a language understanded of the people' . . . We commend the book for the clarity with which the Catholic perspective is expressed, and for the reverent agnosticism which is the inevitable corollary."

SOUTHERN CHURCHMAN: "The result is a work of great value . . . Dr. Hall excels in accuracy of definition and in lucidity of expression, and the reader has no difficulty in grasping his meaning nor in following the steps of his reasoning."

EVOLUTION AND THE FALL

By the REV. FRANCIS J. HALL, D.D., Author of "Dogmatic Theology," "The Kenotic Theory," etc.   Crown 8vo. pp. xviii+225.   Cloth, *net*, $1.50

The author's aim is to show that one may frankly and fully accept the scientific hypothesis that man is descended on the physical side of his nature from the lower species, and may acknowledge that his natural evolution from brute ancestors constitutes an important factor in causing his existing moral state, without incurring the necessity of qualifying his acceptance of the Catholic doctrine of man's primitive state and fall.

His argument involves an elimination, on the physical side, of the speculative philosophy called naturalism, and, on the theological side, of speculative conceptions of original sin that are not supported by really Catholic authority. He seeks to do adequate justice to evolutionary science, being convinced that real science must inevitably fortify one's hold upon really Catholic doctrine.

REVIEWS

CHRISTIAN WORLD, *London:* "It would be good if all theologians who write on the evolutionary hypothesis manifested the same knowledge and appreciation of its strong and weak points."

CHURCHMAN, *London:* Referring to the exposition of the evolutionary theory: "Nothing could be clearer or more helpful than this part of the treatment, especially in its freedom from technical scientific terminology."

GUARDIAN, *London:* "Like all the author's work, the book is cautious and careful, strongly conservative, yet sympathetic with modern conceptions."

CHURCH TIMES, *London:* "We welcome Dr. Hall's book as the work of a man who seems thoroughly abreast of all that is being done in the field of biological science. . . . His work as a teacher has developed in him the gift of clear exposition, and he moves with apparent mastery in this thorny and difficult field."

THE KENOTIC THEORY

CONSIDERED WITH PARTICULAR REFERENCE
TO ITS ANGLICAN FORMS AND ARGUMENTS

By the Rev. FRANCIS J. HALL, D.D., author of "Dogmatic
Theology," etc. Crown 8vo. pp. xviii+247. Cloth, *net*, $1.50.

This volume is written in opposition to the theory that, in
order to assume a real manhood and submit to human conditions,
our Lord emptied Himself of certain divine prerogatives and
attributes during the period of His earthly life.

The writer endeavors to show that this theory is (*a*) a modern
novelty; (*b*) contrary to the Church's œcumenical decree of faith;
(*c*) rejected by Catholic doctors; (*d*) not warranted by the facts
contained in the Gospels of the statements of Holy Scripture;
(*e*) fallacious in its reasoning; and (*f*) perilous in its logical
results. Clearness and simplicity of treatment is aimed at, and
numerous citations are made from ancient and modern authorities.

REVIEWS

LIVING CHURCH: "It is his thorough grasp of those fundamental principles that has enabled Dr. Hall to give us in his
'Kenotic Theory' a theological treatise of more than ordinary
value. It has the singular charm of being direct, to the point,
lucid, and without verbiage from beginning to end. . . . Dr.
Hall . . . lays down, with exactness and precision, the question
at issue. . . . Dr. Hall has done good work in discriminating as
he has done between the views of Kenotic Schools. . . . Nowhere have we seen a better answer to the baseless assumptions
which have been made in England and America to formulate a
complete doctrine of the Incarnation out of a single passage in
St. Paul's writings."

CHURCH TIMES: "The book should be in every circulating
library, and should not be merely read, but studied, as a treatise
which from its merits is a candidate for a place as a handbook
upon an integral question in theology."

LONGMANS, GREEN & CO. PUBLICATIONS

CHURCH AND STATE IN ENGLAND TO THE DEATH OF QUEEN ANNE. By HENRY MELVILL GWATKIN, D.D., Late Dixie Professor of Ecclesiastical History, Cambridge; etc. With a Preface by the Rev. E. W. WATSON, D.D., Regius Professor of Ecclesiastical History in the University of Oxford. 8vo. Pp. viii+416. $5.00 *net.*

"An informed and intelligent student will find in this book what, so far as I know, has never been published in England on a scale both modest and comprehensive—a survey of our secular and ecclesiastical development, in due co-ordination and proportion."—*From the Preface.*

LIFE AND LETTERS OF THOMAS HODGKIN, Fellow of University College, D.C.L. Oxford and Durham, D.Litt. Dublin. By LOUISE CREIGHTON, author of "Life and Letters of Mandell Creighton, D.D.," etc. With Portraits and Other Illustrations. 8vo. Pp. xvi+445. $4.50 *net.*

THE CONVERSION OF EUROPE. By CHARLES HENRY ROBINSON, D.D., Hon. Canon of Ripon and Editorial Secretary of the Society for the Propagation of the Gospel in Foreign Parts. 8vo. Pp. xxiv+640. $6.00 *net.*

"We may congratulate him on his selection of a branch of missionary history so full of opportunity for the valuable work which the missionary world has learned to expect from him. He treats the various countries or races in twenty separate chapters and devotes 33 pages to a bibliography."—*The Times* (London).

THE LIFE AND FRIENDSHIPS OF CATHERINE MARSH. By L. E. O'RORKE. With 5 Portraits and 6 Other Illustrations. 8vo. $3.75 *net.*

A biography, illuminated by much correspondence, her own and others, of the author and philanthropist (1818-1912)—known as an author chiefly by her "Memorials of Capt. Hedley Vicars"; and as a devoted worker in the cause of Missions to Navvies, of the distribution of Bibles to troops in the Crimean, Franco-Prussian, and South African Wars, and of convalescent homes.

FATHER STANTON'S SERMON OUTLINES. From his own Manuscript. Edited by E. F. RUSSELL, M.A., S. Alban's, Holborn. Crown 8vo. Pp. xx+236. $1.75 *net.*

PRIMITIVE WORSHIP AND THE PRAYER BOOK: Rationale, History, and Doctrine of the English, Irish, Scottish and American Books. By the Rev. WALKER GWYNNE, D.D., author of "The Christian Year: Its Purpose and Its History," etc. Crown 8vo. Pp. xxvi+426. $2.50 *net.*

"Just the book needed by theological students and laymen in general, being fully informing and happy in style. . . . Just the one to place in the hands of a non-Church friend who wishes to know the why of the Prayer Book."—*The North East.*